Praise for *Create an Emotion-Rich Classroom*

"A necessary and easy-to-use resource for new and veteran early childhood educators alike. Giroux provides relevant and applicable information using real examples we have all experienced, while also considering children from diverse backgrounds and all abilities. I have 20 years of experience, but already know which chapters I will reread first!"

—**Amanda Vega-Mavec, Ed.D., Director, Academy for Children, El Centro, Inc.**

"A wonderful resource written for teachers by a consummate expert. Through Lindsay Giroux's extensive experience as a Preschool Pyramid coach, she developed classroom planning frameworks (DAPPER and ICARE) that early childhood educators can use to extend their intentional teaching around emotions into the incidental teaching throughout the day. The ultimate purpose is to help young children make sense of their emotions, give them the language to describe what they are experiencing, and teach them to regulate or manage their experiences. Giroux gives practical examples of how to insert social and emotional learning into academic learning experiences, and emphasizes the importance of tracking the data to ensure positive child outcomes."

—**Vivian James, Ph.D., CCC-SLP, NC Preschool Pyramid State Implementation Leader (2007–2020), NC IDEA 619 Coordinator (Retired)**

"*Create an Emotion-Rich Classroom* is a useful and productive tool that will act as a great resource for educators of early learners. Giroux is thoughtful and practical in her use of tips and strategies to assist educators in recognizing, validating, and responding to big emotions in little learners, as well as our own big emotions. The book provides ample opportunities for educators to reflect on and grow their current practices and offers something for every preschool teacher, those who have been teaching social emotional skills for years and those who are first shifting their focus. As early childhood educators, it is our responsibility to teach foundational skills to our students, including recognizing their emotions and the emotions of those around them. *Create an Emotion-Rich Classroom* offers real-world tips to help our early learners find success in the classroom and beyond!"

—**Leigh Anne Bosshardt, M.Ed., BCBA, Infant/Toddler Autism Support Teacher, Red Clay Consolidated School District**

"*Create an Emotion-Rich Classroom* takes you, as an early childhood educator, into the world of emotional literacy as you have never been before. The instructional frameworks introduced in the book allow you to dive deeper into bringing emotional understanding to your young students. The author pulls it all together with frameworks, data tools, assessment, and individualization in a way that makes teaching emotions to young children for understanding so easy. Emotions matter!"

—**Beth Hudson, M.Ed., NBCT, Union County Public Schools (UCPS) PreK Pyramid Model Coordinator**

"*Create an Emotion-Rich Classroom* emphasizes the need for young children to feel safe in experiencing and expressing emotions in early childhood classrooms. This book is a valuable resource for a wide audience of early childhood professionals, providing content to support teachers implementing instruction to create an emotionally rich environment and for professionals supporting teachers to implement best practices. Emotional skills are introduced along an early learning progression, with each chapter building to provide a developmental sequence to support children with recognizing, acknowledging, and regulating emotions. The frameworks used throughout the book support robust teaching, embedding emotional learning and exploration in all aspects of the early learning environment, with added resources to support differentiated instruction and building parent partnerships for a comprehensive approach to promote young children's healthy social and emotional development."

—**Kristine Earl, Ed.D., Regional Consultant, NC Early Learning Network, UNC Chapel Hill**

"In *Create an Emotion-Rich Classroom*, Lindsay has developed an effective approach to promoting young children's emotional development. The text is set out in a systematic manner that makes it easy to read and work through the concepts that Lindsay grounds with research. She has provided lots of activities, scenarios, and examples, with blank forms that can be downloaded. The reflection questions and ideas for engaging families make it a comprehensive approach for addressing social-emotional learning. This is a book that every early childhood teacher and coach should have in their library."

—**Jolenea Ferro, Ph.D., BCBA-D, Department of Child and Family Studies Associate Professor, Florida Center for Inclusive Communities, National Center for Pyramid Model Innovations, University of South Florida**

"Have you ever cared for a child who had such strong emotions that it made teaching them a daily struggle? If so, this book is for you—the adult who cares and strives to teach young children the foundational skills so that they may become more successful in school and in life. Throughout *Create an Emotion-Rich Classroom*, you will find relatable examples, practical strategies, and feasible applications to create spaces that support children on their lifelong journey towards emotional intelligence. What once seemed like a struggle becomes an opportunity to make a difference in the present and future lives of our children."

—**Raquel Lima, M.Ed., Assistant Principal, Clifton Early Learner Academy, Clifton Public Schools**

Create an
EMOTION-RICH CLASSROOM

Helping Young Children Build Their Social Emotional Skills

Lindsay N. Giroux, M.Ed.

Foreword by Mary Louise Hemmeter, Ph.D.

free spirit
PUBLISHING®

Library of Congress Cataloging-in-Publication Data
Names: Giroux, Lindsay Nina, author.
Title: Create an emotion-rich classroom : helping young children build their social emotional skills / Lindsay N. Giroux ; foreword by Mary Louise Hemmeter.
Description: Minneapolis, MN : Free Spirit Publishing Inc., 2022. | Includes bibliographical references and index.
Identifiers: LCCN 2021060833 (print) | LCCN 2021060834 (ebook) | ISBN 9781631986567 (paperback) | ISBN 9781631986574 (pdf) | ISBN 9781631986581 (epub)
Subjects: LCSH: Classroom environment—Psychological aspects. | Social skills—Study and teaching (Early childhood) | Emotions in children. | Affective education. | BISAC: EDUCATION / Behavioral Management | EDUCATION / Classroom Management
Classification: LCC LB3013 .G548 2022 (print) | LCC LB3013 (ebook) | DDC 371.102/4—dc23/eng/20220125
LC record available at https://lccn.loc.gov/2021060833
LC ebook record available at https://lccn.loc.gov/2021060834

Edited by Alison Behnke
Cover and interior design by Emily Dyer

Free Spirit Publishing
An imprint of Teacher Created Materials
6325 Sandburg Road, Suite 100
Minneapolis, MN 55427-3674
(612) 338-2068
help4kids@freespirit.com
freespirit.com

Acknowledgments

In the creation and development of this book, I am forever THANKFUL for those who have offered knowledge, advice, encouragement, and friendship.

A special thank you to:

My **T**eachers—The teachers who welcome me into their classrooms and lives make this kind of exploration and learning possible.

The **H**emmeter Lab Team—Mary Louise Hemmeter and her team at Vanderbilt University took my interest in social and emotional development and morphed it into my life's work.

My **A**lma Mater—The Wellesley Community Children's Center and the Education Department helped me see myself as a teacher. My Wellesley friends and my Wellesley intern, Caroline, have been so supportive as I began to see myself as an author.

North Carolina—I am so glad that I have found my home here. Wake County's Office of Early Learning, our SEFEL/Pyramid Model Implementation Team, my colleagues at Project Enlightenment, the Early Learning Network, my friends, and my parenting support groups all work toward great social and emotional outcomes for children.

The **K**arloff and Giroux families—I am so fortunate to have two families that believe I can tackle whatever I put my mind to.

Free Spirit Publishing—I am appreciative of the opportunity to share this book with the world. I'm honored to be a part of the Free Spirit family.

The **U**nbridled enthusiasm that my team brings to the social and emotional learning of children and adults—Nichole, Angela, Kendra, Jeff, Gay, Patti, and honorary team member Sally: your friendship and your centering of children and teachers make this work so very meaningful. This work is truly better together.

My **L**oves—Russell and Eric Ryan, I am grateful to have you both next to me as we navigate all of life's emotions together. I love you.

Contents

List of Figures

List of Reproducible Pages

See page 224 for instructions for downloading digital versions of these forms.

Foreword

by Mary Louise Hemmeter, Ph.D.

Nicholas Hobbs Chair in Special Education and Human Development, Vanderbilt University

"We don't get mad in this house."

I distinctly remember my mother saying this to me when I was a young child having a temper tantrum. My tantrums often involved crying, flailing my body on the floor, and holding my breath. I think my mother really meant to say, "We don't get mad the way you get mad," but I didn't know what else to do when I was mad. Often when I am in early childhood classrooms, I see young children expressing lots of emotions. They are scared, lonely, jealous, proud, happy, mad, embarrassed, excited, and joyful—just to name a few. However, they sometimes express those emotions with behaviors that adults find challenging, including withdrawing, hitting their friends, screaming at a teacher, knocking over another child's block structure, or running away from the group. You see, they are *little humans with big emotions*, and they haven't yet learned how to respond to situations in which they have these big emotions.

Becoming emotionally literate does not just involve learning about our own emotions and ways to respond to strong emotions; it also requires us to learn about others' emotions, how to recognize emotions in others, and how to support others when they are having big feelings. For example, my friend Sarah told her four-year-old son that I was feeling sad because I was sick. His response was, "Oh no, ML is sick like we were?" His mom said yes and asked, "What do you think we could do to help her feel better?" He looked up at his mom, thought about it with a serious, concerned look on his face, and finally responded, "boom bibbity boom bibbity boom." I believe Harrison knew what it meant to be sad, and he knew what it meant to feel sick— but he *didn't* know what to do or say to help me feel better. Stories like this help us appreciate the complex process of learning about emotions, and highlight the need for effective approaches to supporting young children's emotional development.

The timing of Lindsay Giroux's book is perfect for a number of reasons. Brené Brown, in her book *Atlas of the Heart*, discusses research in which she found that adults were, on average, able to recognize only three emotions and name them as they experienced them. One of the most significant implications of this is that learning about emotions is a lifelong process. All the more important, then, for us to be careful that our expectations for children are developmentally appropriate. The practices in this book can be used to teach children foundational skills that will help them be successful in school and life. Young children will not become emotionally literate

adults without careful, intentional, consistent teaching and support throughout their school years, and we can lay essential groundwork using the strategies and mindsets in this book.

This work is crucial. Young children are being suspended and expelled from preschool at alarming rates—and there is little evidence that those rates are going down. These suspensions and expulsions are almost always in response to behaviors that adults find challenging—such as hurting others, destroying classroom property, running away from the group, or not following directions. And why are these children engaging in such behaviors? Because they are angry, scared, lonely, embarrassed, proud, or experiencing other big feelings. Essentially, young children are being kicked out of preschool because they don't know how to express their emotions in "socially appropriate ways" or how to engage with their peers. And where are they going to learn these skills? At home, yes, but also in school—unless they are suspended or expelled, that is. Even more disturbing than the overall data on preschool suspensions and expulsions is the fact that these exclusionary discipline practices are dispro-portionately applied to children of color and to boys, raising larger issues of how adults can better support all children based on individual characteristics, needs, and experiences.

At the same time, staff wellness is a growing concern in early childhood settings. This is due in part to the COVID-19 pandemic, of course—but it is also a longstanding issue for early childhood teachers. Many of these educators are severely underpaid, receive no benefits, have little support, and work with children whose families are experiencing any number of difficult situations—all while being asked to support and guide the emotional development of our youngest children. This is one reason it is so critical to support teachers as they implement the practices found in this book. Ideally, this requires a commitment not only from teachers, but also from administra-tors. Teachers need time to plan, opportunities for reflection and feedback, and help navigating challenges.

For all these reasons and more, from the minute Lindsay told me she was going to write this book, I was excited to read it—and I could not imagine a better person to write it. Lindsay brings to this work rich experience as a teacher, coach, mother, and student. When she was a student in my lab, she was instrumental in the design of social and emotional activities for a curriculum we developed. I knew any book she wrote would be teacher-friendly, rich with examples, and feasible for and applicable to early childhood classrooms. I want to comment next on what I see as the most exciting parts of the book.

First, it is full of information on effective practices for supporting children's emotional development, with concrete examples of how to implement these practices in early childhood classrooms. Second, Lindsay dispels the myth that focusing on social and emotional skills leaves less time for academics. She does this by providing ideas for how to embed social emotional teaching practices across the day and how to use literacy, math, and science activities as contexts for supporting children's social emotional development as well. Third, she moves beyond the idea of "cute activities for talking about emotions" and explains the importance of considering children's stages of learning and providing appropriate supports for each child. She does this through the DAPPER framework she's created, which both illuminates and addresses the complexity of teaching young children about emotions. Fourth, she acknowledges the role that adults' own emotions play in this process, and offers ideas and supports for teachers to use when engaging in this work. Fifth, she addresses equity, family engagement, the impact of trauma on young children, and other critical issues, both when describing her core beliefs and throughout the book. Finally, she discusses how to address difficult issues that arise when teaching children to express their emotions. She recognizes the need to seek extra support for children when these issues arise, and also gives teachers ideas for how to respond in the moment.

With this book, Lindsay has provided teachers and the field with a valuable resource; the challenge, of course, is supporting the implementation of the practices Lindsay has so brilliantly described. I'll close with a few calls to action—and a few words of encouragement:

1. Be intentional about using these practices with every child. This does not mean all children receive the same thing, but that you consider what each child needs, affirm the beliefs and experiences they bring to the classroom, and use this book's practices to support their individual emotional development. Collect data, reflect on your use of the practices, and make sure each child is getting the support they need.

2. Engage with families in meaningful ways. Learn about how parents support their child's emotions, learn about families' cultural norms related to emotions, and work with families to individualize support to children. Listen to, learn from, engage with, and support families in this journey.

3. Find support for yourself in this work. This might come from classroom team members, other teachers in your building, administrators, related services staff, families, or community advocates. It is not easy work. It takes time, planning, reflection, and feedback. Find others who are equally committed to it, and work together to support every child.

And last, I offer you my gratitude as you take on the challenging and essential job of helping young children build their emotional skills. The time is now to help children learn these skills. I hope that this book will help you in this important work.

Introduction

My first year as a full-time preschool teacher was nothing like I had imagined. After years of working as an assistant in early childhood classrooms on my college campus, I had moved across the country and taken a job where I'd have a classroom of my very own. I was excited to have my own space to try out ideas. I was anxious too; as I awaited the arrival of my first class, I had trouble envisioning how my year would go. But I felt I had done what I could to prepare. I'd set up my room, planned schedules and routines, organized materials, and started to build relationships with families before the children stepped foot into school on the first day.

Some things were brilliant successes. My class responded well to puppet play and songs, and they loved books as much as I did. We had great sensory experiences together, painting with our feet and mixing up slime. Families were appreciative of the developmental notes and photos I shared, and they were great partners in brainstorming and planning for their children's growth. Other things were less successful. The children had a lot of big feelings. There were tantrums when spaghetti was served on pizza day. There were kicks and hits and thrown blocks when a toy was snatched away and when it was time to stop and clean up a favorite activity. I had big feelings too. Between moments of joy, I felt defeated, exhausted, ineffective, and worried.

Emotions Matter

I knew my class needed a lot of social and emotional support, and I didn't feel particularly well-equipped to provide it for them. I wasn't sure how to explicitly teach interaction skills, and I had never had so many children in one group who struggled with handling anger and disappointment. It felt impossible to meet the educational needs of my class without addressing their emotional needs. They needed skills and guidance for handling big feelings and regulating them, expressing emotions in safe ways, and recognizing emotions in others. Emotions matter, and I *knew* this, but I didn't know what to *do* about it.

With support from my coteachers and information gleaned from online resources, I muddled through the year. But I wanted to learn more, make changes, and offer better help to the young children in my care.

A couple years later, I decided to go back to school for a graduate degree, and I wanted to lean into those challenges I had felt so strongly. I studied early childhood special education and focused my research on social and emotional development. I honed my skills in explicit social and emotional instruction and became more confident in my ability to coach children when emotionally intense situations arose.

I couldn't help but think how that first year would have gone differently, and what the benefits would have been for the children, had I known these skills during that part of my teaching career.

In the years since completing my degree, my focus has been on social and emotional learning (SEL), coaching early childhood teachers in both inclusive and self-contained special education classrooms. I have seen amazing, creative lessons on emotional literacy. I have seen children learn to answer "How are you feeling?" with specific emotion vocabulary, and I've seen children select regulation strategies and joyfully announce that they are calm. I have also seen teachers experience many of the same feelings and frustrations I had. They want to meet the needs of their children, and they recognize that challenging behaviors are a result of children not yet having the skills to regulate and express themselves. These educators start to teach about emotions, but often aren't sure where to go next in building skills or being more intentional with instruction. Many curricula encourage reading about emotions, modeling emotions, and using visuals. But when it comes to moving beyond these steps, teachers often feel stuck. What do we do *after* those introductory lessons? What do we do when high-emotion situations arise in the classroom? How do we help children generalize their growing social and emotional skills to other settings, including home?

This book has grown out of my work coaching and training teachers. Within it, you'll find frameworks I've developed to help teachers answer the questions of "What comes after I've read a book and modeled the skill?" and "What do I do or say in the emotional moment to build children's capacity?" You'll notice guided reflections, the same kinds of conversations I have as I coach teachers. You'll read ideas for data collection and prompts for noticing what is working (and what isn't) so you can make adjustments and keep the focus on the children and their outcomes. And you'll see encouragement to make choices that will work for you and your class—because in instruction, as in coaching, there are ample ways to build and reinforce skills. You get to choose your own adventure.

With *Create an Emotion-Rich Classroom*, I have aimed to write a book that would have helped me during that difficult first year—a book that would have given me the skills to understand how to be more effective at teaching about emotions while encouraging me to choose activities and materials that would play to my strengths and create joyful moments in my classroom. I hope this book can do that for you and the children you teach.

Learning from the Past and Looking to the Future

I think now about that difficult first year and the social and emotional needs children brought with them into my classroom. Though many years have passed, I continue to see that young children have many of those same, deeply human needs: the need to feel safety in the routines of the classroom, the need for support with handling disappointment and frustration, and the need to learn prosocial ways to get their peers' attention and express their needs and desires. Like my fellow educators (and parents),

I saw these social and emotional needs increase during the COVID-19 pandemic. The pandemic dealt new traumas to children and their caregivers alike. Illness and death impacted many people. Job loss and insecurity shaped the financial situation of family members and educators. Heightened anxiety about safety hygiene and being near others emerged as a challenge. And isolation for children and families meant children had fewer opportunities to grow socially while adults, too, were disconnected from our own social and emotional supports.

It was a time of profound challenge and loss. And yet, there were glimmers of hope. Along with the healthcare workers and others who acted so heroically to help, educators rose to these new challenges. Teachers worked harder than ever to establish classroom routines as both children and teachers sought stability amid school years disrupted by distance learning and quarantines. To support children craving interactions and connections with others, teachers figured out ways to adhere to social distancing guidelines while teaching how to greet and share with others. Masked teachers encouraged children to read their eyes to learn about facial expressions of different emotions.

The pandemic made teaching these skills more difficult, but not impossible. And while many facets of the pandemic remain difficult to understand and process for adults and children alike, one lesson is clear: Social and emotional learning is more important than ever to support growth and development for all of us as we navigate post-pandemic life.

About This Book

This book's goal is to give you frameworks for planning and implementing a variety of strategies to support the emotional development of young children in your care. It serves as a blueprint to design and build an emotion-rich classroom. Unlike a formal curriculum, which might have a pacing guide of skills and plans for each day, this book provides flexible, adaptable strategies and activity ideas. You can intentionally plan and modify these for your classroom to support the competencies young children are developing during their preschool years. While the content is presented in an order that will allow skills to be built on top of one another, there is not a suggested timetable for how long to focus on one area or skill. Rather, observing children in their interactions and play will support you in knowing whether to teach a new skill or continue practicing and reinforcing the first.

You'll probably notice that there's not a weekly lesson for "Social and Emotional Day." There's not a specific daily lesson for a social and emotional time block either, nor is there an Emotions Unit for the beginning of the school year. These omissions are intentional. Effective social and emotional instruction is woven into the fabric of every school day. It's about teaching explicit lessons, but it's also about responding when a child is upset, modeling when you are frustrated, discussing emotions in storybooks, and asking children to share examples of emotions from their own lives. Just as a print-rich environment intentionally immerses children in a wide variety of literacy experiences, an emotion-rich classroom intentionally surrounds children with a range of social and emotional instruction and supportive interactions.

Social and emotional learning is much more than emotional skills and competencies. Other skill sets, such as social interaction skills, decision making, problem-solving, and self-management, are also components of SEL and, like emotions, they can be taught and are part of lifelong learning. However, I chose to focus this book on emotional skills because of the interrelatedness of emotions and these other skill sets, and how that plays out in the early childhood classroom.

For example, a child I worked with struggled to handle disappointment. We had taught and practiced asking for a turn with a toy in our classroom, and he was able to use his words and gestures to ask. However, those positive interactions quickly took a turn if a peer told him he couldn't have the toy or said he had to wait for a turn. Without the skills to handle this disappointment, he would kick and shout at others. Classmates learned to move away and avoid him when he was in this state, which in turn limited the likelihood of interactions with his peers even when he was more emotionally regulated. Similarly, he struggled with self-management skills such as persistence to meet a goal, because frustration became overwhelming when he met a roadblock during a task. He needed the emotional competencies to allow him to bring a regulated self into social interactions and problem-solving with others.

As you explore this book, you'll notice that social and emotional skills overlap in many areas. For instance, responding to others' emotions lies at the intersection of emotions and friendship skills. Listening to others talk about their emotions and recognizing that they differ from yours is connected to empathy and social awareness. While this book focuses on skills tied to emotions, I hope you get to see and appreciate the growth in children's overall social and emotional development as you create an emotion-rich classroom.

Focusing on emotions as a distinct piece of social and emotional instruction has benefits too. First, it makes instruction specific and measurable, as we home in on very specific individual skills. Second, it allows both teachers and children to gain and strengthen the foundational skills that support other interactions, such as understanding how we feel and knowing how to read others' feelings. Third, emotions influence every choice and decision that we make; they color our perceptions and drive us into action. And fourth, emotions tend to be a topic that teachers wish to dive into, but the whole of social and emotional learning, with its vast importance and wide range of skills, can feel unmanageable. Looking at one distinct strand of skills, and using that strand as a mechanism to practice new frameworks, gives us valuable practice in taking instruction piece by piece.

The emotional competencies featured in this book are:

➤ building children's emotion vocabulary (chapter 3)

➤ learning to read ourselves and others to recognize emotions (chapter 4)

➤ understanding and articulating the causes of emotions (chapter 5)

➤ expressing and regulating emotions (chapters 6 and 7)

➤ understanding others' emotions and perspectives—a key part of empathy (chapter 8)

These competencies are aligned with the skills needed to be an "emotion scientist," as described by researcher Marc Brackett and the Yale Center for Emotional Intelligence. Brackett and his team coined the phrase "emotion scientist" to encourage analyzing emotions rather than judging them, and developed what they called the RULER approach: to **r**ecognize, **u**nderstand, **l**abel, **e**xpress, and **r**egulate emotions. Children and adults can use these skills to better understand emotions in themselves and others and build their emotional intelligence.

The teacher strategies described in this book are based around the Pyramid Model, a framework for promoting social and emotional competence in early childhood education. The Pyramid Model provides evidence-based strategies to promote social and emotional development and prevent challenging behavior. These strategies, important for effective social and emotional teaching and Pyramid Model implementation, are woven into the structure of each chapter. They include teachers modeling their own emotions or ways to appropriately express emotions (Demonstrate and Describe) and using a variety of different teaching strategies to reinforce skills in both small and large group settings (Demonstrate and Describe, Practice, Planned Opportunities). The Pyramid Model also encourages both giving positive descriptive feedback to children about their use of skills and asking children to reflect on their use of these skills (Reinforce and Reflect). Of course, even with robust instruction, teachers will need to individualize some approaches for specific children, changing instructional procedures or materials to make concepts more salient for those children (Differentiation and Advancement).

You might not be in a program that uses the Pyramid Model for social and emotional development, and that's okay too. You'll recognize that these instructional strategies, such as modeling, practicing, and planning intentional lessons, are fundamentally best practices for early childhood education. The structure embedded in the chapters will support you with robust instruction to meet a variety of needs and will provide you with the vocabulary to talk about your instructional practices. You'll also find strategies for connecting with families, along with data collection tools to support children with emerging skills. These will benefit you and your class regardless of curriculum or approach.

The forms in this book are also available at freespirit.com/cerc-forms. For directions on downloading this digital content, see page 224.

In each chapter, there are several suggestions on how to communicate with families about the new skills you are teaching. There are also ideas for soliciting family feedback about the emotion work you are doing at school; this gives families a chance to articulate what is important to them, what their concerns might be (including around social and emotional skills), and what emotional strengths their children are bringing into the classroom. Rather than only sending home information about what you are teaching, allowing families to share their thoughts and beliefs about emotions can make your emotion teaching more effective. Examples and strategies from children's home lives make your instruction more meaningful and connected.

You'll also notice a heavy focus on adult reflection. These reflection prompts are included to encourage you to think about your experiences with emotions in your own life, knowing how interrelated your use of these skills is with your teaching. There are also reflection prompts woven throughout that ask you to consider different aspects of your teaching and your class's responses. Encouraging reflection during classroom coaching is one of my favorite components of my job. Rather than telling teachers what to do, or why a skill is important, reflection allows each of us to identify why a skill matters in our lives and the lives of the children in our classes. Reflection shines clarity on our personal *why* and ties together our actions with the results we see in the class-room. Practicing reflection as you plan and teach will also enhance your ability to help children reflect on their own emotional competencies.

> To begin your reflection on this journey, see the Social and Emotional Skill Reflection Checklist at the end of the introduction.

How to Use This Book

There are many ways to use this book, independently or with others. I recommend using it in whichever way will motivate you to read, reflect, and then implement strategies in the classroom. For some readers, this might mean reading it individually, at your own pace, and taking time to reflect internally without the pressure of a due date or the expectation of sharing your reflections aloud. For others, this might mean creating a book study group to have an accountability framework to encourage you to read, implement, and bring ideas to the table. Consider what structures typically motivate you or allow you the space and energy to try new things.

If you opt to read this book on your own, you might find that recording thoughts and ideas in a notebook as you read can help you revisit and reflect on what you have learned and what you have brought with you into the classroom. Similarly, I recommend that you do take the time to stop and reflect when prompted, as it will encourage you to not only think about *what* you are implementing but also *why* you are working toward an emotion-rich classroom. Documentation of your reflections and instructional decisions can also serve as a record of your professional growth or may become helpful notes to reference if you are working toward Pyramid Model fidelity. And having your thoughts, choices, and plans written or typed out will make creating next year's emotion-rich classroom much easier.

You might choose to read this book with others, such as a group of adults who work in your classroom or a group of teachers at a school. Reading together creates the opportunity for shared study. While you might divide and conquer the content of some books (for example, I read chapter 3 and summarize for the group, and you read chapter 4 and summarize), this particular book does not lend itself to this book study format. Because each chapter contains reflections and instructional decisions that you'll want to make with your own teaching style and your own class's needs in mind, it is hard to reap those benefits without diving into each chapter yourself.

Therefore, other book study formats might work better with the structure of this book. For instance, one such structure would be for all participants to read the same chapter and each complete a "DAPPER Planning Sheet" for their classroom, before holding a book study meeting where everyone shares elements of their DAPPER plans and gives feedback prior to implementing these plans in the classroom. (You'll learn about the DAPPER framework in chapter 2.) Another successful structure could be to have everyone read and begin to implement a chapter's strategies, and then come back to discuss successes and challenges, review child data, and brainstorm next steps to strengthen instruction. To support this work, you can find a PLC/Book Study Guide at freespirit.com/PLC.

One other thing to note: the first time you read this book, I recommend working through the chapters in order. You'll find that the skills rely on the ones before them. Chapters intentionally reference skills, visuals, and activities from previous chapters to build on children's prior knowledge. After you work through the chapters, planning and implementing their suggestions for the first time, you might opt to revisit specific chapters as you plan for a new school year. At that point, this book becomes more of a resource to revisit, reflect again, and revise plans to meet new needs.

Looking Forward

As you embark on the journey to an emotion-rich classroom, I encourage you to envision what you want to create. How would your classroom look if children had the skills to understand emotions, discuss them, and regulate them? What would your classroom sound like? How would your classroom feel if you and the children had these skills?

Most of all, I challenge you to bring an open mind. Exploring your own emotions, reflecting on your experiences with emotions, and working to build new habits of implementation are hard work. Continuing to strive toward creating an emotion-rich classroom requires giving yourself grace. It's normal to feel like you didn't handle an emotionally charged situation well enough, or to feel frustrated when your strategies aren't meeting the needs of your class. A little grace for yourself, alongside reminding yourself of the classroom you have envisioned, will help you move the work forward.

Lindsay N. Giroux, M.Ed.

Social and Emotional Skill Reflection Checklist

It's very challenging to teach a skill that is not easy for you to use in your own life. To improve children's social and emotional skills, you can work to improve your own. Practicing key social and emotional skills allows you to better explain, model, and teach these skills, and encourages empathy as others learn them too.

Take a moment to reflect on each skill in this form, marking your own personal comfort level. Then reflect and mark the columns that represent how comfortable you feel teaching these skills to children.

Social and Emotional Skill	Personally, my comfort level with these skills in my own life:			As a teacher, my comfort level with teaching these skills to children:		
	Not yet comfortable	Somewhat comfortable	Comfortable	Not yet comfortable	Somewhat comfortable	Comfortable
Giving positive descriptive feedback (for example, "You did it. You asked for help when you were frustrated!")						
Receiving positive descriptive feedback						
Talking about your emotions using a nuanced emotional vocabulary						
Accessing calm-down strategies when you have big feelings						
Seeing the intent and desires that drive your actions and emotions						
Responding to others' emotions appropriately (for example, validating and offering support instead of dismissing or minimizing feelings)						
Describing your own emotions, behaviors, and skills (for example, "I was so angry that my face felt hot and my heart was beating quickly. I had to take deep breaths to calm down.")						
Reflecting on your own use of social and emotional skills (such as what worked and what did not)						

→

Reflect on your answers. What do you notice about them?

How will this knowledge help you prioritize areas for your personal growth?

Consider the children you work with. Are you equally comfortable teaching all of them these skills? Are there children you find harder to reach? Why is that? What resources can support you in reaching them too?

What will you need to support your comfort and competency with these skills?

Chapter 1

Six Beliefs About Emotions in Early Childhood

Preschool classrooms are full of displays of emotions, day in and day out.

Crying upon separating from parents.

Squealing with joy when a classmate arrives.

Quaking with frustration when the last piece of a puzzle won't fit.

Cheering when the teacher brings out a new activity.

Hiding behind a bookshelf when a substitute teacher enters.

Shouting when a peer refuses to pass a preferred toy.

Young children are learning how to navigate their emotional worlds. As emotional moments happen, children might be wondering, "What am I feeling? How do I describe this feeling? What can I do to help myself feel better? How does my classmate feel? What can I do to help *them* feel better? When my emotions are too big, how can I regain a sense of control and stability?"

First, imagine that a teacher dismisses or diminishes these emotional moments. She tells sad children, "You're okay," and asks children who are bubbling with excitement to sit down and be calm. She tells a scared child, "There's nothing to be afraid of," and tells an angry child that the problem is a small one and not worth getting upset about. The children might then have different emotions; perhaps they feel embarrassed, shamed, confused, or anxious that their teacher doesn't seem to understand them. The message the teacher is sending, whether intentional or accidental, is that emotions have no place in this preschool classroom.

Now, picture a teacher who has been working to explore feelings and teach emotional competencies to her class. She helps label a child's feeling with clear and specific emotional language: "Wow, you seem really excited to try this activity!" She coaches a child through frustration by offering techniques to help regain a sense of calm. She shares an experience about a time when she felt joyful and describes what it felt like in her body, and she encourages children to use their budding emotion vocabulary to try to explain how they are feeling and what's causing those emotions. While the first teacher is missing opportunities to support emotional growth, the second teacher is seizing those opportunities and fostering that growth. She's using skills and strategies that will help create an emotion-rich classroom where children's emotional intelligence can bloom.

In the emotion-rich classroom, teachers and children actively learn about emotions, explore how they feel, and practice safe ways to express them. Teachers are mindful of their own emotions and model ways to regulate strong feelings. This class is set up to handle the waves of emotions in preschool in a way that the other classroom is not. When a child is upset when separating from family members, the teacher in the emotion-rich classroom feels comfortable acknowledging feelings and has materials to offer that support emotional regulation. Children have learned to notice others' emotions, so a display of joy when a classmate arrives is met with a friendly greeting in response. Children can articulate when they are frustrated about a puzzle, and a classmate or teacher can offer validation and support. While big emotions including excitement and anger will always arise, teachers of emotion-rich classrooms have tools at hand and are prepared to coach children through emotional experiences.

Of course, creating an emotion-rich classroom does not mean we will always have an easy time navigating emotions with children. It doesn't mean that we will handle every situation with confidence, or that we will always keep our emotions in check when we are challenged. The goal of an emotion-rich classroom is not perfection; rather, it's agency and empowerment. Can we feel more empowered to respond to children's emotions? Can children feel more empowered to express how they feel and receive support? Yes! An emotion-rich classroom provides us with ways to create a space for the safe expression, exploration, and regulation of emotions.

The Six Beliefs

The concept of creating an emotion-rich classroom is grounded in six of my core beliefs about early childhood and how children learn. Reflecting on both research and classroom experiences led me to realize that creating an emotion-rich classroom is a combination of teacher strategies and teacher mindset. Understanding that instruction around emotions matters and that *all* preschoolers can learn these skills creates the desire to build an emotion-rich classroom. Recognizing that social and emotional instruction can be embedded into the preschool day—and that it can make life better for both children and adults—also supports the creation of an emotion-rich classroom. Building an emotion-rich classroom starts with understanding these six beliefs, which are supported by research, effective instructional strategies, and intentional teacher reflection.

My six beliefs underpinning an emotion-rich classroom are:

1. Emotional intelligence matters and can be enhanced through teaching. Teaching emotional competencies enhances teachers' emotional intelligence as well.

2. Preschool is an ideal time to focus on social and emotional learning.

3. Focusing on either social and emotional learning *or* academics in preschool is a false dichotomy.

4. Understanding identity and family background will help teachers plan instruction that can be supportive for more children.

5. Instruction in social and emotional skills reduces challenging behavior.

6. Creating an emotion-rich classroom is both a lot of work and a lot of reward.

Belief 1

Emotional intelligence matters and can be enhanced through teaching. Teaching emotional competencies enhances teachers' emotional intelligence as well.

Mrs. Caldwell reads a book about helping friends to her preschool class. She asks children to notice the characters' facial expressions, identifying how they are feeling and who might need help. She follows up with a puppet show in which one puppet, named Milo, picks up a block to help his friend build a tower without asking, and the friend begins to cry. She facilitates a brainstorming session where children identify how to recognize if a friend needs help and how to offer help—as well as clues that someone might *not* want or welcome help in the moment. She records children's ideas on a big piece of paper, and later children revisit the list of ways to help others and practice "reading" the list. Mrs. Caldwell explicitly taught children to recognize expressions and how to be helpful. She later reflects that, in her preparation, she outlined what the steps are for helping others in a level of detail she herself hadn't thought about before. Both children and teachers are learning during this kind of instruction around social and emotional competencies.

Emotional intelligence, a science popularized in the 1990s, focuses on several components of social and emotional learning. These include:

➤ knowing one's emotions and recognizing them in the moment

➤ managing feelings

➤ having emotional self-control

➤ recognizing emotions in others

➤ offering empathy

➤ handling interpersonal relationships

Emotional intelligence is related to lifelong learning, as both children and adults continually have new emotions and unique interpersonal relationships that require the use of emotional competencies. In early childhood education, teachers support children's emotional skills so they can be emotionally competent in both their school and home lives. Children might learn to wait for a turn at the sink at school, just as they might wait in the line at the grocery store. Learning to articulate how they feel when a peer knocks over their blocks is like sharing how they feel when a sibling doesn't wish to share the couch at home. And children aren't the only ones gaining new social and emotional strategies. As educators reflect, discuss, model, and intentionally address emotions in the classroom, their emotional skills flourish as well. Both children and adults mutually benefit from this kind of instruction.

Developing these key emotional skills begins during infancy. When babies cry or fuss, caregivers can choose to be responsive or dismissive. A caregiver who responds to a baby's emotions by matching their vocal pitch, gesturing to them, or comforting them is attuned to the baby, which reassures the child of their emotional connection. On the flip side, a caregiver who does not acknowledge or empathize with an infant's emotions can cause a child to avoid expressing those feelings, which can have dire consequences. During the toddler years, children start to imitate the actions of adults in their lives, whether it's sitting and reading a book like their teacher or brushing their hair like a parent. When toddler caregivers model how to express and regulate emotions, such as taking deep breaths or getting a hug when upset, toddlers see these emotional skills and can begin to understand or imitate them. On the other hand, when emotions are discouraged or ignored by caregivers, teachers, and other adults—whether intentionally or accidentally—the ability and desire to express those emotions can disappear, leaving children without the tools they need to cope with their emotions. Creating an emotion-rich classroom provides a space where expressing emotions is encouraged, instead of dismissed.

Our emotions shift our perception of the world, which influences how we make decisions; when we have more developed emotional skills, we are better able to recognize events that cause emotions, and we have a greater understanding of ourselves, our behaviors, our actions, and the actions of others. In turn, our feelings and those we recognize in others influence our decisions in our social interactions. And in addition to playing a role in the decisions we make, our emotions cause physiological changes in our bodies and brains, influencing both our physical and mental health.

For these reasons and more, a plethora of benefits are related to social and emotional instruction. Research has shown that these benefits affect us from preschool to adulthood and influence all sectors of our lives: from home, to school, to work. Preschoolers, for example, engage in less self-destructive behavior, are physically healthier, are less lonely, and are more likely to have kindergarten academic success when they have age-appropriate social skills and emotion knowledge (Joseph, Strain, and Ostrosky 2005; Torres, Domitrovich, and Bierman 2015). For older children, those who scored higher on measures related to reading nonverbal feelings were the most popular and most emotionally stable and did better in school (Goleman 1995). Having the ability to regulate emotions in high school predicts school success, including higher academic achievement and fewer disciplinary issues (Ivcevic and Brackett

2014). Since a large portion of an emotional message is expressed in nonverbal cues—such as body language, gestures, facial expression, and tone—being skilled in this area leads to better understanding of others and less miscommunication, making navigating social relationships a little bit easier.

For adolescents, those with higher emotional intelligence tend to experience less anxiety and depression and be rated as easier to get along with, both by themselves and by their teachers. Some data suggest that emotional intelligence is also related to higher SAT scores, better high school and college grades, and greater creativity (Brackett 2019). Perhaps this success in school stems from the fact that understanding others' emotions helps take the mystery out of social encounters in class, leaving more energy for other classroom activities. Or students with emotional intelligence might be better liked by teachers, leading to easier academic success. While reasons for the connection between academic success and social and emotional success are not entirely clear, the two *are* clearly linked.

As adults, the benefits of having these emotional skills include better relationships with friends, family, and romantic partners. In the workplace, emotionally intelligent adults are less likely to be anxious, depressed, stressed, or burnt out; they are more likely to have higher job satisfaction, better customer service ratings, high managerial performances, and to motivate and inspire others with their leadership (Brackett 2019). The benefits of emotional understanding are wide-ranging and pervasive, through the many stages of life and a multitude of social contexts.

Beyond school and job success, emotional intelligence supports mental health. Research on the connection between emotional intelligence and mental illness has mostly focused on adolescents and adults, and less on young children. For adults, high emotional intelligence is associated with psychological well-being, and adults with high emotional intelligence seem to be less likely to experience anxiety and depression (James, Bore, and Zito 2012). When elementary-age children participated in studies, researchers found that for individual children there was an inverse relationship between social emotional competencies and mental illness—in other words, having high social and emotional competence predicted lower mental health difficulties, even after researchers controlled for previous difficulties (Humphrey and Wigelsworth 2012). This implies that learning these important skills can support the psychological well-being of children and adults and provide them with additional strategies to handle life's stressors. Teaching these social and emotional skills proactively has benefits; so does teaching them in response to challenges or mental health difficulties.

When a child hasn't yet learned a skill, we teach it, encourage practice, and give feedback and support. Early childhood educators do this with letters, numbers, scissor skills, handwashing, and much more. Children learn those skills and then use them daily for years and years. The same is true of social and emotional skills. In emotion-rich classrooms, these powerful relationship-building skills are taught and practiced, and teachers model and give support. Unlike handwashing and cutting with scissors, teaching emotional competencies requires new exploration for teachers too, as we unpack our beliefs around emotions, examine our ways of dealing with emotions rooted in our own childhood experiences, and work to adjust our comfort levels around sharing emotions with others. To effectively teach handwashing, we practice a routine of discrete steps with children; to effectively teach expressing and regulating emotions, we model attitudes and ways of thinking about ourselves, our emotions, and the emotions of others. As we teach children these skills, our own understanding of emotions, strategies for regulation, and vocabulary to describe how we feel also grows.

As you reflect on this first belief, consider a child you have worked with who has thrived in your classroom. What emotional skills did that child display? How did having social and emotional skills contribute to their success? How did the child learn those skills? Seeing the success that arises from emotional intelligence helps keep us focused on why these skills are so valuable to teach. And as we teach them, we learn about ourselves. Most times, we aren't asked how *we* calm down, or how we feel frustration in our bodies, or how we know a child is sad. Through this work, you will become more intentional about describing and modeling these emotional skills for your class—and this intentionality may lead to some great learning about yourself as well.

Belief 2

Preschool is an ideal time to focus on social and emotional learning.

Ms. Hemond's preschool class starts the school year with a handful of three-year-olds. For many of them, it's their first experience in a classroom with peers. They begin the year intensely focused on materials. While several children might be near each other at the table, they are so focused on their own playdough creations that they don't look at or comment to each other. Children build with blocks near each other, but their play is still mostly parallel. Over the course of the first semester, the novelty of the classroom's range of toys starts to wear off, and the children become more interested in their classmates. All the teachers label what children are doing, and the preschoolers start to notice each other in a way they haven't before. Calls of "Look!" begin as children start to gain their peers' attention and show what they are working on, and some children begin to work together, sharing magnetic blocks to make one large castle instead of two small ones. The social worlds that are small at the beginning of the school year are rapidly growing to include both teachers and classmates.

While the foundation of emotional learning begins at birth, the preschool years are very crucial too. Between the ages of three and five, children begin to have increased interactions and engagement with others, including peers. First, for preschoolers who have not been in group care before, their social circle begins to expand outside the family as they enter school and other community social groups. Second, preschoolers gain play skills, transitioning from watching and observing others to playing collaboratively. Peer interactions provide the context and opportunities for children to learn and practice social and emotional skills. Similarly, the ability to regulate emotions becomes more necessary for preschoolers, given both their brain development and the social expectations and interactions they experience.

Through research and a review of the literature, psychologist Francisco Pons and his colleagues identified nine components of emotional development. They then grouped these skills into three developmental periods during which they are typically mastered by a majority of children. Of the nine, the first three components are mastered between the ages of three and five years, with several others beginning to develop between four and six, further supporting the idea that this preschool period is crucial for social and emotional learning and emotional intelligence (Pons, Harris, and de Rosnay 2004). The nine components and the age at which the majority of children have mastered these skills appear in figure 1.1.

FIGURE 1.1 Components of Emotional Development*

	Component	Age at Which Most Children Have Mastered the Component	Description
Public/External	**Recognition**	3 years	Ability to recognize and name emotions based on expressions
	External Cause	5 years	Ability to understand how external events impact emotions of others
	Reminder	5 years	Ability to understand that while the intensity of emotions decreases over time, things encountered later can serve as reminders that reactivate emotions
Mental/Internal	**Desire**	5 years	Ability to understand that two people might have different reactions, based on their own desires, to the same situation
	Belief	7 years	Ability to understand that an individual's beliefs impact their reaction to situations
	Hiding	7 years	Ability to understand that there can be a difference between the outward expression of an emotion and the actual emotion felt
Reflection/ Rumination	**Regulation**	9 years	Ability to use strategies, including cognitive strategies such as thinking of something else, to manage emotions.
	Mixed	9 years	Ability to understand that a situation may cause multiple emotions, including contradictory emotions, in a person
	Morality	9 years	Ability to understand that negative emotions stem from actions like lying or stealing, while positive emotions stem from actions such as resisting temptation or confessing a transgression

*As described by Pons et al.

As shown in figure 1.1, the first three components that children master in preschool focus on outward and more public components of emotion, such as understanding expressions and causes of feelings. These are typically easier for children to develop, as they can often see emotional expressions and their causes and be reminded of how they have felt in the past. The next three competencies that begin developing during preschool and are mastered between the ages of five and seven focus more on the mental parts of emotions and specifically understanding what others might believe or desire. For example, understanding how different desires impact emotions requires connecting thoughts and feelings with emotions of others. Understanding how beliefs impact emotions also is related to connecting thoughts and feelings, and children need to take perspectives of others to fully grasp this. Around the same time, children start to realize that there can be differences between the emotion someone outwardly expresses versus how they truly feel, such as smiling when given an unwanted gift even if feeling disappointed. The last set of competencies, mastered around nine years old, relates to understanding how reflecting on one's emotions and considering situations from different perspectives can affect emotions.

Pons and his colleagues also determined that the components in each phase emerge concurrently, and that the phases of emotional development build on each other. Thus, preschoolers need to know about the outward expression of emotions such as facial expressions, and also about external causes of feelings, to be able to fully grasp the components that develop next about the internal, mental features of emotions. Chapters in this book are dedicated to facial expressions and body clues and learning to talk about emotions' causes. Other chapters relating to regulation come later and, as behavioral strategies for regulation (such as taking deep breaths to blow a pinwheel) emerge before cognitive strategies (such as reframing a situation to feel differently about it), there's a focus on tangible and physical strategies for regulation.

Imagine the benefits of these components in an early childhood setting:

➤ When Catasha starts to cry in class, she can recognize that she is sad and tell her teacher how she feels.

➤ When Marco arrives at class jumping up and down, he can share that he is excited that his sister is having a birthday party this afternoon.

➤ Jayden realizes that he would be happy if he could ride the tricycle all recess long, but he can also understand that Kathy would feel sad because then she wouldn't get to ride it at all. He considers taking turns instead.

➤ Leilani accidentally bumps Kerianne on the playground. Because Leilani understands that people's beliefs impact how they feel, she can grasp that Kerianne felt angry because she thought Leilani bumped into her on purpose.

➤ Eric knows that thinking about going fishing with his grandpa can bring back that feeling of joy. When he feels lonely, he heads to the art center to draw his trip to the lake.

While social and emotional learning incorporates many skills that go beyond our emotions—including friendship skills, executive functioning, and social problem-solving—several key social and emotional skills do relate specifically to the understanding of emotions. Understanding others' emotions helps build friendships as we respond in supportive ways. Social problem-solving is easier when children can understand how they are feeling, how others might feel, and how and why those feelings might differ. As Pons and colleagues' research noted, starting with the understanding of external features of emotions and then the mental aspects of emotions allows children to build their understanding of others, which in turn helps with other areas of SEL.

Take a moment to reflect on this second belief. Beyond considering why preschool is the ideal time to teach emotions, think about why *your* classroom is an ideal place to learn about emotions. What will children with these skills be able to achieve or explore in your classroom? What about your instruction and personality will support children's emotional understanding? Exploring this book is a step that shows you are willing to expand your knowledge and are curious about this kind of learning. And those are powerful traits to bring to your class!

Belief 3

Focusing on either social and emotional learning or academics in preschool is a false dichotomy.

Ms. Jennifer and Ms. Alex focus on social problem-solving, teaching children how to identify problems, brainstorm possible solutions, and evaluate those solutions to pick one that will be safe and that everyone will feel okay with. They spend time explicitly teaching children how to use visual supports to recognize the steps of problem-solving and they have children role-play problem-solving scenarios. Then children use the problem-solving process during hours of free play, negotiating problems when two children both want to be the cashier at the dramatic play grocery store. Children solve problems when they both want to put the last piece of the puzzle in and when two children want to use the same magnifying glass in the science center. Later, Ms. Jennifer and Ms. Alex work with children on storytelling, allowing them to brainstorm and choose characters and plot lines. Children identify characters, including a unicorn, and write a story of a playground conflict where the unicorn and her friend want to play on different playground equipment. Children identify a solution the unicorn could try, and, with teacher help, they add text features such as a title, illustrations, and speech bubbles for dialogue. Ms. Jennifer and Ms. Alex note how the children have learned the social and emotional content while also learning and practicing key literacy skills and using text to show meaning. Child-directed play time, teacher-directed lessons, social and emotional content, and literacy learning all come together in this preschool classroom.

One of the biggest challenges of early childhood instruction is juggling the plethora of demands on educators' time. The minutes in a day are not infinite, and there are so many skills to practice, explorations to offer, and situations to coach children through. However, these demands sometimes perpetuate false dichotomies. Teachers and programs sometimes feel like they must choose to *either* focus on social and emotional learning *or* academics, or to *either* focus on play-based experiences *or* teacher-directed instruction. We hear these dichotomies when educators speak about their jobs:

➤ *I don't have time to focus on SEL because there are so many other objectives and standards I need to teach.*

➤ *Our program is focused on academics and kindergarten readiness. There's not much time left to devote to other topics.*

➤ *We teach social and emotional skills through real-world experiences. We don't need explicit instruction on those skills because we have many teachable, incidental moments.*

The reality is, there is room for both. In fact, social and emotional instruction increases academic achievement and supports appropriate academic skills for preschool. SEL also works best when taught through multiple modalities—planning for teacher-directed instruction, offering materials to encourage skill development during child-directed play experiences, and providing social coaching when appropriate moments arise.

Beliefs 1, 2, and 5 all highlight some of the ways SEL has intrinsic value for interpersonal relationships and mental health. There are also additional benefits that impact academics and classroom behavior. Research on these academic benefits of social and emotional learning has revealed benefits for young children all the way through college students (Bridgeland, Bruce, and Hariharan 2013; Ivcevic and Brackett 2014; Reyes et al. 2012; Torres, Domitrovich, and Bierman 2015). Preschoolers who have been taught social and emotional skills, such as self-control and identifying and understanding emotions in oneself and in others:

➤ handle frustration better

➤ have more positive interactions and fewer fights

➤ have more impulse control and focus

➤ achieve more academically

➤ are more likely to have later social and emotional success

In an early childhood classroom, these skills translate directly to an easier time with academic content. Picture a small-group math activity where children are working together to build shapes with straws and pipe cleaners, counting angles and sides. A child who can handle frustration is more likely to persist when the sides fall off her triangle. A child who has more impulse control is able to ask another child for a longer straw and wait, rather than snatching it. A child who has learned to get another child's joint attention can share their work and respond to others' comments. These benefits of social and emotional learning allow children to engage more successfully with any other instruction in various content areas.

Some programs fall on the opposite end of the dichotomy, believing that academics can wait, and that preschool is a time that should be solely devoted to SEL, creativity, and play. However, understanding the academic benefits of social and emotional learning helps illuminate how SEL skills prepare children for further learning and dovetail with academic instruction. For instance, when you teach children to recognize emotion expressions, you are building their observational skills, and when you teach children to think about why a peer might feel an emotion, you are building their deductive reasoning. These skills support academic growth, whether in preschool or in later grades, and support children's ability to interact during play and their creative pursuits. Being able to articulate how academic skills and social and emotional skills are linked dispels the false dichotomy and can provide rationale for social and emotional instruction, regardless of program approach.

The academic benefits of social and emotional learning continue for older children. Upper elementary and high school students who receive high quality social and emotional instruction have:

➤ higher achievement scores (11 points compared with students who do not receive this instruction) and academic performance (Durlak et al. 2011)

➤ more positive attitudes toward school and better school behavior

➤ more motivation to learn

➤ better attendance (Bridgeland, Bruce, and Hariharan 2013)

Given the huge role our emotions and feelings play in our everyday life, it makes sense that emotional understanding and SEL have such a large impact on our academic success, as well as success later in life. After all, our emotional states make it easier or harder to focus and learn. Consider a situation where you felt extremely worried or anxious. Imagine a friend or family member tried to teach you a new skill during that situation. How would you have felt? How much of their lesson would you be able to hear and absorb? When we are not emotionally regulated, new learning just doesn't work well for us, whether we are a child or an adult.

Take a minute to identify how SEL relates to your instruction in literacy, math, science, motor skills, and self-help. What skills about observing, thinking, persevering, and working with others will the children in your group bring into their learning?

As you analyze the skills and concepts taught in this book, you'll also notice how these social and emotional skills foster strands of thinking that will support instruction in other content areas too. For example:

➤ Learning new emotion vocabulary words and using them in context practices key literacy skills.

➤ Looking for clues to how you feel or how others feel is a way to practice skills of observation, which are helpful for scientific inquiry.

➤ Talking about the causes of emotions relates to understanding cause and effect.

➤ Considering how your body feels before and after trying a regulation strategy is a form of comparing and contrasting.

➤ Purposeful reflection, such as asking a child to identify how they knew what they were feeling, encourages children to explain their thinking, similarly to when a child explains how they figured out a math question or how they made a prediction about a story's plot.

Just as literacy has been woven intentionally through all components of the day as teachers create a print-rich classroom, this book encourages the same pervasiveness of emotion discussion, growth, and critical thinking.

Belief 4

Understanding identity and family background will help teachers plan instruction that can be supportive for more children.

Ms. Sarah Catherine works hard to build relationships with children and their families. She visits families at home and invites them into her classroom. She hangs family photos in magnetic frames where children can see them on the board or take them down to keep their families close. She has families share about their cultures, and children and their families make lanyards with the colors of their home countries' flags to decorate the classroom. When one child repeatedly struggles to calm down in her classroom, she works with his mom to brainstorm what could help. His mother shares that she often helps him calm himself by speaking in Spanish. Ms. Sarah Catherine gives the mom a small voice recorder where she records a message to her son, reminding him that he is safe and loved at both home and school. He listens to his recording at school as a tool to regulate; his teacher is nearby and his mom's voice is in his ear. Building strong family relationships opened the door for joint problem-solving to support this child, and he saw how his mom and teacher were working together.

Emotions are heavily intertwined with both our life experiences and cultures. Families, as children's primary context for learning, implicitly and explicitly share views about how children show and respond to emotions. Children bring their families' and cultures' beliefs about how emotions should be discussed and expressed into the classroom. As teachers, we carry our families' and cultures' beliefs and our life experiences about emotions into the classroom with us too. All of these factors combine to form and shape children's background knowledge about emotions. Even without explicit instruction, all children come into the preschool classroom with some understanding of feelings. Observing and discussing emotions with children, as well as connecting with families around emotions, will help us know what emotional strengths and skills children are bringing with them.

Researcher Paul Ekman refers to the social norms about which feelings can be shown and when as "display rules." These rules are normed in individual cultures. Culturally influenced display rules might include minimizing the show of emotion, exaggerating what one feels, or substituting one feeling for another (Ekman 2003).

For example, in the United States, males are often encouraged to minimize the expression of sadness by avoiding crying. In some cultures, showing large outward displays of grief at a funeral is socially acceptable, whereas in others the expectation is to minimize those expressions. Children from cultures that have distinct display rules may bring in messages from home to school. They might have been discouraged from showing emotions or might have been encouraged to minimize certain emotions to avoid making others feel bad. Or perhaps a cultural display rule about exaggerating emotions will mean that a child is very expressive, making it easier for peers to identify how that child is feeling.

Creating an emotion-rich classroom also means that teachers and children are learning new display rules for emotions that may have similarities or differences from the rules of their home. For example, a classroom display rule might include making outward emotion expressions so that your teachers and peers can recognize how you are feeling. As the class practices making emotion expressions, children might be practicing exaggerated facial expressions that are different from those displayed by their families. The display rules of an emotion-rich classroom might also be a change for teachers as they shift to be more intentional about modeling emotions and how to express and handle them. Similarly, cultures differ in how they read nonverbal cues to determine emotions of others. For example, cultures have varying norms about eye gaze, and thus looking directly at others to interpret emotional cues might not be a practiced skill for all children and their families.

Knowing that children and families have a range of emotional display rules, which may or may not match the experience of their teachers, leads to more effective instruction. Having open conversations with families about their beliefs around expressing and discussing emotions helps us know how best to work with families. Asking families, in the context of a supportive relationship, to share which emotions they are more and less comfortable with, which emotions they often recognize in their child, and how those emotions are expressed can bring teachers and families together in supporting children's emotions.

Some questions you might ask as you collaborate with families around emotions:

➤ Which emotions does your child display most often when at home or with family members?

➤ Which emotions do you often show or model for your child?

➤ Are there any emotions you feel less comfortable expressing?

➤ Are there any emotions your child expresses that feel uncomfortable to you?

➤ How do you handle anger or frustration? How does your child handle these emotions?

➤ How do you express joy and affection?

➤ What helps your child calm down when they feel upset?

If you support families around emotion topics during workshops or come-to-school nights, you might enjoy activities that encourage families to reflect on emotions. One idea is to give families photos showing emotional facial expressions and have them sort these visuals into three piles: comfortable expressing and discussing these emotions, somewhat comfortable expressing and discussing these emotions, and uncomfortable expressing and discussing these emotions. You can have families work together to identify similarities or invite families who are willing to share why they feel more comfortable with certain emotions and less comfortable with others. Sharing your own examples of which ones are more and less comfortable for you and why can help to connect with families. You'll find other ideas for activities and family support in each chapter to encourage ongoing conversations as you and your class dive into creating an emotion-rich classroom.

A family whose cultural beliefs include minimizing emotions might be less comfortable with engaging in emotion activities at home. Rather than perceiving this as an unwillingness to support school goals, we can view this as a difference between home and school culture and can engage families in problem-solving through possible cultural mismatches. We can also keep in mind how many things are different between home and school. Behavioral expectations, routines such as napping and mealtime, and communication patterns all tend to have differences between home and school for many or most children, and they learn to adjust and follow the expectations of each environment successfully. Similarly, having different expectations around emotions and expressing them in the two environments doesn't mean children won't learn the emotional skills you are teaching; they'll learn cognitive flexibility as they navigate the differences. In addition, some families who have differing cultural beliefs about expressing and discussing emotions might show interest in learning more about your ideas and beliefs around teaching emotions. Reflecting on your own beliefs and comfort discussing and expressing emotions is also useful; your own culture and family experiences influence how you approach emotions in your own life and in the classroom.

Along with display rules, some research has focused on gender-related differences in emotion learning. When studies looked at how families talk to their children about emotions, they found that female children had more discussion around emotions with their parents than male children did (Adams et al. 1995). Parents in these studies also used more emotion words when talking to daughters, and mothers playing with babies expressed more emotions when playing with daughters. Mothers shared more information about the emotional state itself with daughters than with sons. Instead, sons were more likely to hear about causes and consequences of emotions, like anger, rather than the discussions of *how* emotions feel and are experienced that daughters were privy to (Brody and Hall 1993). Other more recent research has found differences too, including parents using more emotional utterances when discussing sad events with daughters than sons (Fivush et al. 2000) and using a higher proportion of emotion words with daughters than sons (Aznar and Tenenbaum 2015).

Of course, we don't know that this is true for the families of children in our care, but having this information can encourage us to be more mindful in how we are speaking and how we're reinforcing emotions. Collecting data on the use of skills and being intentional about giving positive descriptive feedback to all children about emotions helps us ensure we are not reinforcing gender gaps that may exist outside the classroom. At the same time, these gaps could mean that girls have been exposed to a wider range of emotions, or that boys have more ideas about emotions' causes. These might be areas of strength that children are bringing into the classroom.

Find ideas about how to communicate and solicit family feedback about emotions work in chapters 3–8.

This fourth belief is centered around the idea that all families are trying to do the best for their children, and that learning from and respecting families only strengthens the preschool experience for their children. As you reflect on Belief 4, think about a family with whom you have built a strong relationship and have learned from:

➤ What strengths did that family carry with them?

➤ Families show love and caring in a wide variety of ways. How did you know the family loved and cared for their child?

➤ What steps did you take to make the family feel valued in your classroom?

➤ How did you encourage the family to share information about their home, their culture, their beliefs and values, and the goals they hold for their child?

Belief 5

Instruction in social and emotional skills reduces challenging behavior.

In Ms. West's class, a preschooler touches his classmates. He bumps into them, strokes their hair, and jumps on their feet. His classmates are often annoyed, not wishing to be touched or interpreting his bumps as hostile. But his teachers see the connection between social and emotional skills and those behavioral challenges. Ms. West works with her special education coach to plan strategies to teach this child appropriate touching. They model appropriate greetings, like fist bumps or high fives, and they prompt him to ask before touching. Besides working with him on these skills every day, Ms. West embeds greetings in her morning routine where children greet her and practice using their words to get other children to notice and greet them. Before, the child only knew one way to get peers' attention—by touching. He has now learned several different strategies to interact in ways that are more comfortable for all participants.

Young children need social and emotional competencies to be ready for kindergarten and the years beyond. Having social and emotional skills to draw on when things are hard gives preschoolers another path instead of challenging behavior. When children have learned to ask for a turn and wait, they can refrain from snatching a toy from a classmate. When they have learned to recognize anger in their body, they can take steps to get help or calm down, rather than feeling stuck in a tantrum. When they can see and understand that a peer is upset, they can learn strategies to offer kindness and support. These skills are not innate; children need to learn them through modeling, discussion, and instruction. Children with special needs, such as autism spectrum disorder, may require additional support and individualized instruction, using materials and procedures that build upon their strengths, to learn these skills. And this is exactly why early childhood educators have the important job of both teaching about emotions and creating an environment where these skills and competencies are nurtured in all children.

Even though these skills are so important, research over the last twenty years highlights that there are still large groups of children who do not have these critical skills. Only 40 percent of children had the social and emotional skills needed for kindergarten success, according to the National Academy of Sciences (Yates et al. 2008), and in a Baltimore City Public Schools research study, more than 50 percent of kindergarteners did not have these skills (Bettencourt et al. 2018). Similarly, research has found that approximately 10 to 15 percent of typically developing preschoolers will have mild to moderate levels of behavior problems. Additionally, children with disabilities exhibit three times more incidences of serious challenging behavior. Because challenging behaviors often stem from difficulties with regulating emotions and communicating desires appropriately, these social and emotional skills provide replacement behaviors to decrease instances of challenging behavior, which in turn encourages social inclusion. As early as preschool, young children with challenging behavior are rejected by their peers and provided less positive feedback from their teachers, and these negative outcomes persist in later grades. Children with challenging behavior are less likely to be successful in kindergarten, and there is a high correlation between preschool-age aggression and aggression at age ten (Hemmeter, Ostrosky, and Fox 2006). Children need to learn these social and emotional skills to prevent the challenging behavior that occurs due to a lack of social and emotional competencies.

Children who do not have the skill of recognizing others' emotions struggle to understand the nonverbal elements of conversations. Without understanding, they might interpret accidents as hostile. They might not recognize when another child's body language or tone of voice expresses annoyance or frustration, and therefore, without direct intervention, may continue a behavior that is bothering others. They might not recognize that a story a peer is telling is sad and respond to it with excitement or joy. These kinds of responses, which do not consider how other people feel, can lead to unwanted social interactions, such as classmates not wishing to play or peers thinking that they are being teased. Teachers or parents might perceive these interactions as challenging behavior, and not recognize that emotional skills—or a lack thereof—are causing the negative interactions.

Children who have trouble expressing their emotions in expected ways face similar challenges. For a child who expresses joy with high intensity or volume, peers might accidentally perceive that joy as anger, and stay away instead of sharing in it. For a child who frowns, cries, or rarely smiles, other children might struggle to read the child's emotions and not know if they wish to play, want to be left alone, or are in need of help or support. Both situations are challenging in the classroom. Explicit teaching of emotional competencies, social coaching during interactions, and collecting data to target specific skills are all strategies to teach and build new patterns of interactions.

Reframing challenging behaviors to focus on the emotional skills children need support with can help us figure out social and emotional teaching ideas to reduce instances of challenging behavior. This reframing also helps our mindset, as it transforms a daunting problem into a skill that can be taught—and teaching skills is exactly what teachers are amazing at! The frameworks introduced in chapter 2, particularly the DAPPER framework, offer steps for teaching skills like those listed in the "Possible Skill to Teach" column of figure 1.2.

Consider a child you have worked with who has exhibited challenging behaviors. What social or emotional skills did the child need extra support with? Practice reframing challenging behaviors as missing skills. When you share information about

Figure 1.2 Examples of Reframing Challenging Behaviors into Skills to Teach

Challenging Behavior	Possible Missing Skill	Possible Skill to Teach
Bertha snatches toys from other children.	She doesn't know how to ask for something she wants.	Teach her to sign "My turn" when she wants something.
Arlo pushes other children and runs away on the playground.	He doesn't know how to get peers' attention.	Teach him to tap someone's shoulder, say their name, and say "come play."
When plans change, Veronica cries loudly and does not engage in the new activity.	She doesn't know how to handle disappointment.	Teach her regulation strategies and provide a picture schedule so she knows the next step after calming.
When a toy isn't working the way they think it should, Rowan throws it.	They do not know other ways to express frustration verbally or how to ask for help when frustrated.	Teach them how to indicate they are frustrated and get support with the task or with regulating.

challenging behaviors, whether with colleagues or families, keep Belief 5 in mind. Brainstorm what missing skills are related to the challenging behavior and use those missing skills for planning additional supports. As we shift our focus away from the challenging behavior to how to teach the missing skill, we refocus on the child's strengths and our abilities as educators.

Belief 6

Creating an emotion-rich classroom is both a lot of work and a lot of reward.

When she notices that children look sad but don't know what to say when a classmate takes a toy from them, Ms. Gardner leads small-group practice on saying "please stop" or asking a teacher for help. Mr. Harris's class practices breathing strategies every day as part of their morning routine. Ms. Dunkins has her class match felt emotion pictures with emotion words to practice looking at the faces of others. Ms. Kathy uses plastic pockets to have children trace each other's expressions with dry erase marker, encouraging them to notice facial features in a new way. Ms. Patti reads a book about an upset monkey over and over again, talking children through the steps the monkey takes to calm down. Ms. Lisa makes emotion charts and hangs them up in her room so children can self-identify how they feel. These teachers spend a lot of time and energy making materials, planning lessons, and focusing instruction on emotions and how to manage them. And then they see it. A child says, "I'm sad" for the first time. Another child notices a peer's expression and says, "He's happy." A child tells a classmate that she can breathe, and they take breaths together. The children are getting the skills they'll need every day for their rest of their lives and are using them in these emotion-rich classrooms.

Creating an emotion-rich classroom is not particularly easy. Effective social and emotional instruction is most beneficial when it is planned and ongoing and implemented from preschool all the way through high school. While this book focuses specifically on early childhood, the structures featured here set the stage for ongoing growth. You'll find tools for intentionally planning to teach social and competencies, along with support and ideas for social coaching to ensure that children are practicing these as the school year unfolds.

Rather than a brief emotion unit, or lessons on Feelings Friday, this book aims to foster an emotion-rich classroom where these skills are woven throughout the fabric of the days and weeks. This challenges educators to make space, both literally in the classroom and figuratively in their day, to embed rich emotional literacy activities, discussion, and social and emotional coaching.

Teaching social and emotional skills also requires us to reflect on our own beliefs about emotions and our experiences expressing emotions. Just like being aware of our own implicit biases is a step toward being more equitable practitioners, awareness of our own values and beliefs around emotions is a step toward being able to examine emotions in depth with our classes. This sometimes requires mindset shifts—from distancing ourselves from emotions to accepting and working through them, and from feelings of discomfort around unpleasant emotions to validation and support.

> See the Emotion Mindsets Worksheet at the end of this chapter to reflect on your own mindsets around emotions and brainstorm ways to shift them.

This too can be hard. Many of us are used to trying to avoid unpleasant or difficult emotions, or helping children avoid them. If we picture life as a winding path, challenging emotions such as sadness and anger are like mud puddles along the way. Our instinct might be to throw down a towel so children can bypass the muddy spots without getting wet or dirty—like handing a child his favorite toy to prevent him from screaming with impatience for it. Other times we might try to get a child to ignore the muddy spot by pointing out the nice flowers nearby. We tell a child she doesn't need to be sad that it's not her turn to be line leader because she'll be line leader tomorrow. Sometimes we ignore the mud puddles all together, telling children "you're okay" and moving on without hearing how they feel about their wet feet or muddy clothes. These habits of distraction, ignoring, or minimizing may be deeply ingrained in us, even going back to our own childhoods. And leaning on them can be far easier than confronting emotion head-on. But doing the work to break these habits is worthwhile when our goal is to give children the tools they need to go through emotions rather than around them—like handing them rain boots to jump in the puddle or offering them a paper towel to clean up when they make it to the other side.

In reflecting about this concept in a coaching session, Ms. Walker, a preschool special education teacher, described the difference in mindset. "Instead of making them happy or trying to distract them, we can just let them *own it*. They can own that sadness and we can help them work through it."

Working through emotions, even when it's necessary, can be difficult for both staff and children. As emotional experiences are discussed in the classroom, children might disclose traumatic experiences or situations that spark discomfort in us. For example:

➤ A child explains that she felt sad when a relative hit her.

➤ A child mentions they feel scared when seeing their parents hit each other.

➤ A child says he is lonely when his parents are at work and he is home alone.

Identifying additional supports, such as a social worker, counselor, or administrator, for when these situations arise can also help you to feel prepared to handle challenges and make a daunting or upsetting situation a little easier. Reflect and look up your program's established protocols for handling these kinds of disclosures, which can happen when children share about emotions.

➤ To whom do you need to disclose this information?

➤ What do you need to do to both follow established program protocols and get support for the child?

➤ Which coworkers can provide support to you as you navigate these sensitive topics?

➤ What resources do you have to support children who are handling traumatic situations?

Also consider what a supportive reaction to a disclosure of an uncomfortable situation sounds like. Looking visibly shocked may send the message that it wasn't okay to share that information with you. Instead, a validating response (like those discussed in chapter 5) sends the message that you hear and understand. This might sound like, "It's really hard when that happens" or "I can tell that feels scary to you. Thank you for telling me."

Similarly, who can provide emotional support for *you* as you dive into the world of emotions? It isn't always easy to realize that we might feel guilt or shame more than we like, or to reflect and understand that our emotional reactions are tied to how we were raised, how we've been treated, and what we've experienced. Identify a family member, friend, coworker, or therapist who can help you as you do your inner work to build an emotion-rich classroom.

With all the energy poured into this work, the reward is great. Imagine children being able to say, "I'm sad because I wanted to do a different activity" instead of tantruming. Imagine an angry child identifying a regulation strategy that will help them feel better and trying it with your support. Imagine children noticing a peer is upset and asking how they can help. These skills of expressing emotions, regulating emotions, and supporting others with emotions are used by adults daily. This instruction furthers the journey toward being emotionally competent adults. What a gift!

Wrap-Up

Creating an emotion-rich classroom requires our beliefs to align with our actions. We can teach emotions. Emotion work is important and can coexist with other demands on our time. Our diverse emotional experiences have value. These beliefs make up the foundation of the emotion-rich classroom for ourselves and the children we teach.

As you read through the six beliefs needed for an emotion-rich classroom, you might have found that some already align with your views and some challenge your current mindsets or beliefs. Congratulations on beginning to reflect on your own beliefs and emotional skills as you prepare to dive into this process. Understanding that this work is important, challenging, and introspective will allow you to articulate why you are focusing on emotions. Sharing this *why* with your coworkers, your families, and your class will help create a shared vision for your emotion-rich classroom.

This chapter has focused primarily on why this work matters—for children and for you as a teacher. The next chapter will introduce you to the emotion-rich classroom and the structures for teaching and social coaching that will guide your instruction.

Emotion Mindsets Worksheet

Our mindsets and beliefs about emotions are heavily shaped by our upbringing, our culture, and the messages we have received about how to express and handle emotions. Reflecting on the messages you have been sent around specific emotions can be helpful in realizing what mindsets and beliefs you bring into the classroom.

Work through the list of emotions below, noting how you express each one, messages you might have received, your mindset about the emotion (for example, do you avoid, celebrate, accept, minimize, or distract yourself from this emotion?), and what messages your class might receive based on your mindset. The top row is filled out as an example, and at the end of the form you'll find extra rows to add additional emotions for reflection.

Expression	Messages	Mindset	Impact on the Class
I express **sadness** by crying when I am alone.	Big kids don't need to cry; crying isn't productive/ doesn't help.	Avoidance of being publicly sad.	My class might feel ashamed to cry or express sadness if I pass on this belief.
I express **joy** by			
I express **anger** by			
I express **frustration** by			
I express **sadness** by			
I express **fear** by			
I express **pride** by			

$\longrightarrow$

I express **nervousness** by			
I express **love** by			
I express			
I express			
I express			
I express			

Reflect on your answers. What do you notice about them?

Are there some emotions you feel able to celebrate or express freely? How can you encourage your class to do the same?

→

Are there emotions that you have typically handled by avoiding or distracting yourself from them? What countermessages can you create for yourself to become more comfortable with these emotions and, in turn, help children feel comfortable with them?

The goal for experiencing and handling our emotions is to recognize them, express them in a healthy and useful way, and be able to model or share these experiences and strategies with children, as appropriate. With this in mind, ask yourself the following questions:

For emotions where you use *distraction or avoidance*, what strategies could help you focus on identifying the emotion and choosing a way to address it?

For emotions that you *celebrate or accept*, what messages or strategies do you have or use around these feelings, and how could you apply them when you feel less comfortable emotions?

What are some strategies that you feel will help you shift to moving through the emotions you find more challenging? Some ideas might include mindfulness exercises, talking to a friend or family member, reflecting with a therapist's support, or journaling about your emotions and thoughts.

Chapter 2

Planning for an Emotion-Rich Classroom

Ms. Howell's classroom looks like many other early childhood classrooms whose teachers have done some intentional planning around literacy experiences. She has a cozy, inviting space where children can read on oversized pillows. She has a bookshelf with bright book covers facing the children and baskets labeled by topic ("Going to School," "Friendship," "Eric Carle books," "Animals") on the library area's floor for children to rustle through. She has small, pocket-sized board books and poster-size big books. Next to the easel are books about colors, and books about construction sites are on the shelves near the building blocks. Her felt board has felt bears and bowls of porridge, and her puppet shelf has props children can use as they retell popular folk tales and other stories.

Ms. Howell has also displayed the alphabet around the room. Cubbies are labeled with children's names, with the first letter of each child's name in bright blue. Children use alphabet stamps on envelopes and put them in a pretend mailbox. A group of children play at the water table, using magnetic poles to pull out magnetic letters and then match them on an alphabet chart.

Environmental print is everywhere in Ms. Howell's class. She has logos from familiar stores taped to wooden blocks, and children play at pulling their cars up to popular stores and restaurants from the community. Her dramatic play kitchen has real containers from children's homes, including boxes with labels in other languages and clipboards for children to make shopping lists. She has picture and word labels on her bins, so children can independently reference the labels and put away toys in the correct boxes. Her classroom schedule has pictures and words for each part of the day, and the children read it with her from left to right at group time, talking about what activities will come next.

Ms. Howell reads to her class often, with children comfortably seated around her. She shares books from the curriculum her program uses along with favorites from her collection. When Jennifer brings in her favorite book about ballet, Ms. Howell promises to sit with her and look at it during the transition to rest time. "Books We've Been Reading" are proudly displayed on the family bulletin board so families can ask

children about them. Ms. Howell's classroom environment and her enthusiastic tone convey that her classroom is a print-rich one, filled with a love for literacy. A print-rich classroom is not a new idea for early childhood educators. Teachers have long been intentionally planning ways to weave, embed, and encourage a love for literacy, recognizing the impacts that the environment and teacher attitude have on literacy learning.

What Is an Emotion-Rich Classroom?

When we think about an emotion-rich classroom, the same underlying ideas and supports from creating a print-rich classroom apply. Teachers are weaving in emotion instruction, embedding materials and opportunities to learn and discuss emotions during the day, and fostering a culture of emotional exploration. Just like using environmental print to support literacy, an emotion-rich classroom utilizes pictures of emotion expressions and helps children with recognizing and reading facial cues.

Ms. Davis's classroom looks like Ms. Howell's. It has a cozy library, books around the room, a well-stocked writing area, and alphabet activities. But Ms. Davis has created classroom that's both print-rich and emotion-rich. She has an intentionally designed Regulation Station where children can go to access calming materials when needed. Baskets with labels feature "squishy toys," "soft toys," and "breathing toys" like bubbles and a pinwheel. She has designed the space and taught children how to access and handle those tools.

Ms. Davis has emotions all over her room. She has a mirror by the sink labeled, "What feelings do you see?" She has an emotion check-in chart, where children and teachers self-identify how they feel throughout the day. Student-drawn portraits of emotions like happy and surprised and angry are hanging on a bulletin board. Dolls with emotion expressions sit in dramatic play, blocks with different faces are being stacked on a rug, and children at a table are playing feelings bingo.

When her new computer doesn't turn on, Ms. Davis models how to handle emotions, explaining that she is going to take deep breaths to work through her frustration. She reads books about emotions, sharing times where she has felt like the characters and asking children to share their experiences too. When a child is upset, she supports them in calming down, and encourages them to talk about their feelings. She shares children's learning around emotions with families and asks families to share about emotions and regulation strategies that work at home. The work is planned, the materials are engaging, and her responses to children's emotions match her goal of fostering emotional understanding.

Elements of an emotion-rich classroom include:

➤ a variety of materials used to teach emotions, including many visual supports

➤ adult modeling, including modeling expressions and modeling safe ways to handle big feelings

➤ authentic opportunities to practice expressing emotions and responding to others' emotions

> discussions and validation about a wide range of emotions, sending the message that all emotions are okay to have

> a center or interest area created specifically for supporting regulation, including instruction on how to regulate emotions and express them in a safe way

> individualized emotion instruction to meet the needs of all children in the class

> communication to families about emotional competencies that includes soliciting family feedback

Like a print-rich environment, an emotion-rich environment contains materials, instruction, and experiences that are planned with intentionality. A teacher in an emotion-rich classroom is actively fostering emotional literacy, rather than waiting and responding to emotions only as they emerge. Research suggests that all students should receive at least thirty minutes a week of explicit instruction related to social and emotional learning (Gunter et al. 2012). While a time block of explicit instruction related to emotions is helpful for introducing new skills, it's not enough for young learners. Embedding SEL throughout the preschool day, in a variety of contexts with a variety of instructional strategies, will create an emotion-rich classroom where children's social and emotional development can thrive.

An Introduction to the DAPPER and ICARE Frameworks

This book contains two frameworks that support the creation of an emotion-rich classroom. The first is a planning framework to help ensure intentionality in teaching new skills. This framework, called DAPPER, supports planning an initial introduction to a new skill through demonstrating and describing, animating with visuals and gestures, and supporting children with practicing the new skill. Instead of stopping there, the planning framework goes on to make connections to other parts of the day and other contexts to ensure that skill support doesn't end after that first lesson. These connections include ideas for planning opportunities throughout the day and areas of the classroom, extending the learning into other contexts including home, and reflection and reinforcement. This book guides you through using DAPPER to plan instruction around each emotion skill, but DAPPER's application isn't limited to these emotional competencies. I've supported teachers through this kind of planning for a variety of social and emotional skills, including trading materials, asking for turns, greeting peers appropriately, and solving social problems. Knowing how to plan instruction with best practices in mind is the joy of this framework; it gives you a guided set of steps to teach your class any social and emotional skill.

I developed the DAPPER framework in response to teachers' needs. I'd heard many educators articulate that they weren't sure where to go after introducing a social or emotional skill and the visual to support it, and what I've observed in many classrooms supported the existence of this challenge. Teachers were discussing concepts and using many visuals to support children's learning of all kinds of social and emotional skills, including identifying emotions, calming down, and asking for a turn with materials. Amping up instruction to make sure it was consistently integrated throughout the day was the harder piece. A teacher noted, "I taught them how to take turns with materials, but what if no one wants a turn with a material today? How will I make sure they continue to use the skill?" Knowing that this teacher wasn't alone in needing supports to think through continuous instruction and opportunities for her class, I created the DAPPER framework to encourage those practices and skills. Now answering that question is easy; the teacher has put out materials that require turn taking, sent home turn-taking cards to families to support siblings at home, and filmed children using the skill for the class to watch and discuss. The instruction around the social skills goal of taking turns continues on.

The second framework, ICARE, started through my work with instructional coaches. In their role, coaches were often asked, "Did I handle this situation right?" As a coach, I'm often asked that too and, of course, there isn't one "right" answer. Many coaching conversations have focused on the question "What is your goal for these interactions?" Teachers and coaches identified examples such as children practicing new skills, practicing a more appropriate way to do something, focusing on teaching rather than punishing, and working together to calm before problem-solving. Teachers often also say they want children to feel supported and don't want them to feel as if the teacher is "taking sides." From these conversations came the ICARE framework, which gives teachers steps to practice effective social coaching, and gives coaches a tool to use with teachers to reflect on whether a situation worked to meet their goals.

DAPPER and ICARE are not the only ways to approach SEL planning and coaching. Rather, they offer structures to help you keep in mind crucial pieces as you navigate planning and also seize moments for incidental teaching. It might feel overwhelming to think about having two new frameworks to learn and practice, but as you read through them you will probably notice elements you are already implementing or thinking about in your daily work. Also, please note that you do not need to have these frameworks' steps memorized by heart. You can use the "DAPPER Planning Sheet" to keep the categories in mind as you plan and you can review both frameworks using the "DAPPER Summary Sheet" and the "ICARE Summary Sheet."

As for ICARE, a teacher I was coaching opted to print out the framework and hang it on the bulletin board so she had "backup" if she needed support handling a conflict between children. Just like we provide children with visuals and structures to remember routines, such as pictures of handwashing steps, the frameworks provide us with written structures that remind and encourage us to use practices that support learning. Each chapter,

After you read about the DAPPER framework, consider revisiting your reflection notes on Belief 5 from chapter 1. How could you use DAPPER to teach the new skill the child might need?

including this one, has examples illustrating the frameworks to help you see DAPPER and ICARE in real-life situations like those that you face each day in your work.

The DAPPER Planning Framework

Intentionally planning and supporting children's emotional development requires more than implementing a few activities and having several discussions about feelings. Rather, creating an emotion-rich classroom is about high-quality instruction, teaching practices, and responding to incidental moments with social coaching. The DAPPER framework supports teachers in planning robust instruction that extends beyond a whole-group lesson so that teaching social and emotional skills is woven throughout the day. Chapters 3 to 8 focus on specific emotional skills and provide suggestions and options for each DAPPER component, where each letter stands for a specific element of teacher instruction and planning.

D is for both **demonstrate** and **describe**. Modeling is a useful tool for supporting children with learning a new skill, as they get to see that skill in action. *Only* demonstrating a skill, however, would be a missed opportunity; combining demonstration with a verbal description supports children in understanding what they see. For example, instead of asking "Can I play with you?" and having children watch, adding description allows them to hear your thought process and understand the context. "I really want to play with him. He doesn't know I want to play. Maybe I should ask him. I'll go over to him and say his name and ask if I can play." In this situation, demonstrating while describing what the skill is and how you might use it gives children extra context to understand the skill and try it on their own in real situations.

A is for **animate**. Animators take an idea and draw it, and then bring it to life with gestures and actions. In DAPPER, the *animate* step is similar. It incorporates using visual supports and referencing gestures, motions, and signs. While there are many ways to animate a concept, such as videos and role play, the goal for the animate step is to use simple, low-tech visuals and gestures so that children can easily access visuals and be prompted using gestures. Additional supports that show concepts visually are included in each chapter's activity ideas.

Consider your own use of daily visual supports. Maybe you reference a calendar to remember what to get done for the day, or you use a speed limit sign to adjust your own driving behavior. Visuals provide an extra cue in the environment to help remind us of behaviors and routines. Visuals, including gestures and signs, also provide a way to communicate for children who may struggle to find their words verbally. Additionally, visuals provide a stepping-stone toward independence. In the above example of asking another child to play, without introducing visuals or gestures, we might see a child ask another child verbally or not ask at all. With the support of visuals, we might see a child bring a play-related visual to a teacher for assistance. We might see a child bring that visual to another child, or they might use a sign or gesture that we teach before the verbal fluency comes. Teaching visuals, gestures, and signs are all ways to encourage independent steps as children learn new social skills.

P is for **practice**. As new skills are taught, practicing offers children immediate opportunities to try the skills for themselves. It also provides a chance for coaching or feedback from a teacher or peer to promote growth. Demonstrating a new skill without offering a chance for children to try it feels like offering a meal with no plate or utensils. Children might be interested and intrigued by what you've shown them, but do not have a chance to try it out for themselves. Finding opportunities to practice, especially soon after the introduction and demonstration of the skill, encourages children's use of the skill.

Several approaches to SEL focus only on these steps: teach a skill with modeling and pictures, and then practice. These steps do support teachers in planning initial lessons to teach new social and emotional skills, but the big question then is "I taught that first lesson, showed visuals, and every child practiced . . . now what?" There are additional steps that help the teaching move from a single introductory lesson to an ongoing, intentional habit of building a classroom abundant in social skill teaching. These steps are needed to create an emotion-rich classroom. The next three letters in the DAPPER acronym illuminate these additional steps.

The next **P** is for **planned opportunities**. Teachers can plan activities, introduce materials, or prompt children to use their emerging skills outside of the initial teaching and modeling. This serves several purposes. First, children need many opportunities for trying out new skills, becoming more independent with skills, and receiving feedback on their use of skills. Second, planning opportunities is a rich thought exercise for teachers. This kind of planning involves thinking through when and where children might need to use a social skill and anticipating what supports or materials might help them do this successfully. Planned opportunities offer chances for teachers to check in during naturally occurring moments and play-based activities to see where children are with a skill and offer support and feedback. Similarly, planning many and varied learning opportunities for a single skill is a step to embedding the skill into the emotion-rich classroom. Rather than only talking about emotions during teacher-directed activities, planning materials and provocations around emotions offers children new ways to explore the concepts they're learning.

E is for **extend**. Extending new skills you're teaching has several components and involves a variety of contexts and people. When doing this step, you're preparing and encouraging children to practice their skills outside your classroom, and also preparing other key adults to support this practice. This might mean having children use new emotion vocabulary words in a speech therapy session or with an art teacher. It could be extending a skill learned in the classroom to outside on the playground or on the bus. Extending also includes social coaching, encouraging the use of the skills in naturally occurring situations. And because learning extends past the school hours, ideas for connecting home and school around each skill are provided too. Suggestions for family communication, soliciting family feedback, and family activities for working on the skills are featured in each chapter. Families are informed about classroom instruction, encouraged to celebrate children's newly emerging skills, and asked to share information and feedback about what children are learning and what strategies are effective for teaching their child.

And lastly, **R** is for **reinforce and reflect**. Providing positive descriptive feedback when children use a skill and supporting children's reflection on their use of a skill both reinforce the behaviors and growth you wish to see. Positive descriptive feedback means giving children feedback on a desired behavior, with positive nonverbal cues as well. For instance, consider a child in a classroom who walks over to a friend who has fallen and helps them up. You might smile at the helper, or offer a simple "good job." While the smile and the words both offer positive feedback, the child would still have to translate this feedback to figure out how it relates to their actions. Was "good job" for walking in the classroom instead of running? Was it for helping a friend? What "job" is my teacher referring to?

Giving positive descriptive feedback takes out the guesswork, as it connects a behavior or action with the feedback and is specific. "That was kind when you helped her up," also provides positive feedback, illuminating the behavior that was supportive. Similarly, shifting from statements of judgment ("nice" or "good" or "I like how you . . .") to statements that simply describe actions makes them less about complying with adult notions of "good" or "nice" and more focused authentically on the child and their learning.

To turn positive feedback into positive descriptive feedback, comment on the child's specific behavior and, when appropriate, the impact. For example, "Angela, you told me you were sad. Using the word *sad* really helped me understand how you are feeling." "Wow, you remembered the word *disappointed* that we talked about. Yes, the character does seem disappointed when he isn't invited to the party." "You signed '*mad*.' I can tell by your sign and your face that you are really mad." For children who have trouble processing a lot of language, you might limit your positive descriptive feedback statements to just the action—"You said '*sad*'"—and give a big smile or thumbs up to get across that the behavior is helpful.

This feedback gives children a greater awareness of their behaviors and actions. Hearing it in a positive tone from an adult who cares about them sends the message that it is a helpful behavior for the classroom. And getting this kind of feedback also helps a child build their own narrative. "You used your emotion words" translates into "I did it! I used my emotion words and it helped!"

Rather than focusing on external tangible reinforcers, this book will give ideas and examples of how to use your connection with the child and your noticing of the child's skill to send the message of "You did it!"

Taking this even further, prompting reflection allows children to begin to tie together their actions with the naturally occurring social reinforcers, such as how they felt after they calmed down or how a classmate felt when they responded to their emotions.

Figure 2.1 Components of the DAPPER Framework

What are the DAPPER components?	How do I put them into action?
Demonstrate and Describe	Model the targeted skill; verbally describe your behavior and thinking as you work through the skill.
Animate	Use both visuals and gestures to help children remember and access the skill.
Practice	Have children practice the skill, whether through role play or other activities, soon after you introduce it. Give feedback and support.
Planned Opportunities	Intentionally plan opportunities or activities that will encourage the use of the skill. These opportunities can be in any context or content area. Consider reminding children about the skill and how to do it as the activity is beginning.
Extend	Think about and plan how to encourage the use of the skill with different people or in different settings. This includes sharing information with families so children can access the skill at home and using the ICARE framework to encourage using the skills in new contexts.
Reinforce and Reflect	Use positive descriptive feedback to describe when children are using the skill and to celebrate. Ask reflection questions to encourage children's thinking about their skills.

DAPPER in Action: A Classroom Scenario

Chapters 3 through 8 walk you through the DAPPER framework to create a plan for teaching key emotional skills, including recognizing emotions, using regulation strategies, and responding to the emotions of others. For now, let's walk through an example of teaching a new social skill using the DAPPER framework. You'll notice how Mr. George, a public-school preK teacher, uses DAPPER to respond to a challenging situation in his classroom, keeping his focus on teaching the new skills that the children in his group need, rather than only trying to stop a challenging behavior.

Mr. George notices that a couple children are approaching peers and growling at them on the playground. Their peers turn and run away, and the children chase them. Some of the peers are okay with this kind of play. Three other children are talking about how they don't like the growling because it is scary, but they do want to run and play without those sounds. Mr. George sits with his team and plans through how to teach children a different way to ask others to chase them.

Notice that Mr. George did not tackle this brainstorming completely on his own. In this case, he worked with his teaching team who had also noticed the children's responses to the playground growling. Together, they planned out steps to shift the behavior toward the new skill of inviting others to play. The intentionality of walking through the DAPPER framework with his colleagues means Mr. George has a plan for teaching and reinforcing this skill. While the first three steps are part of his mini-lesson the next day (Demonstrate and Describe, Animate, and Practice), he uses the last three steps (Planned Opportunities, Extend, and Reinforce and Reflect) over the next week

Figure 2.2 Example of the DAPPER Components in Action

DAPPER Components	Mr. George's Notes
Demonstrate and **D**escribe	Demonstrate how to call a peer's name, say "Will you chase me?" and then run. Describe behaviors when modeling, such as saying the peer's name loudly enough and from a close enough distance, waiting until the peer is facing you, then saying "Will you chase me?" Describe that some peers might say yes and chase, and others might say no/not want to chase. Model with Ms. Miller saying no and then try with someone else.
Animate	Visuals: Create pictures of the steps of saying peer's name, saying "Will you chase me?" and then running. Gestures: Use hands to beckon toward the body, like saying "come," when asking.
Practice	Do this lesson outside so we can practice right away. In pairs, have a child ask their partner to chase, and have the partner respond. Let them run and then "freeze" and come back over and try again. Maybe use stickers—blue stickers ask green sticker partner first, then come back and have green ask blue next. Then have them try one last time before recess starts, this time asking anyone they want.
Planned Opportunities	Puppet play: Have puppets chase each other. Make movie of visual and asking to chase. Share with the other class that is outside sometimes with us. Send home movie to families to see this new skill in action. Differentiation: Jade will need her own set of visuals to show peers or practice with "chase me" because "Will you chase me?" is a long utterance for her. Let SLP know we are working on this with her.
Extend	Tell Coach Rhodes that we are working on this skill in case it would be useful for PE class. Take visual to PE and outside so that children can access. Share with the afterschool staff. Draw visuals of the steps on the ground with chalk outside and have children help illustrate.
Reinforce and **R**eflect	Reinforce: "You remembered to ask her to chase you!" "You used his name and waited for him to turn to you." Reflect: "Who used *Will you chase me*? today? Did it work? How did your partner feel?"—ask while waiting to wash hands when coming inside.

to make sure that the newly introduced skill is being supported in multiple ways and in multiple settings.

Learning a whole new framework can be overwhelming. Consider which DAPPER components you are already using with your class. You'll likely find that some of the practices are already familiar to you, even if you haven't explicitly used this framework before. Chances are you have used modeling to teach a new skill or have used visuals to animate skills before, for instance.

As you work through the book's chapters and make instructional decisions, you might find it useful to record them on the DAPPER Planning Sheet, which you'll find at the end of this chapter. It's helpful to make quite a few copies of the planning sheet from the start, as you may use one for each skill you teach. Consider keeping your planning sheets together in a planning book or binder. While you might have new children with new needs next year, or you might need to revisit certain skills as the year progresses, you'll have your plans to tweak, rather than starting from scratch.

The ICARE Framework for Social Coaching

One component of extending a skill is providing social coaching in situations where children can use the skill to problem solve. When two children have a conflict, and one ends up with hurt feelings, the children can be coached to use the skill of recognizing and responding to others' emotions. Similarly, when children are having trouble expressing emotions in a socially appropriate way, ICARE can be used to coach a child to try an interaction again with a skill such as using emotion vocabulary or explaining how their body is feeling. For social coaching in the moment, ICARE is a framework to prompt and support children in accessing social skills when they are needed most.

While DAPPER is a framework explicitly for planning instruction, ICARE is about supporting children through problems in a way that fosters connection and encourages the use of emotional skills. ICARE can be a great framework to share and practice with families so they can provide social coaching to their children as well.

I is for **intent**. This is an inner step for teachers as they enter a situation where a child, or multiple children, could benefit from their coaching. The step requires analyzing what the child is trying to communicate with their behavior to determine their intent. For example, Leesa kicked Elizabeth when Elizabeth said, "You can't have this toy. I'm using it." Leesa is likely attempting to communicate disappointment in not getting a turn with a desired material. A child who yells at another child, "You can't come to my birthday party!" is likely attempting to communicate anger or hurt feelings.

When we adults pause to focus on the message behind the challenging behavior, our coaching path becomes clearer. We understand that the child needs help expressing frustration or disappointment more safely or appropriately. If there's one thing that teachers are great at, it's teaching new skills. Analyzing the intent allows us to see the skill that is missing from the situation and gives us clarity in what we can redirect the child to do.

This step also begins the coaching process because it shifts our mindset. Seeing a child hit another child can bring up feelings of worry, frustration, or hopelessness in us. We are concerned about the children's safety, worried about our ability to keep each child in our care safe, possibly frustrated that our instruction hasn't yet been effective for the child who hits a peer, or feeling as if we simply don't know what to do. Seeing the intent behind the behavior shines some empathy on the situation. We might not kick people when we feel disappointed, but we have been disappointed before. We probably can remember a time when we were disappointed and didn't handle our emotions in the most appropriate way. Acknowledging that a child is struggling with expressing disappointment at this moment in time can be relatable for us. Our mindset shifts from seeing the behavior as a problem to seeing it as an opportunity to teach a skill that the child is currently missing.

C is for **calm**. In this step, you'll first check your *own* body to make sure you are calm before entering the situation with the child. If you are feeling too frustrated or upset to be able to see the situation with positive intent, that's a sign that you need to regulate before coaching. Being calm when entering the situation decreases the likelihood for shaming or blaming a child for having strong emotions. Avoiding statements of shame and blame (such as "You don't need to cry about it!" or "If you had just listened to directions, you wouldn't be so upset right now.") opens the door for the child to connect with you and receive your support in working through the emotions. If you aren't calm enough to coach a child through it, handle any immediate safety concerns and then come back to discuss the situation with the child later once you are calm.

Second, help any children who are feeling strong emotions with calming down so that they can access the parts of their brain needed for problem-solving. You might choose to use a calming strategy that you've already taught children (the focus of chapter 6), use the Regulation Station (the focus of chapter 7), or take deep breaths yourself near the child to help the child's breathing regulate. Sometimes children aren't particularly upset but the problem still warrants coaching through it. You can ask children to read their body clues (a skill from chapter 4) to identify that they are calm before moving through the other steps.

A is for **acknowledge**. In this step, you'll offer validation and empathy by acknowledging the child's feelings or desires and describing the situation objectively. The goal of this step is to send the message, "I understand." This can sound like a validating response (one focus of chapter 5), such as telling Leesa, "It's hard when you want to play and it's not your turn." It might also sound like "You were so frustrated that she wouldn't play with you, so you told her she couldn't come to your birthday party." The acknowledgment step is free of judgment. You're sending the message that you get it; you see the intent behind the behavior.

R is for **rewind**. Rewinding means trying the situation again with a prosocial skill. For example, to rewind after Leesa kicked Elizabeth, you might say, "Kicking isn't safe; it hurts. Let's try a different way to handle that disappointment you're feeling." You might offer choices to Leesa if she has multiple tools in her repertoire: using words to express disappointment, going to the Regulation Station to try a calm-down strategy, drawing a picture of how she feels, or perhaps offering a toy to Elizabeth for a trade. For children who are just learning the skill of appropriately handling disappointment, you might only prompt the child to do one strategy, rather than offering choices. Then you coach and encourage the child to try the situation in this prosocial way, offering support so that the child is successful.

E is for **echo**. This step is the recap step, where you offer positive descriptive feedback. You might notice and verbally share what happened and how the child (and other children) responded. "You told her with your words that you were disappointed. Now she knows how you feel, and your bodies were safe when you told her. You did it!" In the example with Leesa and Elizabeth, the focus on echoing is drawing Leesa's attention to the skill she tried and how it worked, rather than lecturing about how kicking isn't a safe choice. This step reinforces the safe, prosocial way to work through problems.

Figure 2.3 Components of the ICARE Framework

What are the ICARE components?	How do I put them into action?
Intent	This step is an inner step. Consider what children were trying to express in the situation. Reframe the situation so that you can see the behavior as representing their need for your assistance to use a more appropriate skill.
Calm	Check your own body to make sure you are calm when entering the interaction. Then help children to calm big feelings if needed before working through the situation.
Acknowledge	Use a validating response to acknowledge what children were wishing for or trying to express.
Rewind	Encourage children to redo the situation using a social and emotional skill you have been working on (such as asking for a turn or expressing emotions with words).
Echo	Verbally, or with visual and gestural support, echo back what happened and what the outcome was. This usually includes positive descriptive feedback for trying the situation in a new way and notes how the situation worked or how the participants felt.

ICARE in Action: A Classroom Scenario

More example scenarios where ICARE can be used to support emotional competencies are in chapters 3 through 8. Unlike DAPPER, which is a planning framework to help you proactively plan out social and emotional instruction, ICARE is a response framework used to harness situations and turn them into teachable moments. Let's look at a sample situation through an ICARE lens.

Henry approaches Cole and asks if he wants to play with trains. Cole says no and turns back to his block castle. Henry asks Rosalina, who also says no. Henry gets increasingly frustrated, and he demands that Noah plays trains with him, instead of asking. Noah tells Henry to stop yelling at him and says he doesn't want to play trains. Henry throws the train he is holding and begins to cry. Mrs. Hambright approaches Henry, keeping the ICARE steps in mind to support him through his emotions and problem-solving.

Figure 2.4 Example of the ICARE Components in Action

ICARE Components	Teacher Response
Intent	Mrs. Hambright realizes Henry is likely feeling lonely and disappointed and doesn't know how to handle those feelings.
Calm	She checks her own body, making sure she is calm before interacting with Henry. She knows Henry created "choo-choo breathing" when they practiced breathing techniques and that this helps him. She sits nearby, taking choo-choo breaths, exhaling like a train. Henry looks up when he hears her, and his breathing starts to match hers. When she sees Henry is calm, Mrs. Hambright starts to offer verbal support.
Acknowledge	"You were really wishing to play trains with a classmate today. It's hard when you can't find someone to play. You seem really disappointed," she tells him. He nods and explains that he really wanted a partner to be the red train while he used the blue one.
Rewind	Mrs. Hambright decides to offer choices to help Henry use social skills they have been practicing. "Would you like to ask another child to play trains now that you are calm and can keep the trains safe? Or would you rather join a friend in another center and come back to trains after nap?" Henry chooses to ask Ms. Bien, the instructional assistant, because "she likes to be the red one when we play." Mrs. Hambright has Henry practice with her through role play. Henry asks, "Will you please come and be the red train with me?" Henry then goes and asks Ms. Bien, who says she will come to the trains after she washes her hands.
Echo	Mrs. Hambright echoes back the situation to Henry while he waits. "Wow, you wanted her to play, and you asked with kind words and a soft voice. She said yes. You calmed your body after classmates said no to get ready to ask someone else. You did it!"

You might notice that there are many ways for Mrs. Hambright to encourage a new skill. She could rewind and remind Henry that when we want to play with others, we can ask to join in their play. She could have had Henry brainstorm ways to use his love for trains to sit at the art table next to Noah and make train art. Like most situations, there's not just one way to help a child rewind to use a new skill. Mrs. Hambright also realized that Henry's frustration made it hard for him to ask appropriately, and thus practicing asking someone to join in might support him with that skill, so she offered it as one of the choices. At its core, the ICARE framework is about regulating our emotions, as adults and children, so we are able to focus our energy on problem-solving and practicing social skills. Rather than teaching a lesson through punishment, ICARE teaches children that adults will help them find a path through the upset.

"The ICARE framework helps children and adults build trust. This creates a pattern where children know that they can go to adults to get support with problems. Trusting adults to help is a skill we want them to have for life."

—Ruthann, preschool special education teacher

Reflect on how you currently coach children through problems in the classroom. What components of ICARE do you recognize when you reflect on your current practices?

For easy-to-reference summaries of DAPPER and ICARE, see the DAPPER Summary Sheet and ICARE Summary Sheet at the end of this chapter.

Formative Assessment in the Emotion-Rich Classroom

Teaching each emotion skill in the context of DAPPER encourages teachers to use many evidence-based strategies. Just like any other skill, you'll want to monitor if children are learning these skills and beginning to apply them. Assessing children's progress may be formal, using an assessment tool your program has, but also can be informal based on observing children during activities, routines, interactions, and play.

Each skill in chapters 3 through 8 has an associated data collection sheet for recording emerging skills and analyzing the data to determine your next instructional steps. You might use your data to:

➤ monitor children's learning

➤ decide what to teach next

➤ group children for small-group practice

➤ individualize lessons for children who need more support

➤ share children's skills with administrators and related service providers

➤ celebrate social and emotional growth with families

➤ document your personal reflection and implementation of instruction

Some skills are discrete. For example, if a child is asked to choose the letter M from three letters, teachers would watch and record that the child did or did not select the correct letter. For social and emotional competencies, skills tend to be less discrete. Because these skills have many steps, yes/no data collection isn't the most useful. Two strategies that may be helpful for monitoring and assessing how children are acquiring these skills are *task analysis* and *levels of assistance* recording (that is, recording what kind of support was needed).

Task Analysis

In task analysis, skills are broken down into their core steps. Teachers can collect data on which steps children complete and which they do not yet complete, jotting down notes, for example, about whether children use visuals, verbal responses, or gestures and signs.

One strategy to build emotional literacy in the early childhood classroom is to have a chart with pictures representing different emotion expressions. Children are encouraged to identify how they feel using the pictures on the chart, and often they place their name or photograph near the emotion that best matches their own feelings. To assess the skill of using an emotion check-in chart, Mr. Powell creates a task analysis with the following four steps. Note that this data sheet captures how one child completes the steps with notes about supports needed, rather than storing documentation for the entire class.

Figure 2.5 Sample Task Analysis Data Sheet

Child's Name: Hector		
Skill Being Taught: Using the emotion check-in chart		
Step	**Does the Child Complete the Step?**	**Notes**
1. Goes to the chart during check-in time	Yes	
2. Picks up own picture	Yes	
3. Places picture under choice	Yes	After I prompt ("Make your choice")
4. Responds to "How are you feeling?" with choice that they have selected	No	Signs happy when asked, but selected calm on the chart

This kind of task analysis allows teachers to reflect on which additional supports a child might need. For this example, Mr. Powell might choose a strategy to support the child with making their choice *without* teacher prompting. The chosen strategy could be extra practice, extra teacher modeling, a visual prompt attached to the picture, having the child watch a video model, or pairing the child with a peer who can support them with routine completion. Or Mr. Powell might choose, instead, to focus on the fourth part of the task analysis to encourage the child to match their signed answer with the emotion they indicated on the chart. He might work with the child to practice emotion vocabulary, encourage the use of signs, or have the child match the emotion receptively by offering visual choices for the child to select when asked what they selected on the chart.

Levels of Assistance Recording

A second strategy for monitoring skill acquisition is recording the support provided for the child. Rather than recording whether a child completes the step or not, the recording focuses on how much assistance or support the child requires. One example might be measuring whether children are able to go to the Regulation Station and choose a calming strategy when upset. Instead of recording yes or no, teachers can record the level of assistance that is needed. For multistep skills, this recording will also include task analysis describing how much assistance is needed for each step.

In figure 2.6, three children's ability to do these steps toward calming down are recorded as independent, verbal, or physical, referring to the support needed from a teacher—none (independent); spoken directions (verbal); or a teacher guiding them, holding their hand, or offering hand-over-hand support (physical). For example, Emmanuel was upset. His teacher asked what he could do about it, and he independently went to the Regulation Station. He then sat there crying, and didn't choose a calm-down strategy or prop. When his teacher prompted him verbally ("Would the frog help you calm down, or do you want to do dinosaur breaths?"), he chose to squeeze a frog toy. Then, without further prompting, he squeezed the toy until he regained a sense of calm. This kind of recording can show the level of support each child in a class needs on one data recording sheet.

Figure 2.6 Sample Data Sheet for Recording Levels of Assistance Needed with Task Steps

Child's Name	Step: Going to Regulation Station	Step: Choosing a Calm-Down Strategy	Step: Using Strategy to Calm Down	Notes
Emmanuel	**Independent** Verbal Physical	Independent **Verbal** Physical	**Independent** Verbal Physical	Chose frog when offered choice; squeezed it and came out of the station after 3 minutes
Reagan	**Independent** Verbal Physical	**Independent** Verbal Physical	**Independent** Verbal Physical	Upset at drop-off, went to station, used sensory bottles, and came out when morning meeting started
Yasmine	Independent Verbal **Physical**	Independent Verbal **Physical**	Independent Verbal **Physical**	Cried when art center was full, agreed to go to station. I held her hand and guided her there, helped her pick breathing choice, and then held her hands to do butterfly breathing. Stayed with her and then came out together.

Each of the next six chapters has ideas on how to collect formative assessment data to guide instruction around emotional competencies. Using this data with members of your team, such as administrators, assistants, and other teachers you plan with, can help you brainstorm next steps for supporting all children in gaining these skills. Using individual child data with members of a child's team, such as related service providers and family members, can help the team decide on next steps for practice and celebrate the growth that your data shows over time.

For blank data sheet templates corresponding to the skills discussed here, see the Task Analysis Data Sheet and Data Sheet for Recording Levels of Assistance Needed with Task Steps at the end of this chapter.

Supporting Families with Their Child's Emotional Development

Three factors play into young children's emotional competency: teachers' instruction on emotional literacy, the child's temperament and individual development, and parental or familial support. While teachers cannot change a child's temperament, instruction on emotional literacy is within the teacher's control, and this book supports that instruction and focus. Observation and data collection, as well as prompts to differentiate instruction, will help teachers provide scaffolding to support individual children's development. The third component of family involvement can be fostered by educators. Teachers can share what they are working on in the classroom, provide resources around social and emotional development, and suggest at-home activities that encourage these skills. Teachers can also incorporate input and information from families about their norms into their in-class instruction to bridge home and school.

Chapters 3 through 8 present examples of how you might summarize new skills in a family newsletter, ways teachers can use videos to help families see the skill in action, ideas for family activities to do at home, and notes about how families can see evidence of emotion learning in the classroom. Family engagement is more meaningful when it flows both ways, with information coming from school to home and from home to school. Ideas about ways to harness families' strengths and solicit their feedback are included in these chapters too.

An Introduction to Terminology: Feelings Versus Emotions

Almost all of us use the words *feelings* and *emotions* interchangeably. This is common in the language we use with children and in the products and tools we use when teaching emotions. You might have a "feelings chart" or an "emotions book," and the differences between the content might be nonexistent. But there are, in fact, differences between feelings and emotions.

The term *emotions* refers to biochemical responses to stimuli in our environment. They are physical and instinctive and are, at first, unconscious. *Feelings*, in contrast, arise from our brain perceiving emotions and giving meaning to them; these are conscious.

In summary, emotions stem from our interpretation of what's happening around us. This can be through sensory input (like hearing a noise), or through a memory we have, or an interaction we have. Emotions are often a warning system; they typically encourage us to act, such as fleeing or fighting, and our bodies respond with physiological changes. Emotions are relatively fleeting.

Feelings, on the other hand, are responses to emotions and are more nuanced. For example, I have a conversation with a friend who keeps ignoring boundaries and I experience the emotion of anger. In turn, I might have other feelings related to that situation and emotion. Perhaps I feel disrespected or underappreciated. Those feelings are my internal reaction to the original angry emotion.

There are also other words that often get thrown into the *emotions* and *feelings* mix that really describe physical sensations. For example, we can feel hungry, thirsty, sick, achy, or tired. These physical sensations represent physiological needs, such as for food or sleep. While we do say, "I feel tired," tiredness and other physical sensations aren't the same as emotions or feelings. A sensation of hunger can lead to many feelings. I might feel excited that lunch is coming. I might feel disappointed that I woke up too late for breakfast. But that hunger itself, technically, is not a feeling.

This chart outlines the six basic emotions identified through Paul Ekman's research, as well as some examples of feelings related to those emotions, and some examples of physical sensations (Paul Ekman Group, n.d.).

Figure 2.7 Examples of Emotions, Feelings, and Physical Sensations

Emotions	Feelings	Physical Sensations
joyful	lonely	hungry
afraid	disappointed	pained
angry	loved	exhausted
surprised	bored	thirsty
sad	excited	drowsy
disgusted	proud	achy

For this book, I'll use the words *emotions* and *feelings* interchangeably, just as most of us do when talking to children. You'll notice that we'll be teaching children to recognize emotions (physiological changes) and to talk about feelings (the conscious expressions of those emotions), rather than focusing on sensations such as hunger. While children might answer "How do you feel?" with "tired," you can encourage them to dive a little deeper. Does feeling tired mean they are disappointed they had to wake up so early? Are they excited to get to rest? Are there other feelings related to the physical sensations they're experiencing?

Roadblocks to Setting Up an Emotion-Rich Classroom

After years of visiting teachers in a hundred different classrooms, I've noticed some common situations where emotion instruction gets stuck. Here are some of these stories for you to consider as you start to set up an emotion-rich classroom and continue to reinforce emotional competencies.

While early childhood best practices include having clear expectations for children's behavior, we want to ensure that rules are not dictating how children feel. Often, you'll see posters with common rules like "use gentle touches" or "walking feet inside," or broader expectations such as "be responsible" with an illustration of a child putting toys away on a shelf. One classroom I visited had followed the general guidelines for having a limited number of positively stated expectations, and one of these expectations was around emotions. Nestled between listening ears and gentle touches was "be happy." The classroom rule dictated how children were supposed to feel. This would be impossible to enforce and, for most of us adults, impossible to model consistently.

This classroom visit was a reminder for me to think through times where we accidentally reinforce the notion that only positive feelings are allowed. For example, the rule of "be happy" implies there is no room in the classroom for other feelings. Feeling sad or angry or frustrated would, technically, be against the rules of the classroom. At other times, I've seen popular classroom decor with similar slogans about "don't worry; be happy" or "welcome to our happy place." Consider the messaging around emotions when choosing rules or hanging up classroom art. Perhaps "all emotions are welcome here" would be a better classroom bulletin board sentiment to reinforce the beliefs on which an emotion-rich classroom is centered.

Consider visiting other classrooms and touring your own classroom space with fresh eyes. Look at classroom rules, classroom decorations, and photographs you have around your space. What messages do you see about emotions? What emotions are not portrayed at all in your classroom?

There are times when our instructional decisions do not match our goals for normalizing a range of emotions in the classroom. One example is the use of happy and sad icons to represent other concepts. In one classroom, happy and sad faces were used to represent yes and no. When children were asked a question of the day, such as "Do you have a pet?" they would put their name under the happy or sad pictures. This is potentially confusing, as you could have a pet, like a cat that scratches you, and be sad about it. Or you might not have a pet and be perfectly content with that family choice. Conflating emotions with yes and no is confusing. Happy isn't a "yes" feeling with sad being a "no" feeling; it is acceptable to be sad too.

At other times, happiness and sadness are conflated with safety or its absence, or are paired with judgment. One teacher led a sorting activity focused on reinforcing acceptable classroom behaviors and unacceptable classroom behaviors. She had children sort picture cards under "happy" or "sad." When she asked a preschooler to place the "clean up" card under happy or sad, she placed it under sad, and shared that she was sad when it was time to clean up. The teacher's intention was that it would be under happy, as a socially acceptable and helpful classroom behavior. In our coaching conversation, we discussed her goals related to the activity and what she was really trying to get at (helpful versus hurtful and safe versus unsafe) and how happy and sad didn't quite match up with those intended messages. The disconnect was clear when the preschooler spoke about her personal feelings, rather than addressing whether the behavior was helpful or hurtful. This teacher and I imagined that there could easily be other disconnects in the day as well. Waiting in the line for lunch is a helpful behavior, but a child might easily feel sad or disappointed to have to wait. Lying on a cot mat at school is a helpful behavior for naptime, but might be a sad time of the day for a child whose body needs less rest. Similarly, a child running around the classroom might feel exuberantly happy, even if the teacher would identify that as a behavior that is unsafe. Using happy and sad can be great discussion prompts, especially when we are letting children choose where and how to sort their experiences. Each of us might put different things under happy and sad based on our own experiences and tastes. But to do this successfully, it's best to take *happy* and *sad* out of activities that aren't truly focused on feelings.

Addressing Roadblocks: Reframing How We Talk About Emotions

There are likely to be times—both in the classroom and outside of it—when we talk about emotions in a way that does not support our mission of creating an emotion-rich classroom. Many of these come from our own childhood, at home or at school, and then pop out of us when we are feeling stressed or overwhelmed. Some of these statements include:

➤ "You don't need to cry about it."

➤ "Stop crying. Dry your tears."

➤ "Get over it."

➤ "That's not a big deal."

➤ "You're okay."

➤ "Babies cry. Big kids use their words."

The underlying message here is, "I know how you should feel, and your sadness isn't appropriate." Similarly, children calling peers "babies" when they cry or get upset sends the message that crying is infantile or not okay. Babies cry to express all their needs. As we develop, we gain tools to express our feelings—including crying, but also speaking, drawing, and writing. Discussion about why we might cry and what feelings our tears can represent (including sadness and happiness) can help normalize that crying is a regular part of emotional expression.

Figure 2.8 Reframing Messages About Emotions

Roadblock Messages About Emotions	Reframed Messages that Support Emotions
Classroom rule: "Be happy."	"Ask for help when your emotions feel too big."
"Welcome to our happy place."	"All emotions are welcome here."
"You're okay. It's okay."	"How can I help you feel better?"
"Babies cry. Use your words."	"You seem sad. Can you tell me why?"
"That's not a big deal."	"That really bothered you."
"If you are going to act like that, you can go to the infant room/principal's office."	"All emotions are okay. Let's choose a safe way to express them."
"I don't like to see you sad."	"Seeing your face gives me the clue you might be sad. Would you tell me about it?"

Teachers can work to address these sayings with intention. The ICARE structure is helpful here, regardless of whether it is another child saying these things or an adult. In the situation that follows, Ms. Saunders uses ICARE to coach a frequent classroom substitute, Ms. Crown, after Rory spilled her milk and Ms. Crown told her, "You don't need to cry about that." Mr. Smith, the custodian, stepped in to handle the mess, while Ms. Saunders and Ms. Crown discuss a different way to approach the situation:

Intent: Ms. Saunders believes Ms. Crown is uncomfortable with the crying and wants it to be over.

Calm: Ms. Saunders notices Ms. Crown's frustration and asks Ms. Crown if she needs a minute to calm. Hearing this, Ms. Crown realizes that what she said sounded harsh and unsupportive. She steps away from the table, washing her hands and taking some deep breaths.

Acknowledge: Ms. Saunders acknowledges that it's hard when children get so upset, and it seems like Ms. Crown wanted the crying to be finished. Ms. Crown nods and says it was really grating to hear Rory so upset.

Rewind: Ms. Saunders reminds Ms. Crown that the way that the class has been working on ending crying is by working through it—handling upset through regulation techniques. She offers the choice of Ms. Crown helping Rory through using some of the regulation tools or watching while Ms. Saunders handles it so she can see how Rory reacts. Ms. Crown chooses to try it and accepts Ms. Saunders's offer to use the classroom's calming menu board.

Echo: After Ms. Crown works with Rory, who successfully calms down through deep breaths and her favorite song, Ms. Saunders makes a point to follow up with Ms. Crown. She asks Ms. Crown to share what happened and reflect on how it worked to meet that same goal of ending the loud crying, but in a more supportive way that helped practice the skills Rory had been working on.

We've all either been on the giving or receiving end of these negative messages, and there's no shame or blame here. Instead, we can plan a new way forward. Which of these roadblocks might you face in your work this year? Are there others you anticipate? Do you have emotion messages in your classroom that you'll want to change? Do you have phrases you wish to intentionally reframe?

Addressing Roadblocks: Checking Our Biases

We've talked about how we can examine our mindsets related to emotions to become more aware of the beliefs we hold about how we name, express, and manage our own emotions. A next step is to consider what beliefs we hold about how others express and manage their emotions. This often means we need to do the hard work of examining our own implicit bias—deep-down, often unacknowledged attitudes and beliefs that can influence how we treat others—and then figuring out how those biases might manifest in the classroom. We all hold biases, and we can all learn to be more aware of them and practice how to not treat others unfairly based on them.

As you respond and support children with emotions, reflect on your reactions. Consider gender, race, culture, language, ability, socioeconomic status, and other facets of identity about which you might hold unintentional biases. It is hard and even painful to admit that we might treat groups of children differently from one another. It can easily bring up feelings of shame. However, it can also be empowering to notice an equity issue and challenge yourself to respond in a way that is more equitable for children and families.

Consider asking yourself reflection questions or working with a coach or trusted coworker to think through possible biases. Related to the emotions work in this book you might ask:

➤ How do the emotion materials and emotion visuals I use represent and honor the diversity of the children in my class, our school, our community, and beyond?

➤ How do I solicit family feedback and offer involvement opportunities to include all the families in my class?

➤ How do I respond to children's emotions? Who gets more or less support? Who gets more or less validation?

➤ How do I continue to view children's actions with positive intent? Do I find this harder to do with some children or groups of children than others?

Here are a few examples of how implicit bias might affect how we respond to children's emotions:

➤ You notice that you frequently coach girls through their sadness and disappointment, but often expect boys to "get over it" themselves.

➤ You realize you are uncomfortable with loud voices, so you often tell several of your louder children to calm down. You recognize that using "calm down" is having negative effects: louder children aren't feeling successful because of the frequent redirection and "calm down" is feeling punitive rather than supportive.

➤ You find that you are struggling to see the positive intent in your ICARE coaching with children who are not the same race or ethnicity as you are.

➤ You reflect and realize that you're more likely to admonish Black girls for expressing their emotions than you are for White girls.

➤ You have a child in your classroom who has significant developmental delays and who successfully calms down by being held, sucking her thumb, or using a lovey from home. You recognize that while you support typically developing children in your group in choosing their preferred calm-down strategies, you often attempt to redirect this child away from her favorite strategies.

➤ You provide positive descriptive feedback to children who speak English more fluently and are less likely to give that same level of feedback to your dual language learners.

➤ You review your family engagement plans and see that your family opportunities are typically during work hours, excluding your working families.

Similarly to how we teach children how to notice their emotions so they can then process and manage them, noticing your own implicit biases is an essential step toward processing and managing them. The teachers who acknowledge and examine their implicit biases can bring intentionality to classroom situations to make them more equitable. For example, a teacher can work to create a system to give positive descriptive feedback to all children each week on a card that gets sent to families. Seeing whose cards tend to be filled out last allows the teacher to rectify the pattern of leaving specific children out. A teacher who recognizes that she often views loud expression as a problematic behavior reflects and realizes that she can offer areas and activities where loud expression is supported, rather than quashed. Another teacher asks her coach to take notes on her responses to children's emotions as she aims to respond to children of all genders with support. Carving out space to reflect on your mindsets, your instruction, and your data can help you identify possible equity problems to solve, ensuring each child is getting the social and emotional support they need and deserve.

The Pyramid Model Equity Coaching Guide (Ferro et al. 2022) has resources and reflection prompts to look at how classroom social and emotional practices can support equity.

Wrap-Up

Take a moment to inventory what features of an emotion-rich classroom you have already started to put in place. Even if you have not yet focused in on emotion instruction, you are likely to have brought emotions into the class in some way. Consider both your instruction and your classroom environment. The following questions might help you reflect on your personal starting point:

> How have you used emotion activities or emotion materials in the past?

> What visual supports do you already have?

> How have you taught children about emotions already?

> What spaces or materials have children been using to calm down?

> What conversations have you had with families about emotional development?

> What emotions have you had, modeled, or labeled in front of children?

Nearly every teacher has done emotion work already, even if it wasn't planned and intentional. If you have worked to build positive relationships with children and their families, you've also begun the work in a meaningful way. We learn best, and can express our emotions more easily, in a situation where we feel comfortable and safe. Celebrate the steps you have taken so far.

Next, identify some next steps from this chapter that have intrigued you. Flip back and take note of ideas, frameworks, or concepts you recognized as important to you or your class. Perhaps you noticed patterns of language that you wish to change, or the idea of using data to enhance your instruction excited you. Or maybe you saw the ICARE framework and are hoping to practice your social coaching. Identifying some steps that have left you feeling encouraged and motivated will help you bring a growth mindset with you into chapters 3 through 8, where you'll be reflecting, planning, and building your emotion instruction toolbox.

DAPPER Planning Sheet

Use this form to plan out how you'll implement the components of DAPPER as you teach children a new social and emotional skill.

Targeted Social and Emotional Skill
Children will be able to:

Demonstrate and Describe
How will you demonstrate the skill?

How will you describe the skill?

In what context will the demonstration and description take place? (Whole group? Small group? Individually?)

Animate
What visuals will you use?

What gestures will you use?

Practice
How will you help children practice the new skill as part of your introductory lesson and soon afterward?

In what context will the practice take place? (Whole group? Small group? Individual?)

Planned Opportunities

How will you provide opportunities for children to practice the new skill after the introductory lesson?

In what settings or contexts will you provide these opportunities?

Extend

How will you extend the learning around this skill to encourage children to use the skill in new contexts?

What information, activities, or feedback will you share with families?

Reinforce and Reflect

How will you reinforce the skill? What would positive descriptive feedback for the skill sound like?

What questions will you ask children to encourage reflection?

DAPPER Summary Sheet

The DAPPER framework is used to plan social and emotional instruction. You can refer to this summary sheet whenever you need a quick overview or reminder of the framework and its components.

What are the DAPPER components?	How do I put them into action?
Demonstrate and **D**escribe	Model the targeted skill; verbally describe your behavior and thinking as you work through the skill.
Animate	Use both visuals and gestures to help children remember and access the skill.
Practice	Have children practice the skill, whether through role play or other activities, soon after you introduce it. Give feedback and support.
Planned Opportunities	Intentionally plan opportunities or activities that will encourage the use of the skill. These opportunities can be in any context or content area. Consider reminding children about the skill and how to do it as the activity is beginning.
Extend	Think about and plan how to encourage the use of the skill with different people or in different settings. This includes sharing information with families so children can access the skill at home and using the ICARE framework to encourage using it in new contexts.
Reinforce and **R**eflect	Use positive descriptive feedback to describe when children are using the skill and to celebrate. Ask reflection questions to encourage children's thinking about their skills.

ICARE Summary Sheet

The ICARE framework is used to socially coach children through situations in a way that reinforces the growth of their social and emotional skills. You can refer to this summary sheet whenever you need a quick overview or reminder of the framework and its components.

What are the ICARE components?	How do I put them into action?
Intent	This step is an inner step. Consider what children were trying to express in the situation. Reframe the situation so that you can see the behavior as representing their need for your assistance to use a more appropriate skill.
Calm	Check your own body to make sure you are calm when entering the interaction. Then help children calm big feelings if needed before working through the situation.
Acknowledge	Use a validating response to acknowledge what children were wishing for or trying to express.
Rewind	Encourage children to redo the situation using a social and emotional skill you have been working on (such as asking for a turn or expressing emotions with words).
Echo	Verbally, or with visual and gestural support, echo back what happened and what the outcome was. This usually includes positive descriptive feedback for trying the situation in a new way and noting how the situation worked or how the participants felt.

Task Analysis Data Sheet

When analyzing a child's ability to complete a task or use a skill, one approach is to break the task down into steps and consider these steps individually, noting if and how a child is able to complete each one. You can then use this task analysis to reflect on which additional and targeted supports a child might need.

Child's Name:		
Skill Being Taught:		
Step	**Does the Child Complete the Step?**	**Notes**

Data Sheet for Recording Levels of Assistance Needed with Task Steps

You can use this data sheet to record children's ability to complete steps toward a social and emotional task, such as calming down, and to note what level of support they need with each step: none (independent), spoken directions (verbal), or a teacher guiding them, holding their hand, or offering hand-over-hand support (physical). You might circle, highlight, place a checkmark near, or otherwise indicate the answer in each box.

Child's Name	Step:	Step:	Step:	Notes
	Independent Verbal Physical	Independent Verbal Physical	Independent Verbal Physical	
	Independent Verbal Physical	Independent Verbal Physical	Independent Verbal Physical	
	Independent Verbal Physical	Independent Verbal Physical	Independent Verbal Physical	
	Independent Verbal Physical	Independent Verbal Physical	Independent Verbal Physical	
	Independent Verbal Physical	Independent Verbal Physical	Independent Verbal Physical	
	Independent Verbal Physical	Independent Verbal Physical	Independent Verbal Physical	
	Independent Verbal Physical	Independent Verbal Physical	Independent Verbal Physical	
	Independent Verbal Physical	Independent Verbal Physical	Independent Verbal Physical	
	Independent Verbal Physical	Independent Verbal Physical	Independent Verbal Physical	
	Independent Verbal Physical	Independent Verbal Physical	Independent Verbal Physical	
	Independent Verbal Physical	Independent Verbal Physical	Independent Verbal Physical	
	Independent Verbal Physical	Independent Verbal Physical	Independent Verbal Physical	

Chapter 3

Building an Emotion Vocabulary

PICTURE THIS All the young preschoolers are gathered around their teachers on a rug for their shared reading time. One teacher takes out a book that features a spider, with a big spider illustration on the cover. Jay-Lin glances at the book, her eyes growing wide. She covers her face with her hands and begins to cry. Her teacher asks Jay-Lin if she is okay; she doesn't answer. "It's okay," her teacher tells her. "This spider is nice." Jay-Lin continues to cover her eyes and her hands start to tremble.

Her teachers are at a loss for what to do. One teacher rubs Jay-Lin's back and whispers to her about what they will do outside after story time. The other begins reading the story. Jay-Lin doesn't take her hands off her eyes until the teacher reassures her that the book is put away on the shelf. While her teachers recognize that Jay-Lin seems scared, they are unsure how to talk about it with her. They try strategies that many of us use in uncomfortable situations. They try to convince her spiders are not scary, dismissing her feelings. They try to physically comfort her and distract her by talking about something she loves, like outside time. Their attempts to minimize her fear do not work, and they avoid talking directly about the fear, worrying that doing so might create new fears in their class of three-year-olds.

Jay-Lin's teachers are not alone. Most of us struggle to pause, validate feelings, and help each other work through them. In fact, I'd bet most of us can think of a time recently as adults where we have said we were worried or nervous about something and have been told that it's "not that bad." Without intentional practice, we often default to dismissing or distracting ourselves—and others—from feelings, rather than working through them.

In this example, Jay-Lin's teachers can start by intentionally using emotion words to create a common understanding among the children. Selecting emotion vocabulary, and teaching these words to their class, will support all children in understanding their feelings and the feelings of others. It will also allow the teachers to see that mentioning and validating these feelings, such as asking Jay-Lin how she feels and being open to talking about her fears, will support all children's emotional understanding. Moving past our own discomfort around emotions is not easy work, but waiting to teach emotions until we are fully comfortable working through them isn't a practical goal. Instead, exploring our mindsets around emotions and beginning to use emotion language in daily conversations are essential steps toward rich emotion instruction. Working through discomfort gives us the chance to become mindful of what supports we need for our own emotional growth. And when the work is hard, we can find encouragement in seeing children's social and emotional development, motivating us to continue creating an emotion-rich classroom to build on our successes and those of the children in our care.

See the Emotion Mindsets Worksheet on pages 31–33 for support with reflecting on your emotion mindsets.

About the Skill of Building an Emotion Vocabulary

In working with teachers, I often ask about their comfort level with talking to children about emotions. Some teachers say they are comfortable and like to talk about emotions of characters in books and have children identify how they feel daily. However, most teachers who have not yet focused on social and emotional instruction say they aren't particularly comfortable. Like Jay-Lin's teachers, they give many reasons, including:

> ➤ not sharing their own emotions because they want to "leave that baggage outside the classroom"

> ➤ not feeling as if there is enough time to walk through emotions whenever they arise

> ➤ not knowing what to say or do when children are having big feelings

> ➤ not wanting the other children to feel upset, sad, or scared when discussing those feelings

> ➤ not feeling like they have the training, support, or resources to know how to teach social and emotional skills in depth

Some of these beliefs might resonate with you currently. Of course, the end goal isn't just to use emotion words with children when they're uncomfortable. The hope is that working through this book will help you to become more confident and comfortable with emotion instruction and reap the benefits of children having new emotional skills in the classroom. As we build our comfort, we notice that:

> ➤ We can't truly separate from emotions when we walk through the classroom door. Acknowledging emotions and taking steps to regulate them provides a model for behaviors we want to encourage in children.

> Practicing regulation with children makes the skill more fluent for them so they can re-engage in classroom activities.

> Peers in the class notice when others are upset, and having tools to respond encourages them to be supportive rather than worried bystanders.

> These skills are life skills, rather than preschool skills. Accurately identifying our emotions, expressing them, and regulating them helps us with our own interpersonal relationships outside the classroom.

Building our personal comfort around discussing, expressing, and regulating our emotions in front of others in the classroom is a big task. In some cases, we're doing this work for the first time and rewriting how we have been navigating through emotions for years. This requires us to give ourselves grace and celebrate each step of progress—just as this book encourages you to do for the children in your care. Take time to reflect on your emotion mindsets and practice talking about emotions. Each step works toward building an emotion-rich classroom and an emotion-rich life for ourselves. What a gift you are giving to the children in your care, and to yourself!

In part, building an emotion vocabulary means being able to label an emotion and connect that label with a matching facial expression. This may seem like an obvious skill. After all, most of us can read children's facial expressions and label them relatively easily. Thinking it is a simple and obvious skill might be another barrier to teaching it. However, we know that reading facial expressions is a necessary skill for children to avoid social problems. For example, a child who cannot read Jay-Lin's facial expressions and understand her fear might hand her the spider book when they are reading together in the classroom library, resulting in Jay-Lin playing elsewhere. A child who does not recognize a peer's surprised face might misinterpret a bump as hostile, rather than an accident. Identifying emotional clues, such as attending to facial expressions and being able to label them with a nuanced vocabulary, helps demystify emotions and emotional interactions with others. Early childhood educators can start this work by teaching children a range of emotion vocabulary words and helping them learn to connect these words with facial expressions and cues.

"I've always talked about emotions with children, but now I'm more comfortable talking about *my own* emotions with children. I tell them how I am feeling: 'Ouch, I feel sad when someone hurts me.' I'm seeing that they are responding. A student came over to hug me when I was feeling sad the other day."

–Joan, preschool special education teacher

Choosing Emotions to Teach

One common question is, "What emotions should I teach?" Researchers have varying ideas. For example, some researchers originally thought that perhaps there were primary feelings, akin to primary colors, that blend to make up other feelings. In Paul Ekman's research, he discovered six facial expressions that are recognized in cultures around the world: fear, anger, sadness, enjoyment, surprise, and disgust (Ekman

2003). Other research notes that the shared expressions of fear and surprise (wide open eyes) and anger and disgust (wrinkled nose) means that there are only four universal emotions (Jack et al. 2016). However, some researchers don't support the notion of primary emotions (Posner, Russell, and Peterson 2005). Some believe in basic feeling families, yet debate remains about what those families should be or what they include. Main families include anger, sadness, fear, enjoyment, love, surprise, disgust, and shame (Goleman 1995). But feeling families do not capture the nuance of more complicated emotions that combine or bridge families, such as excitement, which can contain both enjoyment and anticipation, or jealousy, which can combine anger, sadness, and fear.

While there is no "perfect" list of emotions to introduce to preschoolers, keep the following factors in mind:

First, consider a range of emotions. This range should include those that are easier to understand and those that are more nuanced, those that are considered pleasant and unpleasant, and those that are weaker and stronger (or more and less intense). A challenge that arises when only using four primary emotions (anger, joy, sadness, fear) is that there is not a wide range or multiple examples of pleasant or neutral emotions. While we might consider specific emotions positive or negative, we want to send the message to children that all emotions are natural and okay, even those that don't feel pleasant or comfortable to us. Teaching about, discussing, modeling, and brainstorming around a wide range of emotions ensures that children aren't getting the message from us that some emotions aren't acceptable to talk about or to feel.

One teacher shared that she created a mantra to help children be nonjudging of emotions. She wrote a little chant and shared it with children and families. "Emotions are how we feel and they're all okay. We'll learn to let them out in a safe way." She used this saying to remind herself, too, that every emotion is valid, and that her energy should be channeled toward teaching safe expression, rather than squashing big feelings.

Second, consider the emotions preschoolers exhibit on a regular basis. Excitement is usually very common in preschool, as is frustration. Anxiety or worry also show up often in preschool, and pride is evident as preschoolers share their creations with peers, teachers, and family. Your class might have other unique emotional experiences that you see and recognize. Adding relevant words to your teaching plan based on observation will only make your instruction stronger.

Third, consider adding calm to your list of words to explicitly teach. Calm is a more neutral emotion and not particularly strong, so it often gets overlooked when explicitly teaching emotion vocabulary. However, when children are feeling big emotions, they can work to regulate their bodies to calm themselves and feel better. Exploring what calm means and what it looks like will aid children in understanding the end goal and the benefits to themselves of calming down when their feelings are overwhelming them.

The Starting Point

Think about a coworker passing by and asking you, "How are you?" We often answer in vague generalities, with words like "fine," "okay," "well." Sometimes we answer with a shrug or an "I can't complain." We rarely answer with an emotion word or an explanation of why we feel however we do. Oftentimes we are only specifically asked, "How are you feeling?" when we are recovering from an illness.

A Plethora of Emotions

Take a minute to count how many emotion words in English you can identify.

Now take a moment to consider this: The English language has around two thousand emotion words! How many words did you think of? Two thousand words means there are words to describe all kinds of emotions and even the nuances between similar ones. Considering how many words there are to describe our emotions, it's surprising to think of how little we use them!

There are fascinating words and phrases in every language to describe very specific feelings. For example, *alysm* is the feeling of frustrated boredom that comes from being too ill to do anything. You know that feeling of happiness when you wake up from a pleasant dream? That's *euneirophrenia*. *Dépaysement* is a French word to describe the sadness of not being in your home country. When you're waiting for a visitor to arrive and you keep looking outside in anticipation of their arrival, that's described by the Inuit word *iktsuarpok*. *Dar pena ajena* is Spanish for when you feel embarrassed for someone else. Consider asking children and families to share emotion words from their cultures, languages, or family traditions.

Of course, our answers to "How are you?" depend on the social contexts and our relationships. But our responses might also be rooted in our own discomfort around talking about our emotions. And this means our children might rarely hear anyone answer, "How are you?" with emotion words. Outside of a doctor's office, they might never have been directly asked "How are you feeling?" As educators, using emotion words and sharing how we feel is a starting point for becoming more comfortable discussing our emotions, asking children about their feelings, and effectively teaching emotions in the classroom.

Planning to Start

Reflect on emotion words that come to your mind most quickly or easily. How do you commonly feel? Which words do you often use in your personal life? Which words do you currently use around children? For example, do you often use happy, content, or glad? Sad or disappointed? Scared or frightened? Anxious or nervous or worried? Angry or mad or frustrated? Excited or surprised or shocked? Calm or relaxed?

Plan to use emotion words yourself, both in front of children and in your life outside the classroom. Practice using emotion words to describe how you feel during the day. For example, tell children you feel loved when they paint you a picture, or say that you feel frustrated when you can't find a material you need. When reading, use emotion words to draw attention to how characters feel. When an illustration shows a child crying, label that they might feel sad. When a character notes that they don't understand something, share that they seem to be feeling confused. Which words come up more naturally for you? Which words will you have to be more intentional about using?

Using DAPPER to Build an Emotion Vocabulary

You've taken steps to select important vocabulary words and you've modeled using emotion words in context. Next, walk through the DAPPER steps that follow to intentionally plan how to build children's emotion vocabulary.

Demonstrate and Describe

Vocabulary acquisition, like social and emotional skills, involves both implicit and explicit instruction. Both vocabulary and social and emotional teaching work best when children are encouraged to practice the skills themselves. Similarly, teaching categories of words, and planning for repeated exposures, supports children's vocabulary acquisition. The DAPPER framework provides for this explicit demonstration and instruction of new words as well as planned repeated exposure and opportunities to use new vocabulary.

When teaching new words to children, the five principles of oral vocabulary development, as outlined by Susan Neuman, are helpful (Neuman and Wright 2014):

➤ Identify the words to teach.

➤ Define the words in a child-friendly way.

➤ Contextualize the words, such as using the words in appropriate contexts, giving examples and nonexamples, showing props or pictures, or using meaningful multimedia contexts.

➤ Review words over time.

➤ Monitor vocabulary acquisition and reteach if necessary.

There are several strategies early childhood educators typically employ that support these five principles. We say the word, repeat the word, and continue to use the word in context. We encourage children to repeat the word and use it in context too. We show examples of what the word means—with tangible props, photographs, or pictures, or by looking at visuals and examples onscreen. We attempt to put the word into a category where children might have background knowledge, and sometimes we give nonexamples to support their understanding of what the new word is not.

For child-friendly explanations of emotions you can keep handy, see the Sample Child-Friendly Descriptions of Emotions sheet at the end of this chapter.

For example, consider how Ms. Edwards might teach about crows using these strategies. Then consider how the same strategies might apply when teaching a new emotion vocabulary word like *disappointment*. Notice how the strategies are similar for teaching vocabulary words around both physical objects and emotions, and also consider which strategies are harder to apply to emotion vocabulary. Preplanning child-friendly definitions for each emotion word and some example situations to illustrate each emotion can make introducing a new emotion vocabulary word a little bit easier.

Figure 3.1 Comparing Teaching Strategies for Emotion Words and Other Vocabulary

Strategy	Content Vocabulary Word: Crow	Emotion Vocabulary Word: Disappointed
Defining categories	Ms. Edwards describes a crow as a type of bird with the features of other birds like a beak and wings.	Ms. Edwards describes disappointment as being an emotion, like *happy* and *sad* and *angry*.
Describing	She describes its size and color; crows are usually big, black birds.	She describes *disappointed* as being related to *sad* but elaborates that being disappointed is when you feel sad that something doesn't happen the way you wished for it to happen.
Introducing props	She shows a stuffed crow and a picture of a crow from a book.	She brings emotion visuals and pictures of disappointed facial expressions. She uses her face and body to model the new word. Her eyes and lips point downward, her shoulders slump, and her tone drifts downward too as she acts out and says, "I'm disappointed."
Presenting multimedia	She finds a video of crows building nests to show children.	She finds a read-aloud video of the book *Are You Ready to Play Outside?* by Mo Willems, where Piggie and Gerald are disappointed that it is raining.
Connecting to background knowledge	She ties the word crow back to a book the class read featuring a scarecrow.	She talks about times the class has handled disappointment, like when it rained or when the lunch menu changed and it wasn't pizza day.
Using the word	She encourages the children to say *crow*, repeating the sounds after she says them.	She encourages children to copy her expression, tone, and body language to say and act out *disappointed*, providing physical and visual connections to help her class remember the overall feeling of the new word.
Giving examples and nonexamples	She shows children pictures of birds and asks them to label as *crow* or *not a crow*.	She talks about familiar characters and situations and asks children if the people in the examples would be disappointed or not disappointed. For instance, getting a gift you really wanted or having Dad come to pick you up when you were expecting Grandma.

You've probably noticed a few differences between teaching the word *crow* and teaching *disappointed*. First, *crow*, as a noun, is very tangible; it's easy to find a picture or a stuffed animal and label this particular bird as a crow. While *disappointed* has facial characteristics that may help provide examples, the emotion can manifest itself in different ways and vary from person to person. Second, when teaching *disappointed* and other complicated emotions, we often refer back to other emotion words, such as explaining that it's related to *sad*. This requires first teaching and explaining other emotion words so children can understand the references, rather than simply providing a label for the specific item or expression being taught.

As you plan out your emotion instruction using these strategies, ask yourself:

➤ Do children already know the related emotion words you might use to provide a child-friendly definition or context?

➤ What example situations have you seen children experience that you can reference in your teaching?

➤ What are some clear or obvious examples of the emotion in books, videos, or photographs that could help define or clarify the new word?

Planning What Emotions to Demonstrate and Describe

Do children in your class already understand some emotions well? If so, you could start by reviewing basic emotions that children have some understanding of, and then introduce ones that are new yet related, such as starting with *angry* and then introducing *frustrated*. Teaching a robust group of emotion words means including a range of emotions, as well as weaker and stronger ones. Teaching so many new words and concepts takes time, but providing an understanding of these words and ideas makes the competencies in the following chapters easier to teach. Many social and emotional curricula focus on teaching eight or ten emotions to ensure there are a range. While there is no "magic number," when aiming to ensure that you have a range of emotions and several examples of emotions that feel pleasant and unpleasant, you are likely to have at least six or seven. For example, *happy, excited, calm, proud, sad, scared, worried, angry, frustrated,* and *disappointed* is a list with a good amount of variety and is ten words in total.

> Review the Sample Child-Friendly Descriptions of Emotions sheet to get some ideas of possible emotions to teach.

Draft a list of emotions you want to focus on with your class. Review your list with the following considerations in mind:

➤ Do you have multiple pleasant and multiple unpleasant emotions on your list?

➤ Do you have some emotions that are weaker and others that are stronger?

➤ Does your list include emotions that children discuss or experience often?

➤ Does your list include *calm* to support later work around understanding regulation?

Animate

To teach the new vocabulary words, you'll need illustrations or photographs of each emotion. Knowing children's developmental level and what types of visuals they're familiar and comfortable with will help you select the emotion visuals that will be most helpful. For example, some teachers might opt to select simple line drawings because children already use these kinds of pictures for visual schedules or communication devices. Some teachers prefer real photographs, while others do not because hair or clothing can distract children from the facial expressions. Other teachers have emotion cards that they've already started using as a curricular support with their class.

Review the list of emotions you plan on teaching. Choose a set of emotion visuals, whether from a curriculum kit, line-drawing software, online resource, or elsewhere. Review your visuals with the following considerations in mind:

➤ What kinds of visuals are children already familiar with (for example, line drawings or photographs)? Will the set you are considering build upon their prior knowledge?

➤ Which visuals are least likely to be distracting for children? Are the emotion expressions clear and apparent enough in the visuals to be easily identified?

➤ Does the set have diversity of race, gender, skin tone, body shape, ability, and other physical characteristics? Check to ensure that the diversity is throughout the range of emotions, rather than reinforcing stereotypes by disproportionately associating some groups with positive and comfortable emotions or other groups with negative or uncomfortable emotions.

➤ Do you have visuals for all the emotions you are planning to teach?

Planning How to Animate Emotion Vocabulary

Once you've selected your visuals and reviewed them with the above considerations in mind, it's time to plan out how you will use them for teaching. First, think about the size of the visuals needed to ensure that every child involved in the lesson or activity is able to see the components of the facial expression. For large-group instruction, this often means using large visuals so the whole group can notice the slant of eyebrows or the worry lines on a forehead. Other teachers use medium-size visuals for whole-group instruction but supplement these by also putting a photograph of the visual on a large screen or giving children individual emotion pictures to reference. For small-group or individual instruction, smaller copies of visuals can similarly give children the opportunity to closely reference facial expressions.

Next, be sure to have visuals nearby for more incidental teaching moments. This might mean having a set of pictures readily accessible so you can refer to them as a child is displaying emotions. This could be in the form of an emotion check-in chart (for instance, a sheet with many emotions or a wheel with many small visuals on it) or a set of smaller cards on a lanyard or ring. These visuals will help supplement your words as you ask children how they might be feeling or as you describe what you're seeing in their faces.

At other times, you might find yourself discussing emotions when you do not have visuals handy. Animating also includes pairing new concepts with gestures and body language to help children remember and access these ideas. These signs and gestures can supplement a visual support, or can be used if you do not have a visual ready to provide more context to support understanding. For emotion vocabulary, consider teaching the American Sign Language (ASL) signs for emotion words as you teach vocabulary words, which allows for greater access for children who might not be able to express the words verbally. Often signs for emotion words incorporate facial expressions and body language that will help support the understanding of the word with an additional visual. For example, *sad* in ASL includes moving your hands in specific ways and also making a sad facial expression.

As you use your visuals to teach emotions to your whole class, you might notice some children need differentiated supports. More ideas for differentiation can be found in the "Differentiation and Advancement" section of this chapter.

Practice

The goal of practice is to get children using these vocabulary words. What strategies have you used to teach other types of new words? What has helped children practice and use those words in context?

In the lesson where you introduce a new emotion and new vocabulary, you might consider having an "exit ticket" where you ask each child to choose an emotion word, say it, and make an associated facial expression. For example, in Ms. Edwards's class, she has been focusing on teaching the new vocabulary words and animating with American Sign Language. For a chance to practice, she pairs up children who have more and less skill with expressive language. She gives each pair an emotion card of a word they have been talking about and asks them to figure out the word and the sign for that emotion. She walks around to support each group, observing them use the word and the sign. As children transition from group time to lunch, she has each group share their emotion card, their emotion word, the facial expression, and the sign. Children watch each other present about their emotion, and Ms. Edwards notes which groups needed support to recall their words, expressions, and signs so that she can follow up with more practice.

Similarly, after you have taught several emotions, you might invite children to act one out and have peers guess what emotion is being demonstrated. This works well as a transition activity. After one child acts out an emotion expression, they can transition to the next activity and another child can act out an expression.

Planning How to Practice New Vocabulary

Decide on your activity for children to practice the new word.

➤ Will you have children work in pairs? If so, how will they know who their partner is?

> If you are having children act out an expression in front of the whole class, how will children know when it will be their turn to act?

> Can children all practice the words verbally, or will some be responding with signs, visuals, or communication devices? What materials will you need to support the participation of all children?

> What supports will you need to provide for children so that the practice is effective? Which children might need your assistance?

Planned Opportunities

Children need planned opportunities to continue engaging with the new vocabulary words in context. One example is an emotions collage or an emotions "quilt" made up of large paper squares. In an emotions quilt, your class can collaborate to make large squares for each new emotion vocabulary word as you teach and discuss it with children. To create a square, encourage children to find examples of the vocabulary word in the classroom or in their own life. For example, on little pieces of paper that will be hung on the "happy" quilt square, children might attach happy faces cut from a magazine (with help, if needed). They might draw happy expressions to add to the square. They might write, or have teachers take dictation, about what they know about the word happy and when they might have felt that way. They might take photos of happy expressions on their classmates, bring in happy photos from home, or take photos of book characters who are happy. Similarly, they might look for examples of other emotions such as lonely, calm, disappointed, or excited and use these to decorate more quilt squares.

> If your quilt has multiple squares with different emotions, you can ask children which square their art goes on, prompting them to use the new emotion words or signs.

Other ideas include making class books about new emotion words with examples and pictures. Games that focus on emotions can also help reinforce these ideas. For example, putting emotion faces into a grid to make an emotions bingo board allows children to practice identifying and using the new vocabulary. Call out an emotion, such as sad, and have children find it on their bingo board. As children become more well-versed in emotions, you can modify this game by reading scenarios aloud to children and having them cover up the emotion (or emotions) they think they would feel in that scenario. This advanced game has children practicing recognizing emotions in themselves, the key competency of chapter 4.

Planning Opportunities for New Vocabulary

As you choose planned opportunities to help children practice their skills, answer these planning questions:

> What grouping will work best (whole group, small group, individually with teacher)?

> If choosing a small-group activity, will you group children with similar emotion knowledge to do targeted work? Will you choose a smaller group of children with differing emotion skills so they can support each other and model skills for each other?

> What materials do you need?

> How will you document children's learning as they engage in the activity?

Extend

Extending requires stretching the learning opportunities past the planned group activities and practice you have structured. The goal of extending is to encourage children to use a skill in new contexts, such as during interactions with peers during play, in other spaces outside the classroom, or with other people. For the skill of building an emotion vocabulary, this extending might start when you begin to hear children use emotion words in different contexts, such as hearing a child talking about how the baby is so sad when playing with the dollhouse. You might also hear a child use an emotion word as they retell a story or act out a scene in dramatic play.

One way to encourage the generalization of this skill is to make sure there are visuals available in multiple environments to support children's use of the skill there. For example, if you primarily talk about emotions during group time on a carpet or at a small-group table, consider putting some emotion visuals up in other areas, such as in a block or construction area and in the dramatic play space. Putting other emotion materials out—such as songs or stories about emotions in a listening center, or playdough mats with a blank face template for children to fill in with a facial expression—encourages children to notice and use those vocabulary words in many settings. A child is likely to label the face they make out of playdough or name an expressive face on a puzzle if they have been learning those words and exploring relevant materials.

Similarly, encouraging others to talk to children about their new vocabulary words is helpful too. For example, an art teacher might have children use shapes to make abstract faces and might then ask children about how their art subject is feeling. Speech pathologists might add emotion words to children's communication boards one by one as you teach them in the classroom, supporting children in using these words with another instructor and possibly in a different context. Sharing the new words and sample child-friendly descriptions with families will allow family members to reinforce the use of these words at home too.

Find emotion descriptions to send to families on the Sample Child-Friendly Descriptions of Emotions sheet at the end of the chapter.

Another aspect of extending involves coaching children in the moment to use their new emotion vocabulary words. For example, you might overhear a puppet start crying during a puppet show, and the puppet says, "Come back! Come play!" You might ask the child if they remember the emotion word for "that feeling when you are sad that you don't have someone to play with" and show the emotion visual for lonely. For a child who is starting to use these words more independently, you might simply ask the child to tell you how that puppet is feeling, allowing the child another opportunity to use the new emotion word.

Planning How to Extend Emotion Vocabulary

In what areas of your classroom can you strategically put materials to encourage emotion discussions? What materials can you use? Plan for at least three different materials you can put in three different areas. Continue to add materials over time. Unlike a holiday or seasonal theme where you pack up materials as you switch topics, emotion visuals and materials need to be out across the months and seasons so that children can continue to access them and use their skills.

In addition to materials in your classroom, consider what is needed to support children using the skill outside of your classroom. Which other staff members in your school would be able to reinforce the emotion vocabulary work you are doing? Where in your building, or in outdoor spaces, might you post emotion visuals to help prompt children to use their new words? For example, you could consider hanging emotion visuals at the entrance to your school or program if staff typically greet children and ask how they are doing.

Reinforce and Reflect

One way to reinforce the skill of using emotion vocabulary words is giving positive descriptive feedback as children use new words or show understanding of the new concepts. For example, "You pointed to the *excited* picture. That helps me know how you feel!" Or, "You really noticed the character's angry face. He does look angry that his classmate took his toy." Ensuring that your tone, facial expression, and body language match the feedback you are giving supports children who rely on visual cues to process language.

As children start to recognize and use the emotion words you are teaching, you can begin to ask questions that prompt them to recall and reflect on what emotions they recognized. Some first reflection questions might sound like:

➤ What emotions did you see in this book?

➤ What emotions did you see on your classmates' faces during outside time?

➤ How do you know he is sad?

➤ How does your face look when you are proud?

As you work on additional skills and competencies, you'll notice the reflection questions getting deeper into emotional understanding, rather than focusing on recalling and identifying.

Planning to Reinforce and Reflect on Emotion Vocabulary

Take a moment to think about what positive descriptive feedback might sound like in your classroom for the words you are teaching. Is it easy or hard to come up with examples?

Offering this kind of feedback is a new habit for many of us, so approaching it with a habit-building mindset is useful. What can you do to make this kind of feedback a habit? Consider other times you have built a habit—even if it is a personal habit like daily running, taking vitamins, or writing consistently. Think about what strategies were helpful for you. Did you have others to help you stay accountable? Did you need reminders posted to help you to remember? Did you track your habit? Did you plan for your new habit?

Now consider how to use these strategies to support the habit of giving children positive descriptive feedback.

➤ Do you need reminders or positive feedback starters to help you remember?

➤ Do you need a teammate to hold you accountable?

➤ Do you need to structure a time in your day to give that feedback to children directly?

Rather than assuming you will remember to give this kind of feedback, think through how to add habit-supporting strategies into your day as you build a positive descriptive feedback habit.

> The Building a Habit of Positive Descriptive Feedback sheet at the end of this chapter can help you plan strategies to increase your likelihood of success.

Weaving Emotion Vocabulary Throughout the Day

Next you'll find example activities to further practice and reinforce the use of emotion vocabulary throughout the day's regular activities. Encouraging social interactions and using visuals are big ideas that are woven throughout all of these suggestions.

First, plan some activities that have children working together to further social skills. Structures like turn taking, helping peers, sharing through turn and talk, and asking children to explain their thinking to model for others all build children's understanding while practicing social skills.

Second, consider how to incorporate the use of visuals as you read through example activities. You'll notice that, in this and other chapters, visuals play a big role in helping children remember and connect concepts in new activities. Visuals have many benefits:

➤ Visuals give support with processing after the spoken words are gone. If a child hasn't completely processed verbal ideas or directions, a visual gives additional clues and meaning.

➤ Visuals serve as a reminder of previously taught concepts, just like calendars or to-do lists support us as adults.

➤ Visuals can break down tasks, and pictures or drawings show concrete steps to imitate. For example, "wash your hands" can easily be broken down into visuals for turning on the water, wetting hands, lathering, rinsing, drying, and shutting off the water.

➤ Visuals allow for independence. Rather than having a teacher say each step of the handwashing process, visuals allow children to access clues and cues independently.

➤ Visuals provide a way for children to communicate even if they don't yet have the expressive words to do so. Children can point to an emotion picture to identify how they feel or pick out an activity card to show a teacher what they would like to play with.

Morning Meeting or Circle Time: Play emotion charades. Have children pull an emotion visual out of a bag, make the expression, and have peers guess what the feeling is. Play emotion sign charades on another day with a twist: have children pull out an emotion visual and then make the sign or gesture you have taught. Give emotion visuals to the children who are guessing to help remind them of possible answers. Ask children, "How did you know that emotion?" to encourage reflection on what they noticed about the actor's face or body.

Movement and Music: Put multiple emotion visuals in a bucket or bag. Play freeze dance, where the music plays and children dance. When the music stops, children "freeze" in place as you pull an emotion visual out of the bag. Have children identify the emotion, make the expression, and move in a way that illustrates the emotion. Then start the music again, stopping to identify and act out each emotion. Encourage children to notice the way their classmates are expressing the emotions too by giving positive descriptive feedback such as, "Wow, Vivian! You are moving very quickly to show frustration."

Small Group: Consider drawing big emotion visuals or hanging up emotion visuals around the room. With small groups, have children pull an emotion photo or other visual out of a bag. Have children identify the emotion and then match the emotion photo to the big emotion visuals around the room. You could also use a large computer screen or projector to show emotion photographs. Have children move around the classroom to the emotion visuals that most closely match the photographs they see on the screen.

Transitions: Tape copies of emotion visuals to each side of a square box, such as an empty square tissue box. Ask children to take turns rolling the box like a die and identifying the emotion that lands on the "up" side. Since this game is so short, it works as a transition activity to practice identifying six emotions. For example, roll the box to fill time as children wait for a turn to wash hands for lunch. Rather than selecting who goes next yourself, consider having each child pass the box to a classmate to go next, and then celebrate that children are taking turns.

Gross Motor Skills and Outside Time: Use sidewalk chalk to draw giant emotion expressions on the sidewalk or outdoor play area and encourage children to move to these emotions. One child could call out emotions for the other players to travel to, or children can travel from emotion to emotion and teachers can then ask what emotion they are on to encourage the use of the vocabulary words.

Show children emotion visual cards. Encourage them to move in ways that depict the emotion for them. Perhaps this looks like bouncing or hopping for *excited,* slow pacing for *sad,* or stomping for *disappointed.* For an extra challenge, select an animal from a bag (a picture or a toy) and an emotion card. How would a sad kangaroo move? What would an angry dog look like?

Art: Put out various magazines, newspapers, or catalogs so children can continue to add to an emotion quilt. Consider putting out one pair of scissors or one glue stick per pair of children and encourage them to share materials by asking each other for a turn.

Put out emotion pictures next to art supplies, such as dot stampers or string, and encourage children to make emotion faces with the materials. Encourage children to show and describe their work to others in the class and to their families.

Carve out facial features in a sliced potato to make emotion stampers. Use paint or ink pads to stamp many expressions. Children could also use stampers on index cards to make their own emotion matching game that they could then play with classmates to practice turn taking.

Math: Use emotion stampers to make patterns and have children read the patterns to you, using emotion words (for example, happy, sad, happy, sad, happy, sad). Consider pairing children and giving each child one stamper to make partner patterns. Have children take turns to create an AB pattern or add a third child to the group to create ABC patterns while practicing waiting and taking turns in order.

Story Time: Select books that offer easy-to-understand representation of emotions. Because the focus is connecting the vocabulary word with the facial expression, books with clear photographs or drawings support this skill. For example, *On Monday When It Rained* by Cherryl Kachenmeister features simple text and black and white photographs of a young boy's expressions. Similarly, *Feelings* by Susan Canizares also has simple photographs labeled with one word. Other books focus on specific emotions and can support children in learning related words. For example, *Sad Is . . .* by Cheyenne Nichols and *Baby Happy Baby Sad* by Leslie Patricelli focus in on one or two emotions in more depth.

Consider also being intentional in reading books that are *not* focused on emotions and noticing the expressions on characters' faces. Encourage children to label and discuss characters' feelings. Use characters' situations to remind children of emotion words and ask them to share times they have had that emotion. For example, *The Snowy Day* by Ezra Jack Keats has a scene where Peter feels lonely because he can't play with the older boys. Consider explaining *lonely* and asking children to share when they have felt lonely. Similarly, Mo Willems books often have examples of characters feeling more complex emotions, like jealous and frustrated, where the illustrations give clues to how characters are feeling but the text does not directly state the emotion. Encourage children to suggest what emotions are being shown. As they answer, you could use a sticky note to write down an emotion word, make quick sketch of the associated facial expression, and stick the note to the relevant page of the book. Children can then go back and revisit the book and its emotions.

> "Putting out social emotional materials, like emotion dolls and emotion dominos, really opened a dialogue about emotions . . . between students but also between myself and my students as they explored the materials."
>
> —Leslie, inclusive preschool teacher

Planning to Teach Emotion Vocabulary Throughout the Day

Which activities to reinforce emotion vocabulary appeal to you? What other ideas and materials do you have that would build on the skill of using emotion words and recognizing expressions? As you review activities and materials, plan with the following considerations in mind:

> ➤ For premade or purchased activities, are the visuals easy to identify? Do they portray a range of emotions and people of many genders, races, skin tones, and physical attributes? Make sure to review to make sure that positive and negative depictions are shared across people of all genders, races, and other identities.

> ➤ Spread out your activities across the week and across various settings (e.g., different centers, inside and outside, activities that are facilitated by other adults).

Formative Assessment of Vocabulary Acquisition

Observing children during activities and play can help us figure out if they are able to identify or use these new vocabulary words as we are teaching them. Recording receptive and expressive understanding of the words can be helpful to determine which information children are learning. Rather than quizzing children about emotions, teachers can record information during group practice activities, songs, and play. For many teachers, anecdotal notes are not uncommon as they jot down observations of individual children who are showing new skills. However, gathering anecdotal notes and reviewing patterns for a whole class is more challenging, and it's often harder to use that information to inform your instructional next steps. To help with this assessment, you'll find a sample data sheet for this skill in figure 3.2, as well as a blank template at the end of the chapter. This data collection form will serve three purposes. First, you'll be able to review your data to figure out which children need additional supports or enrichment. Second, the data sheet provides an easy way to see the patterns of what children are learning, allowing you to revisit areas of need for your class. Third, the data provides a clear and simple way to track information to share with families about how their own child is developing new emotional skills.

The sample data sheet in figure 3.2 shows one way to collect information about children's emotion vocabulary and the efficacy of your instruction. On this sheet, children's names are listed in the left-hand column. Emotion words being taught in class are in the other columns. For each emotion, the teacher can choose *Receptive* or *Expressive* when a child uses a word or answers a question. If you do not have an opportunity to assess a child's understanding of a word, that cell in the table would be left blank. If you have not heard a child use a particular word correctly, and they are unable to receptively identify the word, you would mark "not yet" to indicate that they child has not yet shown an understanding of the vocabulary word.

Receptive identification means the child shows you they understand the language they are hearing without using the words themselves. Instances of receptively identifying an emotion would be pointing to a picture depicting surprise when asked how a character felt, or a child passing a proud visual when asked "Can you pass me the proud face?" Expressive identification means the child uses a word or sign to express themself through vocabulary. Examples of expressively identifying an emotion would be using an emotion word or emotion sign to answer a question, such as "How do you feel?" or using the word or sign during play.

For example, Ms. Edwards asks Olivia what verse of "If You're Happy and You Know It" she would like to sing. Ms. Edwards holds up the visuals for happy and sad, and Olivia answers "happy." Ms. Edwards marks off that Olivia has an expressive understanding of *happy*. Later, she hears Clark announcing that the baby is sad and making crying noises when playing with the dollhouse; she notes that he has an expressive understanding of *sad*. When she asks Raquel to pass her the angry puzzle piece, Raquel finds angry and hands it over; she marks that Raquel has a receptive understanding of *angry*. Ms. Edwards's teaching partner takes anecdotal notes during a small-group emotion matching activity, and Ms. Edwards transfers these notes to her data sheets as well.

Figure 3.2 Sample Data Sheet for Recording Receptive and Expressive Use of Emotion Vocabulary Words

Child	Emotion Word: Happy	Emotion Word: Sad	Emotion Word: Angry	Emotion Word: Calm
Eric	Receptive **Expressive** Not yet	Receptive **Expressive** Not yet	Receptive Expressive Not yet	Receptive **Expressive** Not yet
Raquel	Receptive Expressive Not yet	**Receptive** Expressive Not yet	**Receptive** Expressive Not yet	Receptive Expressive Not yet
Olivia	Receptive **Expressive** Not yet	Receptive **Expressive** Not yet	Receptive Expressive Not yet	Receptive Expressive Not yet
Clark	Receptive Expressive Not yet	Receptive **Expressive** Not yet	Receptive Expressive Not yet	**Receptive** Expressive Not yet
Binh	Receptive **Expressive** Not yet	Receptive Expressive Not yet	Receptive Expressive Not yet	Receptive Expressive **Not yet**
Sankalpa	Receptive Expressive Not yet	**Receptive** Expressive Not yet	Receptive **Expressive** Not yet	Receptive Expressive Not yet
Zavier	**Receptive** Expressive Not yet	Receptive Expressive Not yet	Receptive Expressive Not yet	**Receptive** Expressive Not yet
Tessa	Receptive **Expressive** Not yet	Receptive Expressive Not yet	Receptive Expressive Not yet	Receptive Expressive **Not yet**

You can find a blank template of this data sheet at the end of the chapter.

At the end of the week, Ms. Edwards reflects on her data sheet as she begins to plan for next week. She realizes that she does not have a lot of data for *angry*, so she plans to be more intentional on collecting that data next week. She also notices that most of the children were using the words *happy* and *sad*, but were not yet using *calm*. So she decides to plan some targeted activities where children will help sort pictures into buckets labeled "calm" and "not calm." She selects photos that have a range of emotions for the activity, noting that she'll be able to ask children who have mastered the four emotions she has taught to share what they know about the "not calm" emotions portrayed. She'll also be able to show children two pictures at a time, of calm and not calm, and have them receptively identify which is calm if her prompts for expressive responses are ineffective.

Planning for Formative Assessment of Vocabulary Acquisition

Draft a plan for your formative assessment.

> Which words are you planning to collect data on?

> Are there activities or materials for play that would encourage children to use the words naturally in routines?

> What times of day will work best for gathering data to support your instructional decisions?

> When will you review your data so that you can use the information to plan your next instructional steps? For example, if you do your lesson planning on Friday mornings, consider reminding yourself to review this week's data on Thursday so that you can plan accordingly for next week.

Differentiation and Advancement

Reviewing data can lead to intentionally planning more opportunities to practice the skill and meet a wide range of developmental needs in your class. Which children in your class are going to need individualized procedures or materials to make the vocabulary you are teaching more accessible? What kinds of supports have been useful for developing the vocabulary of those children?

Some children, such as those on the autism spectrum or those with anxiety, might find that noticing specific facial expressions doesn't come easily. Consider creating scripts to describe the facial features that go with each emotion. For example, jot down on the back of your happy visual, "eyes open, mouth is a smile." For angry, "eyebrows down, mouth tight" might help add an additional layer of description. "Eyes wide open, mouth wide open" might support describing surprised. Using these descriptive clues alongside the visuals of emotions and basic definitions supports children in being able to look and analyze expressions to identify them.

For children with visual impairments, consider making visuals high contrast, such as light paper on a dark background. Consider adding facial features with textures, such as foam for smooth lips, or twine for eyebrows, to allow for tactile exploration of the expressions.

Some children will come to your class with a wide range of emotion vocabulary words. Advancing their skills can look like asking more in-depth questions that encourage them to model thinking out loud about how they recognized an emotion. What facial clues did they use? What context clues from the book or situation helped them understand? This practices a more advanced skill of understanding and being able to describe the *why*. For children with advanced vocabularies, you might find that offering other emotion words related to the ones they know is a way to grow this skill. Teaching *elated* or *devastated* to a child who has a good grasp on *happy* and *sad* can help them begin to understand not only categories but relative strengths and intensities of emotions.

When my son was in preschool, I tried to expand his vocabulary by teaching him *embarrassed*. He wasn't sure he had ever felt embarrassed until one day I received a call saying he wasn't feeling well and I went to pick him up. When I arrived in his classroom, he turned to me and said, "Mommy, I get it now. When I threw up on the playground and everyone was looking at me . . . I felt so embarrassed!" Introducing a more complicated word ahead of time allowed him to access the word when he needed it later.

Planning for Differentiation and Advancement

Create a plan for children who might need individualization. Use data and observations to identify specific children for whom you will intentionally plan individualized supports.

➤ What instructional procedures for learning words are helpful for the children you have identified? For example, consider whether these children tend to imitate words you provide to them or whether they have typically spontaneously used words when requesting materials. If children will imitate words that you provide, how can you plan to prompt them to use emotion words in the classroom? If children spontaneously use words to request things, how can you practice emotion words so they come more naturally to them? If children use assistive communication devices or picture boards, how can you incorporate these new words into their communication systems?

➤ What materials or visuals have been successful? Can you build on their strengths by creating similar visuals or using similar materials that children are familiar with?

➤ What interests them? For example, if trains hold their interest, can you use trains with facial expressions to support or enhance their learning? If they use language to request bubbles often, can you put emotion faces on the bottles of bubbles to encourage them to identify which one they would like?

➤ How can other staff members, related service providers, or family members collaborate to develop and implement ideas for helping these children?

Troubleshooting Around Building an Emotion Vocabulary

Consider ways to troubleshoot the following questions or obstacles you might run into as you teach this skill.

"What do I do when children label every smiling expression as happy *and every expression without a smile as* sad*?"*

This comes up in many classrooms as children first start to classify emotions. A child who labels excited, surprised, and proud as *happy* is noticing new facial expressions and beginning to relate them to happy, which is a more familiar one. Celebrate this recognition with positive descriptive feedback. This could sound like, "You noticed that she has a smile and wide eyes" or "You knew that this smiling face means that he isn't feeling sad or angry."

Consider revisiting how you have been describing these other emotions. Using those definitions, revisit the nuances. For example, proud is like happy, but is related to feeling happy specifically about something you accomplished. Using little stories can help children label emotions more descriptively. "She painted this picture all by herself. Feeling happy that she did it means she is feeling proud." Compare pictures of happy and proud together. What is the same about those faces? Are there noticeable differences in the visual representations? You might also consider having children sort into piles those emotion expressions that seem positive and those that do not, and then highlight similarities and differences between grouped expressions.

"Some children label pictures of sad *as* crying*. Some children see a peer crying and assume they are sad when sometimes they are mad. How do I encourage them to connect crying with a range of emotion words?"*

"Crying" is a common answer I hear in classrooms too when children are asked to identify emotions based on a picture. Again, children are noticing the facial features, which is a skill we are working on building. So we can start with recognizing that skill, which might sound like "You noticed there are tears on his face. You were really looking to figure it out!" Next, help children understand that crying and tears are only one clue to figuring out how a person feels. Explaining that we need to look for other clues, and redirecting to looking at the person's mouth, eyebrows, or body language, can be helpful.

You might ask children a crying-related question of the day, and you might model with an answer of your own. Have they ever felt so scared they cried? Have you ever felt so happy or proud or loved that you cried? Maybe you've had tears of frustration too. Crying can be a part of many emotions, so digging deeper to look for more clues can be useful in figuring it out. Chapter 4, focused on recognizing body clues, can also help children be more aware of how to read body language to determine emotions.

My four-year-old niece was watching a video of a hamster in a maze. He made it out and she began to cry. "I'm just so proud of him. These are happy tears," she explained. Talking about how we may tear up when emotions overwhelm us, rather than only when we are sad, helps give children an understanding of "happy tears" and other emotions crying might represent.

Family Engagement and Support

As children learn new social and emotional competencies at school, you can strengthen the school-home connection by sharing information, ideas, and activities for families to try. Most teachers send printed or emailed newsletters talking about the weekly or monthly happenings in the classroom. Including blurbs about the social and emotional instruction occurring at school helps families see that these skills are important in the classroom. Effective "social and emotional snippets" may include the skill you are teaching, the impact on children, and some ideas of what you have been doing to support the skill.

A social and emotional snippet related to teaching new vocabulary might look like this:

> *This week, we have been learning new words to describe our feelings. Having more emotion words in our vocabulary means we will have an easier time describing how we feel or how others might feel. Many children already understood sadness, so we expanded our vocabulary this week with more specific words that are related to sad. This week we focused on disappointed (when you are sad that what you were wishing for didn't happen) and lonely (when you are sad that you don't have anyone to play with). To learn these emotion words, we practiced looking at faces and describing what we see (for example, mouth in a frown and eyebrows curving down). You can see our emotion quilt with many pictures illustrating our new emotion words hanging in our room by the sink.*

Seeing skills in action can be powerful for families. Video clips can serve as a model, showing families a skill so they can reinforce it at home. Similarly, a video clip allows them to see the new, emerging skill in action. The clip can also help foster communication between children and family members about instruction at school as they watch and discuss it together. After receiving appropriate permission to take videos of children and share them with families, consider sending home video clips of children showing the emotion visual, sharing the word, making the expression, and showing the sign or gesture. This could make up a little "video dictionary" of the new words for your class. Also consider asking families to share about emotions in their home languages, using videos to share the words and show facial expressions that match the words.

Besides sending home information about what social and emotional skills children are learning at school, teachers can share suggestions for family activities to practice these skills. As you teach children new emotion vocabulary and introduce new pictures, support families by sending them copies of the emotion visuals you are using at school. Consider sharing ideas for using the visuals at home, such as reading a book with their child and asking their child to match a character's emotion to the visual. Encourage them to talk with their child about the emotion cards and to model talking about their own feelings. You can also ask families to look in free magazines, newspapers, or store fliers to find emotion expressions. They can encourage their child to cut them out while talking about the emotions and then bring them in to add to an emotion quilt or emotion book.

Sending information to families communicates that the subject is valuable to you and important for preschool success. However, it doesn't necessarily create feedback loops where families can also provide feedback and support to teachers. For each emotion skill, consider soliciting family input to make your instruction more relevant to families' individual contexts. For example, during the weeks where you focus on teaching new emotion vocabulary, consider asking families if there are specific emotions they would like their child to learn about. Ask families in person, send home a questionnaire or an email, or put "poll boxes" out where parents can put a token into the box with the choice that most resonates with them.

After sending information to all families, and soliciting family feedback to help support your instruction, reflect on how to share the data you've collected. This might include telling families which words their child is using, how they have learned a new sign, or an observational note about their participation in an activity.

> "I went to the school's open house and my daughter's teachers talked all about math, science, and literacy. The fact that they left out social and emotional learning sent the message that it was not as important to them as the other areas. That was hard because I believe so strongly in social and emotional teaching and learning."
>
> –Patti, a preschool special education teacher and parent of a preschooler

As you work on building the habit of giving positive descriptive feedback, consider writing these examples down so children can share the celebration of their progress with their families. For example, in Ms. Nida's classroom, her weekly note sheet for families has three sections. First, she relays any major happenings of the day (a story they read, an activity a child enjoyed). Second, she provides a column for parents to write back any comments or concerns or stories from home. Third, there's a section specifically for sharing a celebration of the week for the individual child. Ms. Nida and her teaching partners look for examples of growth in children and then share at least one celebration for each child on the week's sheet, including celebrations like "Ivy noticed her classmate was upset and offered a hug" or "Terrance has been using emotion words in conversation. Today when he was offered a snack, he told us that he was sad that it wasn't graham crackers."

Sharing information about the vocabulary you are teaching at school sets the stage for you to continue sharing with families information about all the emotional skills you will be teaching as you create an emotion-rich classroom. Soliciting family input—such as inviting families to share emotion vocabulary from their home languages—positions families to contribute their knowledge and offer suggestions to inform your instruction. Building structures of ongoing communication ensures that you are fostering a sense of partnership and community with your families to support children's social and emotional growth.

Wrap-Up

Congratulations on reflecting, planning, and teaching your class new words to grow their emotion vocabulary! Having more words, or more precise words, to describe how they and others are feeling makes communicating easier. That easier communication decreases the likelihood of challenging behavior resulting from not being understood or being misunderstood. After all, most of us feel upset or annoyed when we are angry and a friend says mistakenly, "You seem so sad about that." We all seek to be understood and have our emotions recognized and validated. Learning words to describe emotions allows us to say how we feel, correct others when our emotions are mislabeled, and start to tame our physiological responses.

Having and building an emotion vocabulary leads into the next skill: detecting the emotions we're feeling and connecting them to a label. Rather than saying we feel "bad" or "good," we can provide more specific details as we look for body clues. While chapter 3 supported answering the question, "What are emotions we might feel?" this next skill, the focus of chapter 4, gives the answer to, "How do we know what emotions we feel?"

Sample Child-Friendly Descriptions of Emotions

You can use this sheet as a quick reference when helping children begin to understand, recognize, and label emotions. Some of the sample explanations in this chart relate complex emotions to simpler ones (for example, connecting disappointment to sadness). It helps to teach or review the less complex emotions first (happy, sad, angry, scared, calm), as children are more likely to have background knowledge and exposure to these words and ideas.

Emotion Word	Facial Expressions	Sample Explanation	Example Situation
Happy	Eyes open, smile	When you are happy, you feel good about something that is happening.	"I feel happy when I get to snuggle with my dog."
Excited	Eyes open, smile, raised eyebrows	When you are excited, you feel really happy about something that is going to happen.	"I feel excited when I get to go to my friend's house."
Sad	Mouth in a frown, eyebrows down, sometimes tears	When you are sad, you feel upset or unhappy.	"I feel sad when I miss my mommy. I wish I was with her."
Angry or mad	Eyes narrow, mouth tight, eyebrows down	When you are angry, you feel really upset about something happening that didn't feel right to you.	"I feel angry when I get pushed at the park."
Scared	Eyebrows arch upward, eyes wide open, mouth open	When you are scared, you feel like something bad is going to happen. Your body usually wants to get out of the situation.	"I was scared when the snake was slithering toward me. I was scared it would get too close, and I wanted to be away from it."
Calm	Eyes relaxed, mouth straight or resting	When you are calm, your body is relaxed. You aren't really feeling any strong emotion.	"I feel calm when I read a book. My body and my face are relaxed."
Disappointed	Mouth in a frown, eyebrows down	When you are disappointed, you are sad that something you were wishing for didn't happen.	"I wanted to go outside to play but it was raining so I couldn't. I felt disappointed."
Worried or anxious	Eyebrows down, worry lines on forehead, teeth clenched tight	When you are worried, you don't know what will happen, but you are scared that something bad *might* happen.	"I didn't know what would happen during bedtime but I was worried that there would be a loud storm and it would scare me."
Proud	Eyebrows up, smiling, chin up, hands on hips	When you are proud, you feel happy about something you have done a good job on.	"I felt proud when I finished the puzzle all by myself."
Frustrated	Eyes narrow, mouth tight, eyebrows down	When you are frustrated, you feel angry about something that isn't working the way you wanted it to.	"I felt frustrated when I couldn't fix my bicycle. I tried three times and I couldn't get the wheel back on."
Confused	One eyebrow raised, nose and forehead scrunched, lips tight	When you are confused, you don't understand what to do.	"I felt confused when I didn't hear the directions. I wasn't sure where I was supposed to sit."
Surprised or shocked	Eyes wide open, mouth wide open, eyebrows raised	When you are surprised, something happened that you did not expect.	"I felt surprised when I opened the door and my grandma was there! I didn't know she was coming over."
Lonely	Mouth in a frown, eyebrows down	When you are lonely, you are sad that you don't have anyone to play with or spend time with.	"I felt lonely when all my friends were in the sandbox and no one wanted to play on the slide with me."

Building a Habit of Positive Descriptive Feedback

Providing positive descriptive feedback is new for a lot of us. You can use this form to make a plan for building a habit of giving children this feedback as they learn and practice the social and emotional skills you're teaching.

What is a habit, professional or personal, that you have successfully created for yourself?

Consider the list of habit-building strategies below and identify any you've used before to successfully create a habit, or add other strategies to the list.

- ☐ Scheduling (planning a time to do the habit)

- ☐ Goal-setting (defining a very specific, measurable goal)

- ☐ Monitoring (keeping track of your progress)

- ☐ Partnering for accountability (having another person check in on your progress)

- ☐ Finding your *why* (being clear about *why* the habit matters to you)

- ☐ Setting reminders (using written notes, phone reminders, alarms, prompts on lesson plans, or other methods)

- ☐ Scripting (planning exactly what you would say or do to complete the habit)

- ☐ Promising (letting others know to expect something from you)

- ☐ Others:

→

Choose strategies from the above list that have worked for you in the past. Consider how they would look if you applied them to forming the habit of giving positive descriptive feedback to acknowledge children's use of skills. For example:

➤ Planning a time in your day, like a celebration circle, to share positive descriptive feedback (scheduling)

➤ Having your phone alarm or other alert tell you several times a day to stop, observe, and give positive descriptive feedback (setting reminders)

➤ Creating a display with clear pockets for each child; giving feedback verbally and also writing it down and putting in pockets to quickly monitor who has received feedback (monitoring)

➤ Letting families know you will send home celebrations of children's progress with these social and emotional skills at the end of each week (promising)

My plan to make positive descriptive feedback a habit:

How will I know if my plan is working or if I need to try additional habit-building strategies?

Data Sheet for Recording Receptive and Expressive Use of Emotion Vocabulary Words

To assess children's progress with building their emotion vocabulary, record whether each child can *receptively* identify the various emotion words you have been teaching (by pointing to a picture of the correct word when prompted, for example) or *expressively* identify them (such as by answering "What emotion is this?" with words or signs).

Child's Name	Emotion Word:	Emotion Word:	Emotion Word:	Emotion Word:
	Receptive Expressive Not yet	Receptive Expressive Not yet	Receptive Expressive Not yet	Receptive Expressive Not yet
	Receptive Expressive Not yet	Receptive Expressive Not yet	Receptive Expressive Not yet	Receptive Expressive Not yet
	Receptive Expressive Not yet	Receptive Expressive Not yet	Receptive Expressive Not yet	Receptive Expressive Not yet
	Receptive Expressive Not yet	Receptive Expressive Not yet	Receptive Expressive Not yet	Receptive Expressive Not yet
	Receptive Expressive Not yet	Receptive Expressive Not yet	Receptive Expressive Not yet	Receptive Expressive Not yet
	Receptive Expressive Not yet	Receptive Expressive Not yet	Receptive Expressive Not yet	Receptive Expressive Not yet
	Receptive Expressive Not yet	Receptive Expressive Not yet	Receptive Expressive Not yet	Receptive Expressive Not yet
	Receptive Expressive Not yet	Receptive Expressive Not yet	Receptive Expressive Not yet	Receptive Expressive Not yet
	Receptive Expressive Not yet	Receptive Expressive Not yet	Receptive Expressive Not yet	Receptive Expressive Not yet
	Receptive Expressive Not yet	Receptive Expressive Not yet	Receptive Expressive Not yet	Receptive Expressive Not yet
	Receptive Expressive Not yet	Receptive Expressive Not yet	Receptive Expressive Not yet	Receptive Expressive Not yet
	Receptive Expressive Not yet	Receptive Expressive Not yet	Receptive Expressive Not yet	Receptive Expressive Not yet

Chapter 4

Recognizing and Labeling Emotions in Self

PICTURE THIS Kamari, a four-year-old, goes over to the emotion check-in board in his classroom. He holds a card with his name and photo on it and considers his options. He sees *happy, sad, angry,* and *scared.* He looks in the mirror that is near the board and contemplates his reflection. His teacher comes over to see what his emotion choice will be. Kamari tells his teacher, "I'm not happy. I'm not crying. I'm not angry. I'm not scared." He thinks about it again and asks, "What's the word for the regular one? I just feel regular."

As children learn emotion words and can identify emotion pictures, they can talk about emotions more freely. However, it is still hard work to be able to reflect on how you feel and translate those feelings into words. This is exacerbated by the fact that we all feel and express emotions differently. Some of us cry when we are happy or mad, rather than crying only for sadness. Some of us feel anger as heat in our bodies, while for others anger manifests as a clenched jaw and tight fists. Children need to be coached to reflect and notice how emotions feel in their own bodies and how their facial expressions reflect these emotions.

About the Skill of Recognizing and Labeling Emotions

Sometimes, when we are feeling particularly sad or experiencing other difficult feelings, emotions seem like a burden we can't shake. When coping with overwhelming emotions, it's hard to see the bigger perspective. From an evolutionary point of view, emotions are designed to send us impulses to act. With our emotions come biological responses, rooted in human evolution over time. For example, anger sends blood to our hands to strike, our heart rate increases, and adrenaline is released to give us energy. Feelings of surprise come with a lifting of the eyebrows to allow us to see

more and let more light into our retinas, helping us figure out what is going on. These biological responses combine with our cultural and life experiences to determine how we, as individuals, react to various emotions.

Of course, our emotions often register as facial expressions. Paul Ekman's work, mentioned in chapter 3, found that expressions of certain emotions are largely the same across cultures. Similar research looked at other emotion clues and how they are perceived. For example, in a study of eleven cultures, participants from all cultures were able to match sounds and emotions (Cordaro et al. 2016). Listening to tone of voice and vocalizations is another clue to support recognizing how we, and others, feel. Knowing that our bodies are going to experience physiological changes because of emotions allows us to examine the situation, and these clues from our bodies, to better understand how we feel. Focusing our attention on perceiving our own emotions allows us to accurately label them, which lessens distress and activates the brain's region for emotional regulation. When we can recognize our own emotions and find the vocabulary word to assign a label to them, we can harness our own power to regulate.

The Starting Point

For teachers, one challenge is identifying all the ways we recognize emotions in ourselves. Reflecting on how we recognize our own emotions can help guide our instruction with children. For example, how do you know you are feeling really frustrated? How do feelings of anxiety show up in your body? We tend to focus emotion instruction on looking at facial expressions. While expressions give helpful clues, our emotions are felt in the rest of our body too. We might also identify our feelings by recognizing physical sensations, hearing changes in our voices, or noticing our breathing. Perhaps our body's sensory needs, such as feeling jittery or feeling like we need to yell to release energy, can also provide clues to labeling and understanding our own emotions.

Consider four components to recognizing emotions in yourself:

➤ facial expressions

➤ physical sensations

➤ vocalizations

➤ sensory needs

Planning to Start

Practice identifying what excitement, anger, sadness, and other emotions feel like for you so you can effectively describe the clues and help children recognize emotions in themselves too. Jot down notes on the four components so you have ideas of what to model or discuss, based on your own experiences.

Figure 4.1 Sample Recording Sheet to Identify How Emotions Show Up for You

Emotion	Facial Expression	Physical Sensations	Vocalizations	Sensory Needs
Excitement	Raised eyebrows, smile	Butterflies in stomach, limbs feel "vibratey"	Higher voice, faster speech	Movement, deep breaths
Anger	Frown, clenched jaw	Hot face, feel like crying	Voice gets louder and higher	Privacy and space
Sadness	Lowered eyes, downturned mouth	Pit in stomach, feel like crying	Quiet, low voice	Warmth, hugs

Using DAPPER to Teach Recognizing and Labeling Emotions

> You'll find a blank template of this recording sheet at the end of the chapter.

You've reflected on ways your emotions show up in your own body, considering your facial expressions, physical sensations, vocalizations, and sensory needs. Now you'll use the DAPPER framework to plan how you will teach your class to recognize their emotions based on these same categories of clues.

Demonstrate and Describe

Now that you have an idea of how you recognize your own emotions, it's time to demonstrate and describe for your class. Choose an emotion that you have already discussed with children and bring the visuals you used when teaching that emotion vocabulary with you to this lesson.

Explain that you are not sure how you feel, but you think your body will give you some helpful clues to recognize it. Model and demonstrate your emotions using facial expressions and words. Tell them explicitly that you feel the emotion in your body too. Model looking into a mirror to see your face and describe the expressions you see. Talk about how the emotion feels in your body—how your breathing is, whether your body feels hot or cold or jittery, how your stomach or muscles might feel.

Model how your thoughts or vocalizations might sound. For example, you might describe that your voice feels like it will be loud like a shout, or grumbly. Or perhaps you are frustrated and just feel like "ugggghhh," or you are excited and you feel like shrieking. If your body has a sensory need, describe this too. Perhaps embarrassment has you wishing to hide, or your anger makes you feel like stomping or pushing.

Explain that our bodies give us many clues about our feelings, and that we can figure them out like a detective by listening carefully to what our face, body, and voice are telling us. Model thinking out loud about what you know and identifying the feeling. You might also model eliminating some feelings. For example, you might look at your emotion visual for calm and narrate, "Hmm, I'm not calm. A calm body doesn't have a racing heart or downward eyebrows" before putting the calm card in a pile of "not it" cards.

Thinking out loud is often a strategy we use when teaching young children. It is powerful for them to hear our thought processes while watching us walk through a situation. Thinking out loud about what we notice in our body, those physical manifestations, is another example of how thinking out loud can support learning.

How did your class respond to this? Was your thinking out loud ("My breathing is fast and my eyes are wide open.") more engaging for them than simply describing the skill ("We can look at our face and breathing to get clues about how we feel.")? Reflect on why modeling and thinking out loud might engage children differently than a discussion of the skill.

Planning to Check in with Your Body

This kind of description and modeling involves self-awareness and the practice of "checking in" with your body.

➤ How can you encourage this practice during the day to make it easier for you and your class? You might opt to try guided meditations that focus your attention on sensations, you might encourage children to feel their heartbeat after dancing or sleeping to notice those differences, and you might practice "body checks" to talk about how your body feels in general.

➤ What ideas do you have that can support the practice of checking in and noticing clues from your body, voice, and face?

Animate

One support that can be helpful when teaching this skill is a visual reminder of how children can get clues from their bodies that help them recognize their emotions. The Body Clues Map is a visual way to encourage children to think about how their face looks, how their body feels, how their voice sounds, and what their body wants to do (sensory needs such as wanting to run, hide, or cover their ears).

You'll find the Body Clues Map at the end of this chapter.

Introduce this map of body clues and ask children to help you remember how you were feeling earlier when you modeled and described your emotion. Consider using a blank copy and recording the clues with children, in words or pictures. Then have them help you figure out how you were feeling, using the emotion vocabulary visuals. Celebrate their hard work being "emotion detectives" to help you recognize and label your emotion!

Animating the concept also includes adding gestures or signs. Since the general idea is to take a moment to stop and think about your body's clues, one gesture option would be to motion to your head for "think" and then motion to your body to represent "think about your body." Once you teach a little chant with gestures, it becomes easier to prompt children. For example, when you say, "We're going to think about our bodies" and gesture for *think* and *bodies*, children will start to recognize that prompt as a cue to begin to reflect or get the visual support needed to further this skill.

Think about visual supports that can help focus children's attention on four types of body clues. Reflect on what visuals children are already familiar with and which have been successful for teaching other routines. How can you use those strengths to support teaching and learning this concept?

For example, if children use a visual schedule where pieces are pulled off as they happen, consider adding pieces like that to the Body Clues Map. If children are used to the structure of numbered steps, consider adding numbers next to each piece. If social stories are successful, consider using the visual to walk step-by-step through the body check-in process to help with fluency. If children are drawn to props, could you add visual cues to a doll to make a 3D Body Clues Map?

Planning How to Animate Body Clues

Plan to modify the visual support for your class. Consider each of the following factors and possible modifications, keeping children and their prior knowledge in mind. Note which statements are true for your class as a whole and which modifications might support individual children.

➤ Your class is familiar with visuals with multiple components.

➤ Your class is familiar with visuals with pieces that can be moved or taken off.

➤ Your class is familiar with visuals that have numbered parts to review in order.

➤ Your class is familiar with social stories and would benefit from viewing the visual like a book with pages for each part of the check-in.

➤ Your class is familiar with using 3D props to support learning.

➤ Your class will need black-and-white or high-contrast visuals.

➤ Your class will need full-color visuals to stay engaged.

➤ Your class will need individual small copies of the visuals for easy access.

Based on your answers about your class's prior knowledge and skills, identify and make the Body Clues Map version that will best build on their interests and abilities.

Practice

One practice opportunity for this lesson would be to choose an emotion that children are familiar with (anger or excitement might be easy ones to think through together). Ask children to "act out" these emotions and then encourage other children to share the clues they notice. Depending on the size of the group, this might be done as a whole group, with children sharing some of their clues, or you might pair children to work together to talk about it, with adults providing support for pairs who might need additional scaffolding. For example, Tara and Courtney are given the emotion visual for frustrated. They come up to the front of the group and begin to stomp their feet and growl. Their teacher, Mr. House, asks the other children to describe the clues they see, and Brandis raises her hand to share that they are stomping and Tara's eyebrows are wrinkled. Mr. House asks Tara and Courtney to share how their bodies felt inside when they were acting out frustrated, encouraging them to describe less visible clues.

In another classroom, Mrs. Suggs has introduced the idea of paying attention to body clues to her class of four-year-olds. She is ready for them to try it themselves. Knowing that her class loves Fishing Day, where they bring the water table outside with fishing rods and magnetic fish, she decides to plan another Fishing Day for the day of her emotion discussion. At group time, she tells the children they might feel their emotions in their bodies when she tells them about something special. She shows them the visual and reminds them to think about the clues their bodies are sending so they can recognize their feelings.

She places a special star on her classroom schedule next to outside time and she announces the Fishing Day plans. As she anticipates, the children are visibly excited. Several jump up and down and one shouts, "Yes! I love Fishing Day." Mrs. Suggs gives space for their reaction, and then asks questions to prompt their reflection and recognition, holding up the visual reminder of the clues. "How does your body feel when you think about Fishing Day today?" she asks. She asks them to listen to their breathing and feel their heartbeat and reflect on whether it is fast or slow. She asks what voices they had when they heard the news, and the child who shouted is able to share that his voice felt really big, like it needed to come out. Other children share that their bodies had energy and wanted to jump, and a little girl shares that her body "was ready to do the fishing right now." Mrs. Suggs holds up an emotion chart that she has been using with the children and asks them to recognize and name their emotions as they transition out of the group time.

With this practice, note for children that emotion clues can vary among people. While one child might feel like jumping up and down with excitement, another child's excitement might look very different. That's why it's important to start learning our own body's clues to help us understand how we feel, and then we can tell others how we feel so they can understand or help us if we need it.

Planning How to Practice Recognizing Body Clues

Decide how you want to structure the practice that will accompany your introductory lesson. Considerations might include:

➤ Do children need more time and practice to understand what the body clues to recognizing emotions are?

➤ Do you have children in your class who are already recognizing and labeling their own emotions accurately? Would having them model be helpful for your class to see another example in action?

➤ Do you have children in your class who have big displays of feelings who would be willing to share what their bodies and voices are "saying" about their emotions? Some children might not wish to share, but others might like to process a big emotional experience; once they are calm, they can describe how they were feeling.

Planned Opportunities

You've taught children about the idea of listening to their bodies' clues to recognize their emotions. You've shared visual supports and modeled and practiced identifying some of the emotion clues. It's time for some additional practice opportunities to support children's recognition of their own emotions.

Of course, we cannot plan when children will have emotions that that they'll need to recognize and process. Instead, we can set up opportunities for continued practice and discussion. For example, one opportunity is creating a routine of an emotion check-in. A check-in is a structure in which children work to recognize their own emotion and then reflect on how they are currently feeling. This can look like individual charts or a group chart. Setting up a time (or times) to check in during the day allows the process to become more fluent and gives teachers the opportunity to give support and feedback. Then, when children are experiencing emotions or after they have worked through emotions, a teacher can encourage them to check in—something that will, at that point, be a practiced skill.

Many teachers choose to use an emotion check-in as part of a transition. For example, children put away their backpacks, wash hands, and then do the check-in chart that is located near the handwashing sink. Other teachers work it into a routine, such as clean up, check in, come to circle. How can you work an emotion check-in chart into your daily routines? Reflect on times of your day where this might make sense.

Check-in charts can look very different depending on the needs of your class, available materials, and personal preference. For example, Ms. Brown has a chart with hook and loop strips on the back of a bookcase. Children place their photo on the strips under the emotion that they are feeling. In Ms. Almeida's room, children's photos are dragged next to an emotion picture on a Smart Board. In Ms. Dunkins' class, children are asked to check in by pulling an emotion piece off a chart. In Ms. Hackmann's room, children use clothespins to put their name on a large emotion wheel. In Ms. Saechao's class, children have individual emotion wheels in their cubbies and they each "set" their wheel as part of their morning, midday, and afternoon routines.

Don't forget to check in yourself! It gives you a chance to model the check-in process and take a moment to slow down and recognize the emotions you are bringing to the day. Have the names, pictures, or clothespins ready to go for daily classroom staff to make modeling easier.

Regardless of the format, establishing a check-in routine means that children spend time every day checking in with their body and emotions. Rather than simply asking children to identify how they feel, practice asking other reflective questions: "How do you know?" "What clues helped you figure that out?"

Another option is to explicitly encourage children to remind themselves of the types of body clues before doing an emotion check-in. This could look like putting the clues visual as Step 1 and a mirror as Step 2, and then doing the identifying of the emotion as Step 3 in the emotion check-in routine.

Another planned opportunity could be intentional discussions and deep dives into clues around specific emotions, using the Body Clues Map. Children, with adult support at school or at home, can help draw or write out what clues their body gives them related to certain emotions. You might choose to put these into a book that children revisit to explore how emotions feel for them and how they can recognize them in their bodies.

Planning for an Emotion Check-In

As you plan for your emotion check-in, there are many decisions to make to get the system up and running.

➤ Will you make a whole-group chart or individual charts?

➤ If you make individual charts, would you have a chance each day to stop by and review children's individual check-in charts? When will you do this? How will you follow up with individual children about the emotion they selected?

➤ If you make a whole-group chart, where might it be located? It should be easily accessible for children, but also viewable for teachers. If you want to review it with children at group time, perhaps locating it nearby or making it portable would support that goal.

➤ How many children can fit around your chart to work at it? Is there a transition where children can stagger their time at the check-in chart to avoid wait times and crowds?

➤ What time(s) of day will be best for the check-in? How do children know the pieces of your routine? Do they have a visual to remind them? Did you teach by practicing? How will you teach and prompt children to check in as part of the routine?

➤ What materials will you need to model the check-in process? If you make individual check-in charts, make ones for staff too. If you make a whole class chart, make sure you include staff names or pictures so you can model and take part.

Extend

It's easier to talk about our body's clues when we are not in the middle of waves of feelings crashing down on us. To extend this skill of recognizing and labeling our own emotions, we need to coach children through using this skill while they are having big feelings.

In Ms. Suggs's class, Jayden is working, brow furrowed, with a shape sorter. He pops the circle piece into the round hole and smiles with pride. Next, he easily pushes the star piece into the star hole. He grabs the octagon piece and attempts to push it into the hexagon hole. He tries once, rotates the octagon, and pushes again. When the piece doesn't fit, frustration rises. He throws the shape sorter into the toy shelf and begins to cry. Ms. Suggs goes over to use the ICARE approach to coach Jayden through the situation, with a goal of supporting the skill of recognizing and labeling emotions.

Intent: Ms. Suggs approaches Jayden. She analyzes his intent. He is frustrated and he doesn't yet know how to recognize and label his emotions or ask her for help. She reminds herself that he isn't throwing the shape sorter with the intent to break it. She enters the scene calmly, with an intent to support and teach.

Calm: Ms. Suggs knows that Jayden will often sit in her lap for help calming down, so she sits down next to him to offer him support with regulation. He crawls into her lap and she takes slow and steady breaths of her own, and his breathing starts to match hers. She continues intentionally breathing until he looks up at her, crying finished, and states, "I threw the shapes."

Acknowledge: Ms. Suggs acknowledges how he was feeling. "You were having trouble getting the shape in the hole and you weren't sure what do with your big feeling."

Rewind: Ms. Suggs thinks about what could have happened differently and what skill Jayden is working on. She chooses to reinforce the idea of using your body's clues to recognize and identify the emotion. If she can help Jayden match the words with how he is feeling, and encourage him to ask her for help, she can support him with frustration going forward.

She asks Jayden if she can help him figure out his body's clues. Together, they look at the Body Clues Map. She prompts him to think about what happened with the shape sorter. "I couldn't get it in," he explained to her. She asked him where he felt his emotion in his body. He pointed to the hands of the visual. "Oh, yes, your body gave you a clue through your hands."

"I threw it," Jayden explained, and he pointed to the eyes when Ms. Suggs asked where else he felt his feelings. "Oh yes, you did start to cry too." Ms. Suggs repeats back key parts of the conversation to Jayden: "Your hands felt like throwing, and your eyes felt like crying, and you couldn't get the shape in the sorter. What feeling do you think that was?" Jayden pointed to the mad emotion visual, and Ms. Suggs elaborated. "Yes, you could feel mad when you can't put the piece in. And you felt the mad in your hands and in your eyes. Another feeling like mad is frustrated. It means you are mad or upset when you are trying something, and your plan doesn't work."

Echo: Ms. Suggs models how to say, "I feel frustrated." Jayden practices saying, "I feel frustrated!" She echoes back what they talked about. "When your tries aren't working and you feel upset in your hands and tears in your eyes, you might be frustrated. You can say 'I feel frustrated!' and I will come and help you handle it."

In this situation, Ms. Suggs waited for Jayden to calm and then individually worked through talking about the body clues they discovered in that situation. She helped Jayden tie those clues to possible feelings, like mad or frustrated, and then encouraged him to practice declaring how he feels so that a teacher can help. This in-the-moment coaching supported Jayden with using the tools and techniques the class had been practicing during a real situation and his very real feelings.

Planning to Extend Recognizing Emotions

Part of extending children's understanding of how to recognize and label their emotions involves having relevant materials readily accessible, like the Body Clues Map or visuals of emotions. Plan where you might be when children need to be coached through those supports.

➤ Are your visual supports readily accessible for social coaching?

➤ If not, where do you need extra copies? Are there specific areas that would benefit from having these materials?

➤ Do you need to have them on you, like on a lanyard or clipped to a belt loop?

➤ Who will get them when you need them? Will you get them? Will you make a plan for another adult to bring them to you when you are supporting a child through a situation? Would you like to create a classroom job that involves a child bringing the Body Clues Map or other visuals to you when needed?

Reinforce and Reflect

To reinforce the skill of recognizing one's own emotions, teachers and other adults can encourage and prompt children's reflection. For example, a teacher might ask, "How do you feel?" and then go beyond that starting point to encourage the child to explain how they knew they were experiencing that specific emotion, allowing them to share their thought processes. They might ask questions about why a child is feeling a specific thing ("Why are you feeling frustrated today?") and help children connect what happened with how their body responded. This reflection also ties into recognizing the emotions of others, as children can more easily recognize some of the expressions and body clues they see in peers after focusing on their own with intention.

Besides consistent practice and support with the skill, providing positive descriptive feedback when children work to recognize their emotions is helpful to support and encourage their growth. For a child who starts attending to his own reflection in the mirror, this could sound like "You remembered to look at your face for a clue!" Perhaps a child starts picking up a visual when thinking through emotions. "You got your supplies to be an emotion detective today! Looking for clues is so helpful!" Or maybe a child shares that she knows she is frustrated because she feels it in her hands. Noticing that she is reading her clues and expressing her feelings might sound like, "You did it! You used your body clues and figured out how you are feeling!" This noticing specifically supports children in connecting the steps they are taking with the desired outcome.

Planning to Reinforce and Reflect on Recognizing Emotions

Brainstorm reflective prompts that might encourage children to reflect on their emotions and their body clues. For example, "Which body clue helped you know you were sad?" How might you use these prompts to encourage reflection? For some teachers, written reminders are supportive, so having reflection prompts near the check-in chart or on the agenda for emotion check-ins is useful. For other teachers, creating a routine of reflection—such as having a child share about their emotion, why they felt a specific way, and what clues they discovered—every day as a part of group time or snack time helps build the habit, especially as children will remind you if you forget a piece of the routine.

Jot down some reflective prompts you will try. Ask yourself questions like:

➤ Where should you record these prompts to have them ready?

➤ At what time of day will you be intentional about encouraging children's reflection?

➤ How will you know you are meeting the goal of providing reflective prompts to your class?

As you add another layer of positive descriptive feedback into your emotion teaching, consider what kind of positive feedback you have been giving for labeling emotions. Are there phrases or sentence stems that seem to be helpful or more natural for you? If you are already saying, "You did it! You recognized *proud*," how can you use that same structure to give positive descriptive feedback around the new skill of recognizing their own emotions?

Recognizing Emotions Throughout the Day

Consider the following examples of ways to further practice and reinforce emotion recognition throughout the day and during a range of activities.

Morning Meeting or Circle Time: Have children "act out" some of their emotions. As they do, film their responses. Later, play the clips for children and have them identify which emotion they were acting out. How did they recognize the emotion from the video of themselves? What body clues did they notice?

Pair children up and give each pair a puppet. Have children pick an emotion visual and use their puppet to show body clues—how does their body look and feel? What voice do they have? Encourage partners to work together to act out the body clues for the puppet, including using the puppet's "voice" and narrating how the puppet's body feels.

Music and Movement: Practice checking in on breathing and heart rate. Have children feel their heartbeat when calm and try again when they're excited or after exercise. Talk about the difference in heart rate and breathing patterns and how that can change and help us figure out how we feel.

Sing "If You're Happy and You Know It" using different body clue verses that children help you develop. For example, "when I'm excited and I know it, my heart beats fast," "when I'm angry and I know it, I want to stomp," or "when I'm proud and I know it, I want to shout hooray!"

Small Group: Consider doing shared writing or creating class books about body clues. For example, you could make a "When I am excited . . ." book in which children share how their body feels with words, drawings, or photographs.

Transitions: During a waiting time, such as a transition where children are waiting to wash hands or to get jackets, hold an emotions scavenger hunt where children look for characters in books and try to read their body clues to find specific emotions. This expands the notion from recognizing feelings in themselves to recognizing them in others. Consider pairing children to look together, which will also help them work on skills like sharing a material and discussing emotion clues.

Gross-Motor Skills and Outside Time: Make a tracing of a body—yours or a child's—outside with chalk. Have each child color or decorate where they feel an emotion. For example, on a "frustrated" body, children might color or sign their name on the feet if they feel like kicking, or by the mouth if they feel like yelling. This could also be done inside with large rolls of paper. Consider taking photographs to document the children's work before the chalk is washed away.

Art: Use gingerbread people cookie cutters with playdough. Have children use small loose objects, like sequins or acorns, to show where in their body they feel specific emotions, like anger or anxiety. Encourage children to show others their playdough creations and describe where they feel their emotions to their peers.

Math: Consider polling and graphing children's body clues related to specific emotions. For example, ask children to think about when they are really angry. Do they yell or do they cry or do something else? To make an easy bar graph, give each child an interlocking block, with all children's blocks being the same size and shape. Write or draw your choices on paper or the board and have children "vote" by stacking their blocks in front of the option that is most like them. Compare the stacks of blocks. Which one has the most? Which has the least? If you like, you could add to this graph by inviting families or other members of your school community to share what body clues help them figure out their feelings.

Story Time: You might plan opportunities for children to pretend they are characters in books and have them explore what body clues look like for the characters. For example, when reading *The Chocolate-Covered-Cookie Tantrum* by Deborah Blumenthal, you might ask children to pretend to be Sophie and examine what those clues are for her (for example, crying, feeling exhausted, and feeling like the world is spinning). Practice using the Body Clues Map visual and presenting all the prompts for children to answer as if they are Sophie. Other books with displays of strong feelings and clear body clues also work well for practice.

Planning to Recognize Emotions Throughout the Day

Which activities to reinforce body clues identification appeal to you? What other ideas and materials do you have that would build on this skill? Do you have mindfulness or meditation resources that encourage participants to focus in on bodily sensations? As you review activities and materials, plan with the following considerations in mind:

➤ Do you have examples of activities where children recognize body clues for emotions other than strong upset or anger (such as excited, calm, or lonely)?

➤ Have you chosen activities focused on a wide range of body clues? Instead of only focusing on facial expression, do you have ideas for activities related to vocalizations or sensory needs?

➤ Spread out your activities across the week and across different settings (different centers, inside and outside, activities that are facilitated by different adults).

Formative Assessment of Emotion Recognition

Observing children during an emotion check-in, and at other times when they are feeling strong emotions, can help give us valuable information about how they are able to recognize their own emotions. One skill is being able to check in and find some of the clues their bodies send to alert them to their emotions. A second skill is being able to use those clues to identify one of the emotions from their emotion vocabulary. Collecting this data allows us to reflect on strengths and gaps in our instruction, encourages our individualized planning for children, and gives us data to share about growth and emerging skills with families.

The sample data sheet in figure 4.2 shows one way to collect information. Remember that children, when in the peak of big feelings, will find it hard to reflect on their feelings and clues. However, children who are slightly triggered or children who have regained calm can be encouraged to talk about what they were feeling and what clues and messages they were receiving from their bodies.

On this sheet, children's names are listed in the left-hand column. The other columns indicate different types of body clues children might use to identify their emotions. You can either mark the box when you observe a child using the strategy (the child looks in their mirror at their own expression when asked how they are feeling) or when you hear a child talk about the body clue in relation to an emotion.

("I get so hot when I am angry." "Her heartbeat probably is fast when she is excited.") The second-from-right column allows the teacher to note whether the child self-identified an emotion that matched with their body clues. If the child did so, the right-hand column has space to record what emotion they chose or verbalized.

For example, Ms. Suggs is supporting Malachai with the emotion check-in at the mirror. He came into school scowling and angry about how his breakfast went that morning. He approaches the chart, looks in the mirror, and puts himself under angry. When Ms. Suggs asked which body clues helped him figure it out, he said he was yelling all morning and his voice still felt "mean." She recorded the interaction on her data sheet. Since he used the mirror to check his facial expression, and acknowledged his voice was a clue, she marked both "facial expressions" and "vocalizations." He also chose an emotion choice that matched his affect, so she marked that he did identify his emotion. She added a note that it was *angry*.

Later, when Ms. Suggs talked with Samyra about her birthday party and how it felt, Samyra described how she was excited by acknowledging that she kept jumping up and down, her body wanted to move, and her voice was yelling, "Happy birthday to me!" Ms. Suggs checked off physical sensations, vocalizations, and sensory needs and jotted down *excited*. From their discussion, Ms. Suggs knew that Samyra was able to read those body clues and understand how they were related to her birthday excitement.

Figure 4.2 Sample Data Sheet for Recording Children's Understanding of Body Clues

Child's Name	Facial Expressions	Physical Sensations	Vocalizations	Sensory Needs	Identification of Own Emotions	Emotion or Emotions Identified
Malachai	x		x		x	Angry
Cameron	x				x	Happy
Finley	x				x	Happy
Samyra		x	x	x	x	Excited
Zara	x				x	Sad

For a blank copy of this data sheet, see the end of the chapter.

At the end of the week, Ms. Suggs reviews her data to use it to support instruction. When she sees a couple of children are only able to identify emotions based on their facial expressions, she selects those children for some small-group time to revisit other body clues and practice together. She makes sure to verbally recognize when she sees a body clue. For example, when she sees Zara hiding behind her dad when there was a different teacher than usual at drop-off, she later talks to Zara about how it seemed like her body was wishing to hide, and that sometimes that gives us a clue that we are afraid or nervous or shy.

Planning for Formative Assessment of Emotion Recognition

Draft a plan for your formative assessment of this skill.

➤ What times of day will work best for gathering data to support your instructional decisions around this skill?

➤ Which emotions do you wish to collect data on? If there are specific emotions you want children to practice recognizing, what activities or resources will you need to encourage that skill with regard to those emotions?

➤ Can you embed data collection into certain times of day in your classroom, such as when children do the emotion check-in or when you are asking your reflective prompts? Who will collect this data?

➤ When will you review your data so you can use that information to plan your next instructional steps?

Differentiation and Advancement

You may need to extend a skill's practice and application to meet a wide range of developmental needs in your class. To differentiate your instruction for children who have a harder time understanding visual representations or icons, you might consider working with the child's family to take pictures or videos of the child when feeling common emotions like happy, excited, angry, or sad. Then you can use that documentation to help the child look for those clues to recognize their emotion expressions, whether through facial expressions or other body clues.

Or, for a child who needs more structure, consider converting the visual support into separate steps about how to check in with your body about emotions. This could look like a visual routine that presents several steps in a row and allows children to pull off pieces or turn them over after reflecting on each one. Some children might be just starting with the basic skill of looking in a mirror to explore their own facial expressions. Celebrating with a clap, "hooray," or a smile each time the child uses the mirror can help build positive associations for children who have trouble with eye contact and referencing a mirror.

For children who can describe their bodies' clues and accurately label their emotions, consider providing more advanced work. You might encourage them to write and record the clues they notice for more complicated emotions and work individually with them to compare and contrast this with the ways other emotions manifest.

Planning for Differentiation and Advancement

Reflect on your data from the week. Are some children able to identify and talk about body clues during activities and real-life situations? If they are developing this skill, what activities have you done that were most salient and memorable for them?

Create a plan for children who might need individualization. Use data and observations to identify specific children for whom you will intentionally plan modified or individualized supports.

> ➤ What instructional procedures for encouraging awareness of their bodies have been helpful for the children you have identified? For example, consider what strategies helped with identifying sensations such as hunger or sleepiness or needing to use the bathroom. If a child recognizes and articulates these bodily needs, how might you use that skill to help a child recognize emotions? Families might have valuable insights and ideas to share.

> ➤ What materials or visuals have been successful? Can you build on children's strengths by creating similar visuals or using materials they are already familiar with?

> ➤ What emotions are most relevant and important in their day-to-day experience? Which ones do they feel often, or which ones do they seem to tune into when seen in other people? Consider starting with these.

> ➤ Which children have this skill? Would they benefit from activities such as helping others with the skill, recognizing more subtle or complicated emotions, or documenting their ideas? Plan a strategy to challenge them.

Trauma-Sensitive Emotion Coaching

Recognizing body clues can be challenging, particularly for children who have experienced abuse or other trauma. Setting up specific structures in your classroom can help encourage trauma-sensitive emotion coaching. Knowing how to get support for yourself as you support children is also important for you to be able to keep doing this work.

First, choose and teach a way for children to opt out of activities that make them feel uncomfortable. How can children let you know they aren't feeling safe? One option is to teach children to say "pass" if they wish for their turn to be skipped. In other classrooms, children can go to the Regulation Station if they feel like they need a break. If a child is upset when exploring body clues, and you have children paired up to share, how will you invite children to articulate that they aren't comfortable? Teaching children how to opt out of an activity is important, but also keep an eye out for discomfort among children who haven't spoken up. If a child is unable or unprepared to tell you they are feeling unsafe, but you notice it, you can ask the child if they wish for a pass or ask the child to be your partner and focus the activity on your emotions, modeling rather than asking the child to do the activity themself.

Second, offer choices. For example, rather than telling children they have to close their eyes when focusing on how they are breathing, offer the choice of keeping eyes open or closed before you begin the activity. Rather than having every child talk about body clues for sadness or fear, you might ask children to pick an emotion to share about, giving them the option of choosing one that might feel more comfortable for them.

Third, remember that predictability helps create a feeling of safety. Letting children know what you are going to be talking about or working on ahead of time can help make it feel predictable and potentially less threatening. Giving reminders of skills you have taught, such as using the Regulation Station when upset (the focus of chapter 7), helps foster in children a feeling that they know what they can do to access help if needed.

Fourth, keep in mind that triggers related to trauma are often not obvious, to teachers or children. A child whose trauma has triggered a stress response in their body might not know how they are feeling or why. While we will encourage building the skill of understanding the causes of emotions (the focus of chapter 5), if a child is unable to identify specific causes, we also can and should accept that, rather than insisting on them having an answer each and every time we ask.

Last, remember to get support for both the child and you. Glance back at your reflections and thoughts from Belief 6 in chapter 1.

➤ Who can offer support to a child who is navigating traumatic experiences?

➤ Who do you need to discuss this with in your program?

➤ Similarly, who can support you as you do this work? Who can you ask for help as you navigate your own feelings and emotions when trauma surfaces, either for you or children?

Troubleshooting Around Recognizing and Labeling Emotions in Self

Consider ways to troubleshoot the following questions or obstacles you might run into as you teach this skill.

"What if a child can't tell me how they feel and I guess wrong?"
Many of the teachers I work with wonder about this. They don't want to mislabel a child's emotions, and at the same time they want to make sure they are using emotion words with children to add context and help teach those words. There are some ways to strike a balance between mislabeling a child's emotions and not using those emotion words at all.

For example, you might describe the child's face and body. "Your eyebrows are down, and your lips are going down into a frown." Showing them their face in the mirror can help so they see those clues to their emotion too (which is a big focus in this chapter). One option is to use the language of uncertainty. This might sound like, "You seem sad" or "You might be disappointed." Some children will nod, shake their head, or find another way to indicate if you got it right.

In a classroom of four-year-olds where all the children are on the autism spectrum, the teaching team had worked really hard on teaching children *sad, mad, calm,* and *happy.* When a child was crying, the teacher described his face and said, "You seem sad." He turned to her and said, "mad." Communicating verbally wasn't easy for him, but he had practiced with those words and was able to correct her when she got it wrong!

Another strategy is to be very honest and say that you aren't sure. "I think you might be sad that it's not your turn to play with the speech pathologist, but maybe you are mad." You might describe the body clues that you see too. Offering the two options that you are considering with visuals might encourage the child to point or gesture or look at one of the cards to give you an indication, but even if they don't do this, you are still modeling the skills of looking for body clues to how someone is feeling and trying to match those clues with the vocabulary words you are teaching.

While teachers often worry about misidentifying children's emotions, sometimes children misidentify their own emotions. This might happen as children learn and practice new vocabulary, but usually leads to self-correction over time as they master emotion identification. Teachers are often concerned about the scenario in which a child picks an emotion they like, rather than how they seem to be feeling. For example, a seemingly happy child in a classroom where I was coaching said, "I'm so mad. Grrrr!" and then laughed about it every day for two weeks during emotions check-in. The teacher had questions for me: Should she point out that the child's facial expression and body language didn't match her choice of angry? Should she let her pick angry because it's the one she wished to acknowledge every day?

I choose to navigate these situations by thinking though my goals so I can align my responses to them, and I encouraged the teacher to do the same. My goals include:

➤ Children becoming comfortable identifying their emotions

➤ Children recognizing their emotions

➤ Children having the space to share their emotions and others respectfully listening

Outlining these goals helps rule out some responses. Saying, "You should put happy because you have been laughing and playing all morning" contradicts the goal of having emotions validated and respected and sends the message that the child isn't in charge of self-identifying. Similarly, "You pick angry every day. Try choosing a different one" doesn't match those goals either.

Some responses that align better with the identified goals include:

➤ "I see your face with your tight eyebrows and I hear your growl. Those are ways we might look or sound when we're angry." This response validates that she is matching those clues with the emotion of anger.

➤ "You were angry, and now I see you laughing like something is silly. Take a look in this mirror. Did your emotions change?" This also reads her body and expressions, narrating those, and emphasizes that emotions do change.

➤ "You are wishing for us to know that you feel angry. After this check-in, we're going to practice our calming strategies, and then you can check your body to see if they helped." This encourages another round of practice with recognizing her own emotions.

Many children will also pick happy every single day. Perhaps that is truly how they self-identify or maybe they are not yet comfortable choosing a different emotion. Consider your goals to guide your responses in those moments. You might opt to continue to label, describe facial expressions, and teach children about other emotions individually outside of the emotion check-in. You might be intentional in your modeling to send the message that all different emotions are okay to have and discuss in the classroom. Or you might choose a response that encourages the use of a new skill and validates the child's response.

Be mindful about checking in with yourself, as well. Are you bothered when a child picks happy every day, even when they might feel differently? Are you bothered when a child picks angry or sad every day, even when they might feel differently? Reflect on whether it's a challenge for the child or for you. We want to accept all feelings rather than focusing on changing them. Sometimes a child saying they are sad every day makes us uncomfortable because we want the child to be happy in our class. Remember, we aren't responsible for the child's emotions, but we are responsible for how we respond to them. Be sure not to shame or embarrass a child for their emotion check-in response, and consider talking to the child, the child's family, and other colleagues who can offer support if a child truly is angry or sad every day.

Family Engagement and Support

Sharing information with families about body clues and emotion recognition builds on the information and strategies sent home about building emotion vocabulary in chapter 3.

A social and emotional snippet in a newsletter or weekly email might look like this:

This week, we have been practicing recognizing our own emotions by being detectives and looking for our body's clues. Some of these clues are found when looking at our facial expressions in the mirror, checking in with our body to notice where we feel tension, listening to how our voice sounds, and paying attention to what our body wants or needs to do. For example, seeing a scowl on our face, screaming, and feeling like we want to stomp our feet are all clues that tell us we might be feeling angry or frustrated. We practiced talking about our body's emotion clues and then identifying our emotions on a feelings check-in chart. You can see the chart in our room near the entryway. There are extra clothespins to add a feeling if you'd like to do the check-in with your child at drop-off or pick-up.

With appropriate permission to share, consider sending home video clips of children using the Body Clues Map and talking about or acting out their emotions. Explain the different kinds of clues you have been teaching children and send home videos of children trying to identify them. You can also ask families to send videos to you of their children feeling big emotions so you can watch them with children and talk about clues together.

Support families in creating an emotion check-in chart for home. They might make one just for their child, or they might make one for the whole family to use. Consider providing modeling or videos to support families in understanding how you use this structure at school and how they could use it at home. Working together to make an emotion check-in chart for home can be a great activity for a family workshop or home visit if families are interested!

You might also encourage children to ask their family members about their own body clues that help them identify emotions. You could ask families to record some of their examples, and have children share in class. It can be another reminder that we all feel emotions in different ways, and our clues may even be different from those of people close to us.

Remember to solicit family input and feedback. Are there resources they are looking for as they work with their child on recognizing emotions? Ask families what they have noticed as they talk about emotions at home with their child. Share your celebrations of what you notice their children doing in the classroom.

In addition, now that you have been sending home information in various ways—through snippets, videos, and home activity ideas—consider asking families which of these ways they prefer to get social and emotional information. Collecting that feedback can help you figure out where to focus your energy. If most of your families

"My child's virtual teacher shared her own experience of frustration and talked to her students about how she was feeling hot inside. I learned new language to use with my children about how emotions feel in their bodies, and my daughter was able to share how her teacher felt and why."

–Genevieve, a parent, describing the benefit of hearing the language teachers were using in the classroom. Sharing the language around body clues with families can help them continue these conversations at home.

prefer videos to written support, consider sending a video example of an activity instead of written ideas and directions. Being responsive to family feedback continues to foster the positive relationship you've worked hard to create.

Wrap-Up

Congratulations on reflecting, planning, and teaching your class how to recognize body clues to their emotions! Being able to recognize the physiological signs of emotions, and then finding the appropriate emotional labels, allows children to make sense of their feelings and sensations that can sometimes feel out of control. When we don't connect our physiological changes with our feelings, we often cannot regulate our emotions successfully. We might try to "fix" the sensations, such as taking off our sweater when we are hot, without realizing that a strategy to regulate our anger or anxiety would more effectively help our bodies. Understanding how we feel allows us to pick strategies to support regulation, and knowing we have tools to handle our feelings effectively makes emotions more manageable.

Thus, recognizing our body's clues leads into the next skill: understanding the causes of emotions. We have recognized what emotions we are feeling, and we know the words to label those emotions. While chapter 4 focuses on "How do we know what emotions we feel?" chapter 5 answers the question "Why do we feel the way we do?"

Body Clues Map

My body wants to:

My voice sounds:

My face looks:

In my body, I feel:

Recording Sheet to Identify How Emotions Show Up for You

Use this simple chart to jot down how emotions feel and manifest for you. Reflecting on your own expression of feelings will help you guide children as they learn to spot the clues and recognize emotions in themselves.

Emotion	Facial Expressions	Physical Sensations	Vocalizations	Sensory Needs

Data Sheet for Recording Children's Understanding of Body Clues

As children practice and build the skill of recognizing and understanding their body clues and how they connect to emotions, you can use this sheet to record your observations and data. Mark whether children are able to notice and interpret each type of body clue in themselves and whether they use that information to identify emotions.

Child's Name	Facial Expressions	Physical Sensations	Vocalizations	Sensory Needs	Identification of Own Emotions	Emotion or Emotions Identified

Chapter 5

Understanding Causes of Emotions

PICTURE THIS Nichole is in the construction center. She is working on building a gigantic tower of rectangles, with triangle blocks around the top. The tower reaches her shoulders, and she is slowly and carefully adding another triangle to the top. She steps back to admire her work and realizes there's one spot left for a triangle topper. Checking the block shelf, she realizes there is not another triangle for her to add. She turns to see if there are any on the floor, and she notices that Leslie and Ana have a large pile of triangles, rectangles, and cylinders that they are pulling from to add to their house. Nichole puts out her hand and asks for a triangle. Ana responds, "You can't have it because we need it for our house."

Nichole turns and looks at her tower, with the one empty space on top. She looks at the pile of five triangles on the floor that Leslie is sweeping closer to her body. Nichole takes a couple steps toward Leslie and Ana's building area and, with one swift kick of her sneaker, knocks their house over. Leslie begins to cry. Ana stands up and screams, "You aren't my friend anymore!" in Nichole's face. Nichole begins to cry too and runs to the Regulation Station, while the classroom teacher approaches the other girls in the construction center.

There are a lot of big emotions right now in the classroom. There are three upset children, a mess in the construction center, and several other children who are watching to see how the situation unfolds. The teacher, overwhelmed, addresses the emotions she sees. "You are upset because Nichole kicked over your blocks," she says to Ana and Leslie. She offers the two girls a basket of calming tools, and then heads toward Nichole. She asks Nichole what happened, but Nichole is crying too hard to answer. She tells Nichole it isn't okay for her to kick over a tower if she is angry, and that she can calm down and use her words instead of kicking. Nichole, still upset, continues to cry, and her teacher isn't sure where to go from here. While she felt equipped to support Leslie and Ana in acknowledging their emotions and offering tools to

help, she didn't see the situation unfold in its entirety, and that leaves her feeling at a loss for how to address it with Nichole. She jots down a note to remind her to ask her instructional coach about this later—"How do I support children through emotional situations when I don't really know why something happened? How do I encourage Nichole to explain the cause of her upset so I can help her through it?" The teacher realizes that understanding more about what caused the feelings can help children connect emotions with strategies, like feeling lonely and finding someone to play with or feeling frustrated and choosing regulation tools. She wishes to help Nichole articulate the cause of her upset so that she can listen, acknowledge, and validate, and help Nichole plan for more effective strategies than kicking over her peers' creations.

About the Skill of Understanding Emotions' Causes

Once children have an emotional vocabulary, they can use those words to describe how they are feeling, which helps us get insight into the behaviors and responses we see and what might be helpful in regulating or handling those feelings. Using body clues can help children become more accurate in recognizing and applying the correct emotion label too. Another step in the process is understanding *why* they might feel a particular way, or why another person might feel a particular way. Understanding causes of emotions allows us to better understand our feelings and see patterns in our behavior.

Understanding the causes of emotions is complicated, for children and for adults. For example, I tend to be snippy and short-tempered when it's time to go in the morning. I get easily frustrated when my son is moving slowly or when he can't find his second shoe. Stepping back and asking myself why a shoe is causing frustration, and what about this situation is uncomfortable, helps me gain additional perspective. In this case, the frustration is really stemming from anxiety about the possibility of being late and looking as if I do not value the time and commitment I have made to the teacher with whom I have a morning appointment.

Children's understanding of emotions might be less nuanced than that example, but we do want to encourage children to start thinking about and expressing causes behind emotions. This might look like a child saying, "I was mad because the menu said pizza and then it was sandwiches." It could look like a child saying, "He never wants to play with me," allowing us to help the child understand that feelings they might have in this situation are loneliness or rejection. Or perhaps the understanding is in relation to another child or a book character; "She might be worried on her first day of school because that's how I felt when I came to school."

Nichole's teacher can get a better sense of how to support children through scenarios by encouraging her class to develop the skill of understanding emotions' causes. Doing this can also help her see patterns of emotions emerging, which in turn can lead to new instruction. She could ask Leslie and Ana, when calm, how they think Nichole was feeling and why she felt that way. She could also ask Nichole how she felt, and what caused that feeling. Hearing Nichole explain that she was frustrated because she couldn't complete her plan, or share that it seems to her that Leslie and Ana always say no when she asks for a block or asks to join their game, helps her teacher coach her through these problems. The strategies in this chapter aim to encourage children to start talking about causes of emotions, and to give teachers the tools to elicit responses and understanding to better support children through big feelings.

The Starting Point

Imagine you had stayed at work late one evening, planning a new lesson and sensory experience for your class. You had bins ready for color mixing with cornstarch and water and had selected one of your favorite books about colors. You've overheard children talking at the art station about mixing watercolors and watching the water change colors, and you're imagining how engaged they will be with the activity building off a current interest. Thinking of their little faces and messy hands has you feeling excited and proud about the preparation you have put in.

Now imagine that you get called out of your classroom for a meeting and the person providing coverage finds the bins and puts them out for play time. You return to the room and the materials are used up, there is cornstarch everywhere, you didn't have a chance to read the book or introduce the materials, and it's time for lunch and nap. You get home at the end of the day and share with your family how you felt really disappointed to not get to see your plans through. Your family members respond with, "It's okay. You can buy more cornstarch and try again," and "Could be worse. My coworker broke her leg at work today!"

Reflect on how you would feel if this situation happened to you and those examples were how your family responded to your plight.

> How do you feel when other people don't seem to understand or hear your emotions?

> How does it feel when you are wishing for validation and instead get advice for how to solve the problem?

> What kinds of responses are helpful when you have had a hard day?

> Are you hoping for advice at that moment, or do you want a response indicating that the other person hears your struggle?

When responses to our feelings don't address the emotion or its cause, we often feel misunderstood or frustrated. Three strategies are helpful here and can apply to our work with children. First, considering the possible emotions of others and asking clarifying questions can help us understand and be supportive. For example, paraphrase emotions to check for understanding; asking "So, you felt discouraged when you found the materials had been used?" allows the speaker to share more about how they felt so we can respond in a way that isn't dismissive. Second, thinking through and articulating the causes of our own emotions helps us and others develop a better and fuller understanding of feelings and their causes. Third, practicing validating responses creates a connection between two people and helps ensure that next steps are offered in a way that is supportive for both parties.

Also consider your personal experiences with emotions.

➤ What are your personal reactions or biases that might get in the way of offering a validating response?

➤ Are you more likely to jump into problem-solving instead of validating?

➤ Is your tendency to explain why it isn't a big deal or why it isn't worth getting upset about (in other words, minimizing or dismissing the emotions at play)?

➤ Consider how others respond, or have responded in the past, to your emotions.

Being aware of these experiences and tendencies can make you more mindful of how you respond to emotional situations in your classroom and help you learn to shift your inclination to validating.

Review the Emotion Mindsets Worksheet to reflect on your emotion mindsets and chapter 2 to consider your implicit biases that influence your responses.

Planning to Start

Think of a child's emotionally charged situation that is hard for you to relate to; maybe this situation is one where you just aren't sure why it is a big deal for a child. For example, a child might be upset because they wanted the blue cup instead of the red cup. When we reflect on the cause of the emotion, we are more likely to be able to offer genuine responses. While it might be hard to wholeheartedly mean it when you say, "It's disappointing to get the blue cup instead of the red," thinking about the underlying cause of the emotion (not getting what you want) makes it easier to have empathy. "It's hard when you can't have something you want" is a sentiment that we can all relate to.

Consider the cause of the emotion in that situation and other common emotionally charged situations in the classroom. Reflect on what validating response you might offer that will address the cause of the emotion and spark your empathy. What kinds of responses seem most natural to you?

To help plan for examples that you can use for modeling the skill and responding in emotional moments, you can make a chart like the one in figure 5.1.

Using DAPPER to Teach Understanding Emotions' Causes

You've now reflected on your responses to emotions, and you've practiced developing responses that support and validate the emotions of others. The next step is to use the DAPPER framework to support children in exploring the causes of emotions and responding with understanding.

Figure 5.1 Common Situations, Emotions, and Possible Validating Responses

Common Situations	Underlying Emotion	Possible Validating Response
Wanting to be line leader when it's not their turn	Disappointment	"It's hard to wait for your turn when you really wish to help."
Missing Daddy	Fear, sadness	"You were wishing Daddy could stay and be with you. It's hard to be apart from someone we love."
Not wanting playground time to be over	Disappointment	"You love the playground so much that you don't want to leave."
Can't get the puzzle pieces together	Frustration	"You're having a hard time getting those pieces together."
No room at the lunch table for sitting next to a friend	Jealousy, loneliness	"It doesn't feel good to feel left out of the group that is eating at that table. You wanted to be a part of their conversation at lunch."

Demonstrate and Describe

First, demonstrate how to think and share about the causes of emotions. As you do emotion check-ins or other discussions about emotions, be consistent in labeling your emotion and also identifying a possible cause. For example, "I'm feeling happy because this morning I was wishing for everyone to come to school to play, and you are all here," or "I am feeling disappointed today. I was expecting to go outside to work in the garden and the storm means we have to stay inside to be safe."

One way to think about causes of many emotions is outlining what you wanted or expected and then what happened. While this is simplistic, it is helpful for modeling in a way that is relatable for preschoolers. Thinking about common preschool situations, we see disappointment when children want to go to a favorite center, but it isn't their turn. They are frustrated when they want something to work, like a piece fitting into a puzzle, and it doesn't. There is sadness when they want time with Mommy and it is time for school. There is anxiety when they expect their teacher to be at school and there is a substitute. While young children feel many emotions and their causes may be different, there often is an unmet desire or expectation behind feelings.

Second, practice your validating responses. Consider holding a teacher theater session where you and a colleague act out understanding emotions so children can see this in action. Have the other adult share how they feel, and respond by asking them questions to figure out why they feel this way. Then use validating responses that send the message that you understand how they are feeling. These could sound like:

➤ You were really wishing for a turn on the tricycle and outside time ended.

➤ You were excited for a turn at that center; it's hard to wait.

➤ You didn't want this fun time to end.

➤ You seem frustrated that the game didn't work out the way you wanted.

➤ You thought it was a stay-home day, and it's a school day. It's hard when things are different from what we thought.

If a child tells us how they are feeling, then we can use that in our validating responses. If they identify that they are sad, we can use their language in our response. "You're feeling really sad right now." If they can identify a cause, we can use that in our response too, either directly ("You're feeling really sad that he laughed at your picture.") or indirectly by paraphrasing ("You feel sad when you feel like your classmates are teasing you."). When a child can't tell us how they are feeling, even when we offer the tools and supports of chapters 3 and 4, we can take our best guess and use the language of uncertainty ("You seem sad right now") or we can ask based on body clues ("Are you sad? I see tears and a frown on your face.").

"I wanted my students to know that it's okay to be sad or angry and that I am here to listen or offer support. I felt like I didn't quite know what to say, but then I worked with my coach to practice validating statements. My students know that I hear them and that in our class, there's a place for all feelings."

—Kim, inclusive preschool teacher

While we don't necessarily expect every preschooler to be able to respond to others with validating responses, teachers can practice and model this so that children see how the emotional interaction might come together: labeling feelings, discussing causes, and having their feelings acknowledged, with calming first if needed.

Planning to Demonstrate and Describe the Causes of Emotions

Sketch out what your Demonstrate and Describe lesson will look like. When putting on a teacher theater session to demonstrate this skill for your class, considerations could include:

➤ Who will be role-playing with you?

➤ What emotion will you demonstrate?

➤ What questions will you ask to understand the emotion and its causes?

➤ What are some validating statements you might use to respond?

➤ How might you offer support to handle the emotion during the role play?

Animate

Animating adds a visual and gestural component to the skill to help make it more salient. While we can't fit every possible cause of emotions on any visual, we can offer children popular ones to help them articulate their own feelings. One way to do this is by using the Emotion Causes Flip-Book. This visual's format allows for potential causes to be reviewed and considered individually. Unlike a menu with all the options visible, presenting these one at a time allows children to ponder the situation and the cause and determine if there's a match. "I wanted someone to play with me" can help if the emotion came from feeling happy or excited about a playmate, or feeling sad or lonely when excluded from play. "I expected something different to happen" might be related to the cause of anxiety or disappointment. "I did not get what I wanted" might be related to frustration, anger, disappointment, or sadness.

Take a look at the Emotion Causes Flip-Book Template at the end of this chapter. What other causes can you think of that need to be added? A flip-book, bound with a binder ring, allows you to add more pages as you determine common causes. Children can also illustrate their own "cause pages," which could be added to the class book or become part of individualized books for specific children. Reflect on what other pages might be supportive for children to identify causes.

> At the end of this chapter you'll find an Emotion Causes Flip-Book Template that you can print or customize for your group.

Because the main skill for understanding our emotions in this chapter is that of asking why, you might find the ASL sign for "why" useful to prompt the question, "Why am I feeling this way?" Using the gesture, in combination with your verbal prompts, can help children remember what to start thinking about. Why am I feeling this way? Why might this character be feeling this way? Why might my teacher or friend be feeling this way?

Planning How to Animate the Causes of Emotions

Take a moment to be intentional in planning out your work around animating the causes of emotions.

> ➤ What other pages or information do you want to add to the Emotion Causes Flip-Book?

> ➤ Will you add these yourself, have children or families work on them, or some combination?

> ➤ Where will you store your flip-book so it is accessible both to you and to children?

> ➤ Will you need more than one book to ensure that this tool is readily accessible to everyone?

Practice

Have children practice the skill of understanding emotions' causes. Consider having children talk with partners so adults can move from group to group, listening and facilitating discussion. You might find it easier to encourage practicing by offering a prompt or sentence stem. For example, Ms. Griffin pairs up children and offers the prompt, "I felt frustrated when I wanted _____ to work and it didn't." She has the prompt written and reads it with the class. Then she models saying, "I felt frustrated when I wanted the printer to work and it didn't print my pages." She holds up the frustrated emotion visual and uses her facial expression and tone to animate. She encourages the pairs of children to talk with each other and identify a time they felt frustrated because something didn't work the way they wanted. She plans on trying a similar prompt for excited ("I felt excited when I was looking forward to having fun _____.") during snack time, encouraging children to share people or events that felt exciting to them.

Other possible prompts could be:

> I felt sad when I missed _____.

> I felt worried when I thought _____ might happen.

> I felt surprised when _____ happened and I didn't expect it.

> I felt calm and relaxed when I _____.

Providing validating responses and encouraging children to discuss causes of emotions also gives children a way to start attributing positive intent to others. Melissa, a preschool special education teacher and mother, shared how this made a huge difference in her daughter's emotional regulation. At a theme park, her daughter noticed that princesses were patient and kind, even when children were cutting the line or crying. Melissa explained the idea of the "princess spirit," outlining how the princesses were offering positive intent to understand others, like recognizing that a crying child might be tired or bored and a child cutting the line might feel disappointed about the wait time. Melissa continued to model positive intent, offering possible causes of emotions, until her daughter was able to summon the "princess spirit" to see situations as multifaceted.

Of course, princesses aren't the only option for discussing and practicing offering positive intent. When my son was younger, we modeled this skill by noting that a cranky cashier might have a bad headache yet be trying their hardest, by observing that a child at the park who didn't want to play might be feeling shy, and by considering that a barking dog might be feeling scared when neighbors walk by. Talking about possible causes of emotions—and acknowledging that we don't always know how others are feeling but can decide to make the assumption that everyone is trying their hardest to navigate their day the best they can—is a practice that supports relating emotions to possible causes and giving grace to others.

Planning How to Practice Causes of Emotions

Plan how you might encourage children to practice talking about the causes of emotions.

> What possible prompts will you use to encourage discussions around causes?

➤ What structures do you have during your day where you talk about emotions? Plan out when you will offer prompts for discussions. How can you add "Why are you feeling that way?" into existing routines like emotions check-ins?

➤ Consider possible areas of need. Are there emotions you have taught that you think children may have more difficulty connecting to possible causes? Reflect on why you think children have those feelings during the school day or at home. How can you model talking about these trickier emotions and incorporating them specifically into planned opportunities?

Planned Opportunities

Encourage children in your class to combine several learned skills together to practice getting a deeper understanding of emotions. For this planned opportunity, ask members of your school community (adults or older students) to come in to receive help from your class with understanding emotions that they might have had. Ask your guests to show on their faces and with their bodies how they felt during the situation. Encourage children to ask questions about the guests' body clues to try to label emotions. Have the guest confirm the feeling they are expressing.

Next, encourage children to take guesses as to possible causes. Why would the guest feel that way? What are some events or situations that might cause that emotion? This is a big brainstorming session to help children think about body clues and emotions and come up with possible causes. Ask the guest to give some clues. Where were they when they were feeling this way? Use the Emotion Causes Flip-Book to encourage children to ask questions, like "Did you want something you didn't have?" or "Were you expecting something else to happen?"

Have your guest finish the "game" by revealing what the situation was, and what the cause of the emotion was. Of course, there is no way for children to identify the exact causes of all the possible feelings. The goal for this game is to practice using clues and synthesizing information to come up with relevant possibilities, and to practice using the flip-book to help narrow down causes as well.

Planning Opportunities for Exploring Causes of Emotions

To continue with planning additional opportunities, reflect on times when emotions tend to come up in the classroom.

➤ What are these situations? List several that are likely to pop up in a week.

➤ How can you encourage children to identify causes of those scenarios? Would these situations lend themselves to role play or puppet shows to encourage thinking about the causes? Would discussion or shared writing be a way to capture those causes?

➤ Are those causes reflected in your Emotion Causes Flip-Book, or could you make extra pages to capture them?

Next, review your plans for the upcoming days or week. Note when there might be opportunities to talk about causes of emotions. Perhaps there are activities you think might bring excitement or books you plan to share that will lend themselves to these discussions. You could place reminders on sticky notes in books to prompt you to remember to discuss those causes.

Extend

Identifying emotion causes is one of the easier skills to extend throughout the day, as you can practice the skill of identifying causes in unrelated situations with the same kind of language. For example, "When the wind blew, the paper fell off the easel" or "I am hungry because I did not eat my whole breakfast this morning." Encouraging children to think through the causes behind events or circumstances, such as why the slide is wet in the morning, supports similar thinking skills as examining emotions and relating cause and effect.

"When our school was focusing on persistence, I told my class we were going to watch a 'funny video of a dog and his ball.' The dog dug and dug in the couch cushions to try to get the ball out. When the video ended, a child chimed in and explained, 'That wasn't funny, Ms. Jenkins. The dog was probably sad that he couldn't get his ball out!' He understood that not being able to play with a favorite toy would probably cause sadness for the dog. He was getting it!'"

—Ms. Jenkins, inclusive preschool teacher

Another way of extending this skill is for children to practice it with new people or in new settings. Telling other adults who work with your class that you are working on identifying causes as a way of understanding emotions allows them to support the work. Consider following up on children's time with others by asking them how they felt in music class and why, or how they think the occupational therapist felt during their session and why they might have felt that way. A portable flip-book can also help children use the visual support to identify emotions' causes when they are outside your classroom.

Coaching children through emotions allows us to practice validating responses and encourage them to identify causes. The A in the ICARE framework is the spot to acknowledge a cause or a desire, offering children validation and a chance to talk more about their own emotions:

Hamza and Davion are playing together outside, chasing and laughing. When Davion gets a drink of water, Hamza hides behind a tree. Davion calls out for Hamza, and Hamza doesn't answer. Davion begins to cry. Ms. Griffin approaches Davion to coach him through the situation.

Intent: Ms. Griffin considers the intent and cause of Davion's behavior. She read his body clues as he called for Hamza. His eyes were wide, and his tone of voice was urgent. She recognizes that he seems scared to have lost his playmate.

Calm: Davion often responds well to physical touch. Ms. Griffin asks if he wants her to rub his back, and he nods and leans in. She takes deep breaths and his breathing regulates to hers. The crying subsides.

Acknowledge: Ms. Griffin starts with, "You seemed scared." Davion nods. She adds a prompt of "Tell me about it." This encourages Davion to identify emotions and causes. "I lost Hamza," he tells her. She uses a validating response. "You wanted to play with Hamza and you couldn't find him. That was scary." He nods again.

Rewind: Ms. Griffin asks Davion what would help him solve this problem in the future. He says he will tell Hamza that it was too scary when he couldn't find him. He chooses to articulate how he feels and why to Hamza so Hamza understands. Ms. Griffin helps facilitate the conversation. She also encourages Hamza to describe how he felt. He explained that he felt silly, like hiding was a silly game. He didn't know that Davion would feel sad.

Echo: Ms. Griffin echoes back that sometimes two friends have different emotions about the same situation. Hamza felt like hiding was a silly game, and Davion felt scared that he couldn't find Hamza. Ms. Griffin notes that Davion wants Hamza to hide only when they are playing hiding games, and Hamza agrees.

Planning to Extend Understanding Causes of Emotions

Note which children in your class can identify some causes of their emotions. For children who cannot yet do this, be intentional about acknowledging possible causes as well as you can in social situations, and then asking if you got it right. Most children will correct us if we say they seem sad when they are in fact frustrated, or if we attribute that frustration to the wrong incident.

Plan for how you will coach children who are not yet identifying or sharing about the causes of their emotions.

➤ What visuals will you need to offer a "best guess" about the cause of an emotion?

➤ Would picture supports about possible causes help? Might you also need props to represent those causes?

➤ How do these children communicate whether you are right or wrong? Can they verbally tell you? Would they respond better to picture choices for yes and no?

Reinforce and Reflect

Using validating responses reinforces children's skills of talking about and describing emotions. The feeling of connection that comes from being understood can be a powerful motivator. Positive descriptive feedback also reinforces the skill of talking about the emotion. This could sound like "You described what happened, and that helped me understand" or "You figured out why you felt angry. Way to go!"

We can encourage children to reflect on their new skill through intentional questioning. Our questions may encourage them to think about articulating their thought processes around their feelings, or highlight the benefits of understanding their own emotions or those of others. Possible questions include:

- How did you figure out what caused your emotion?

- If that situation happened to you, would you feel the same or different as this character? How do you know?

- Have you ever had a different feeling in this situation? Is this how you usually feel when X happens?

- Now that you know the cause of that feeling, what could you do?

Planning to Reinforce and Reflect Around the Causes of Emotions

Take a minute to reflect on how your positive feedback and reflective questioning is being received. Are children responding positively? Are they able to talk and share about their emotions when you ask follow-up reflection questions?

Think about when you are asking these questions. Are children calm enough to receive your message and process it? If you feel like they aren't, reflect on how and when you are doing this "reinforcement" piece and consider how you might try it differently to ensure that children are calm and receptive.

Discussing the Causes of Emotions Throughout the Day

Consider the following ideas for integrating this skill throughout the day and encouraging the discussion of emotions' causes during many activities.

Morning Meeting or Circle Time: Consider bringing puppets to group time. Have puppets tell a story about something that happened to them. Walk through the Emotion Causes Flip-Book with children, having them give the puppet the words to connect their emotion to the cause. For example, a frog might have been at the pond and wanted to play but he didn't want to get into the water. Frog looked around for friends who wanted to play in the sand, but everyone was already in the water. Have children work together to help Frog say, "I felt lonely when I couldn't find anyone to play with." Choose many kinds of emotion scenarios, including some that are like experiences in your classroom. After trying this activity several times, invite children to pair up and come up with puppet emotion stories to share with the class.

Movement and Music: Have children brainstorm reasons for emotions to sing a new version of "If You're Happy and You Know It." Use the familiar tune to sing different scenarios and how a child would feel. For example, "When my cat scratches me, I feel sad. When my cat scratches me, I feel sad. When my cat scratches me, when my cat scratches me, when my cat scratches me, I feel sad." Another verse might be "When Grandpa hugs me, I feel loved. When Grandpa hugs me, I feel loved. When Grandpa hugs me, when grandpa hugs me, when Grandpa hugs me, I feel loved." After singing the verse, encourage children to add their own creative movements to it. It might help to pair up children to act out the scenarios and the emotions.

Small Group: Young children tend to really enjoy lift-the-flap books. Consider using cardstock folded in half horizontally with the fold at the top. Have the "top" or "front" page describe a situation, such as "When I am invited to a birthday party, I feel . . ." or "When my grandma gets on the airplane, I feel . . ." Then have children open the page (or lift the flap), draw their emotion expression inside the fold, and label it. This kind of project helps children think about and identify the causes behind emotions, and the completed cards can be displayed or played like a guessing game.

To further children's understanding of causes behind emotions, you can ask them to look at the fronts of cards and guess what emotions their peers might have identified under the flap. Encourage further thinking through questions like "Why do you think she might feel happy about that?" or "If that happened to you, how would you feel?" You can support children as they ask the illustrators of each card follow-up questions about their emotions, and you can practice offering validating responses as children share.

Transitions: For a quick transition activity, consider playing the "surprise game." As a child is ready to transition to a new activity, have them pretend to hold an invisible box with a present inside. Encourage them to slowly open their present, and then you tell them what it is. "Get your box, take off the lid, peek inside . . . it's a _____!" You can use food ("It's a banana!" "It's an onion!"), you could use animals ("It's a snake!" "It's a mouse!" "It's a ladybug!"), or you can use an object like a toy or a book. Then ask the child how they would feel about the thing in the box and why ("I feel disappointed because I don't like to eat onions."). Then have the child transition to the next activity. If you want the transition to move more quickly, with small groups transitioning together, ask anyone else who would feel disappointed to go with first child. Then call on another child to share how they would feel and why.

Gross-Motor Skills and Outside Time: Gross-motor games tend to lead to some big emotions. Consider being especially mindful of situations that come up on the playground and elsewhere and socially coaching children to talk about their emotions while offering validating responses. For example, being pushed down the slide, having to wait for a turn on the bicycle, falling on the grass, kicking the ball over the fence, and winning or losing a running race are all opportunities to practice the skill of identifying emotions and their causes.

Art: Use a large piece of butcher paper or poster board to create a collaborative art project on emotions. Have children vote on an emotion to work on. If they choose "surprised," label the artwork "We feel surprised when . . ." and have children draw on it to make a collage of causes they can think of for feeling surprised. To add another element to the project, consider having children take photos of each other's surprised faces to add to the collage, or encourage them to pair up and draw each other's surprised expressions. This practices both observation skills and teamwork.

Math: Understanding causes of emotions means we also understand that emotions come and go as situations change, as we regulate, or as our needs are met. One connection between this and math is that we have a lot of feelings in a day or even in one morning. Consider using a simple recording sheet to show children how to track their own emotions during an activity or time block. For instance, if children are about to play a board game, ask them before the game starts how they are feeling and why, and note those emotions on the recording sheet. Put the sheet in the center of the play space and encourage children to add to it themselves (with dots or tally marks) when they are feeling another emotion. Then ask children in the middle of the game and at the end of the game to identify emotions and their causes. Continue to record this information on the sheet, and talk about the data with the group. How many emotions was the group feeling? How many marks were there, total? Did emotions change over the course of the game? Why did children have those different emotions?

Story Time: When reading a book, point out a character's body clues to label the emotion they may be feeling. Then ask the children to help identify why the character might feel that way, by reviewing the pages in the Emotion Causes Flip-Book. Read each flip-book page and show the group the illustrations, asking the class if they think each statement could be true for the character. If children identify a couple causes as true, ask them to support that with a part of the book (whether text or illustration) that offers insight into the emotion's causes.

Planning to Understand Emotions Throughout the Day

Which activities around understanding emotions appeal to you? What other ideas and materials do you have that build on this skill? As you review activities and materials, plan with the following considerations in mind:

➤ Do you have examples of activities, stories, or role play where children recognize causes for emotions—especially emotions other than strong upset or anger (such as excited, calm, or lonely)?

➤ Are there other activities you do in your classroom that encourage discussion of cause and effect and will reinforce this concept and language? For example, using a watercolor resist technique (drawing with white crayons on white paper and then painting over the drawing with watercolors) makes neat patterns *because* the paint doesn't coat the crayon marks. Testing out various materials with magnets leads to discussions of magnets being attracted to surfaces *because* they are metal. Make notes to yourself to talk about causes and effects during activities outside of planned social and emotional instruction to further support this learning.

➤ What key words or phrases in home languages would help children access these lessons and ideas? Make a list of them to ask families to translate, or invite families to share their own ideas.

> ➤ Spread out your activities across the week and across different settings—such as in a variety of centers, inside and outside, and during activities that are facilitated by other adults.

Formative Assessment of Understanding the Causes of Emotions

As you work on the skill of understanding emotions by thinking through what causes them, a simple recording sheet can help you track which children are connecting emotions with causes. This can then help you plan targeted activities to encourage these skills in children who need it.

Ms. Griffin talks with a small group of children about emotions as they make pages of a lift-the-flap book. As they talk, she makes notes in a data sheet, shown in figure 5.2. She notes that Waylon said he was mad when lunch wasn't what he wanted, and Meredith was happy when her family adopted a kitten. She also saw that Alex selected sad but couldn't think of a cause. Ms. Griffin encouraged Meredith to help talk through Alex's feeling, and Meredith reminded Alex about how sad he was when he wanted the Potato Head toy and she said no because she was using it. Ms. Griffin notes that Alex needed help, and that Meredith was able to identify the emotion and cause of Alex's emotions, not just her own emotions.

Figure 5.2 Sample Data Sheet for Recording Children's Thoughts About Causes of Emotions

Child's Name	Identifies Causes of Own Emotions	Identifies Possible Causes of Others' Emotions
Waylon	Mad (wanted different lunch)	
Beth	Shy (points to "wanted to play" in the flip-book)	
Alex	Needs Meredith's prompting to remember when he was sad	
Meredith	Happy (family adopted kitten)	Alex was sad (wanted a turn and she said no)

Later, Ms. Griffin looks through the notes she took during the activity. She could see that children were starting to have the language to talk about the causes of their emotions. She noticed that Alex needs more support. He can currently point to the emotion card and say the emotion label, which means he is identifying the emotion, but he did not identify a cause even when using the Emotion Causes Flip-Book support. Ms. Griffin plans to be intentional with helping Alex label his

For a blank template of this data sheet template, see the end of the chapter.

emotions in the moment and helping him articulate possible causes as the moments occur to see if that helps build his skill.

Beth was able to point to a page in the flip-book to show Ms. Griffin and her peers that she wanted to play with a friend when she felt shy. She connected shy with wanting to play with others. While she cannot yet do this verbally, the visual cue allowed her to articulate causes. Ms. Griffin plans to be consistent in using the flip-book with Beth, but also considers taking photos or videos of situations for Beth, giving her additional visual representations and supporting her in discussing causes of her feelings. Taking these quick anecdotal notes has helped Ms. Griffin design the next week's instructional plans for her class.

Remember to review your data to ask:

➤ What does the data suggest about children and articulating causes of emotion? Who needs more practice and support?

➤ Who can articulate probable causes of their emotions and those of others, using body clues and context clues?

➤ Based on your data, what next steps should you take for whole class instruction?

➤ What next steps might you plan to support individual children with advancing their skills?

Planning for Formative Assessment of Understanding the Causes of Emotions

Draft a plan for your formative assessment.

➤ What times of day will work best for gathering data to support your instructional decisions?

➤ Which activities will lend themselves to collecting data about emotions' causes? Will you collect this information during check-in or during group activities?

➤ When will you review your data so that you can use the information to plan your next instructional steps?

Differentiation and Advancement

Understanding the causes of emotions is complicated. How many times have we, as adults, known that we feel angry, yet not been able to pinpoint exactly why? How many times have we struggled to identify why a situation makes us anxious, and had to think further about underlying causes or past situations that might be influencing our current feelings?

Among children, expect a range of ability in how well they can articulate causes. Reviewing the underlying skills at work can help remind you of which children will likely need support. For example, a child who struggles with reading other people's body clues is probably also going to need more help with identifying possible causes of others' emotions. After all, if you don't correctly identify how someone is feeling, then chances are your best effort in figuring out a cause might also be incorrect.

After reviewing and supporting children with precursor skills, consider offering targeted supports that match each child's strengths:

➤ Use the visual of the Emotion Causes Flip-Book to think about each possible cause.

➤ Be intentional about verbally labeling an emotion when the child isn't able to do so. "You looked frustrated when she took your toy and wouldn't give it back."

➤ Simplify your statement into one with fewer words and gestures or visuals. Show the frustrated visual and give the cause: "She took your toy; frustrated."

➤ Use scripts to support a child in learning a repetitive structure. "I felt X when Y." Model and have children repeat after you to practice saying causal statements.

➤ If a child uses one-word utterances, start a sentence about emotions with your best guess and leave the cause for the child to fill in. "You felt mad when you didn't get _____." Have the child identify what they were wishing for with a word or by gesturing.

➤ Encourage children to "show you" what caused an emotion if they cannot say. Can they point to a center or a toy or a visual to express what caused their feeling?

➤ When talking about causal statements, add gestures. "I felt frustrated when she took my toy" could include making a frustrated expression and acting out a child snatching a toy.

➤ When talking about causes of emotions for book characters, stop and point out facial expressions and other picture clues. Consider thinking out loud to model how you figure out what may have caused the emotion.

➤ If a child cannot identify a cause for their emotion, you can take your best guess and verbally offer the child a causal statement: "You feel calm when you get to hold your blanket."

Also keep in mind that we really must be calm to allow our brain to do problem-solving and analytical work. If a child is too upset about a current situation, calming has to come before we ask them to plan next steps. Help the child regulate, and then use validating responses or ask them to share about the situation to encourage dialogue.

Some children will pick up on this quickly and be able to clearly relate many emotions to their causes. Going deeper with reflection, such as having them reiterate how they figured it out, helps them practice vocalizing their own thinking. You can also ask them to draw parallels. When you felt the same way as this character, what did you do? What helped you? Do you think that might help this character? Why or why not? When children have facility with this skill and are ready for more challenge, you can encourage them to dive deeper into thinking about causes of others' emotions and planning ways to respond to others' feelings (the topic of chapter 8).

Planning for Differentiation and Advancement

Create a plan for children who might need individualization. Use data and observations to identify specific children for whom you will intentionally plan modified or individualized supports.

> Review data and observations for the children who need extra support. What skills do they currently have around emotions? Which skills are still emerging?

> Then review the list of possible targeted supports. Match a support or two with each child, based on their strengths and developmental ability.

> Plan when you will offer these targeted supports for children who need them. If there are several children with the same targeted needs, will you work with them together in a small group? Will you opt to work with them individually in the context of large-group activities?

> Next, review data to determine which children have this skill and are ready for further learning. Plan out questions you might ask to prompt deeper reflection and exploration.

Troubleshooting Around Understanding Causes of Emotions

Consider ways to troubleshoot the following questions or obstacles you might run into as you teach this skill.

"What if a child identifies abuse, neglect, or maltreatment as the cause of their emotions?" It is possible that a child might relate emotions to serious experiences they have had, including abuse, neglect, or witnessing violence. Remember to listen without judgment and offer validation. A simple, "That sounds like it was really scary for you" can let the child know you hear them and understand the emotion that they are telling you about. After responding in a way that assures the child that

Review Belief 6 of chapter 1 for planning around this situation.

you heard and understood, remember to jot down what the child said and then follow your school's procedure for reporting these disclosures.

"How do I talk about the causes of emotions without assigning blame?"
We want to be able to talk about the causes of emotions, but we don't want to use these discussions to shame or blame others. For example, sometimes the reason we are frustrated is related to our class talking over us as we try to read a story. However, saying something like, "You are making me so mad because you're talking over me" starts to insert blame into that modeling that doesn't serve us well. Similar to developing statements that are validating and acknowledging, think about what you wanted and use that as a way to articulate your emotions. "When you're yelling over my words, I feel frustrated. I wanted to share this book with you and I can't focus." This subtle difference shares the same message—frustration and its cause—without putting the weight of your emotions on children by saying they are *making* you feel a certain way.

When we focus on the people who "make" us angry or annoyed, the power shifts. As Dr. Becky Bailey explains in her book *Easy to Love, Difficult to Discipline,* "When you place someone in charge of your emotions, you place that person in charge of you." If I decide that someone is "making" me angry, then the solution is either for that person to go away or for them to stop doing annoying things. Neither one of those solutions is focused on me and what I can do, such as redirect behavior, take a calming break, or ask for help.

While emotions can be triggered by others, ultimately we are responsible for identifying, recognizing, and managing our own feelings, and using messages that focus on us underscores this idea. That doesn't mean we shouldn't address situations in which others are hurtful to us, and we want children to see how their actions impact others. But our emotions are ours, and focusing on the needs and desires that cause our emotions empowers us to problem solve and redirect.

You might have children identify that *you* are the cause of their emotion. "I'm sad because you were mean to me and didn't let me have my turn." You can reflect back what they wanted or what they didn't like without having to be defensive. Shifting this to "You're feeling sad because you really hoped for a turn on the easel and the list was too long for your turn today" helps children learn to discuss causes in a way that focuses on what was going on for them.

Take a moment to practice this shift. Consider the following examples and brainstorm some of your own.

Figure 5.3 Shifting from Shaming and Blaming to Reframing

Shaming and Blaming	Reframing
"I'm sad because you aren't following rules to keep the classroom safe."	"When you run inside, you could get hurt, and that feels scary to me."
"She made me so mad because she hit me."	"I felt angry when she hit me. I want to feel safe in our classroom."
"You make me so happy when you listen to my words."	"When you listen to my words, I know that you hear how to use the new materials. I feel happy that I can share these materials and we can use them together safely."

Often when we use shame or blame to describe the causes of emotions, we are attempting to change behavior. For example, we might announce, "You make me really sad when you don't listen" in hopes that children will feel badly and change their behavior. It often is more effective to own those emotions, and then use positive redirection to help shift behaviors that aren't helpful. This could sound like, "When no one is listening to me, I feel worried that you won't hear my directions for being safe." For the first example in figure 5.3, redirection might include showing children the visual for walking feet, playing slow music and encouraging them to move in slow motion, or asking individual children to hold your hand and walk with you to stay safe. Rather than hoping children will feel badly that they are "causing" your upset, you can acknowledge your emotions and their source, and then take active steps to support children or yourself in changing the situation.

Family Engagement and Support

A social and emotional snippet related to teaching understanding the causes of emotions might look like this:

This week, we have been trying to understand our emotions. We have learned to recognize emotions and label them. Now we are focusing on why we might feel a certain way. Maybe we are excited to come to school because we know we will read a favorite story. At other times we are sad to come to school because we wish to be at home with our family. Identifying what we feel, and why we are feeling that way, is one goal. We are also learning that we feel different than others. One classmate might feel excited about tacos for lunch, while another classmate might feel sad that it isn't spaghetti. We have different emotions caused by our different experiences and perspectives.

Videos can also be helpful for families to see children talking about the causes of their emotions. Imagine dropping off your child at school when they are upset. You leave, feeling worried about how your child is doing. Then suppose you get a video message from your child explaining that he was sad because he missed you, but his emotion changed when it was time to go outside, and now he is feeling happy. What a gift of reassurance this would be—and also a gift to see and hear your child being able to express the causes of his emotions!

There are so many ways to include families in discussions about emotions and their causes. You can consider having families share examples of causes of their emotions and can add to the classroom's collage of emotions. You can invite families to participate in the game where you identify possible causes of the emotions of guests. You can ask families to recommend books or shows they read or watch with their child that feature emotional situations so you can consider using them in the classroom for practice. You can also ask families to share common causes of their child's emotions so you can use that information to reinforce concepts and give children relevant examples.

One fun activity is to have children work with an adult at school to complete simple statements about their family. For example, "My mom is happy when _____." "My uncle is excited when _____." To customize these statements, you can work with families to identify the important people in their child's life. Similarly, you can include school community members. "Mrs. Broyles is surprised when _____" or "Ms. Ward is calm when _____." This activity can be quite funny and creative, and sharing the answers with families can be a celebration of their child's learning at school.

Wrap-Up

Congratulations on reflecting, planning, and teaching your class to better understand emotions by identifying causes! We have all felt confused about our emotions, unable to articulate why we are feeling a certain way. But this skill allows us to share why we are feeling an emotion, and that clarity has the added benefit of helping us problem solve or get support to handle the emotion. Talking about causes can help children realize that emotions vary from person to person—and even within the same person—as different situations arise. As we encourage children to talk about emotions and their causes, it also gives us a chance to practice our validating responses and let children know that we hear, we understand, and we care.

Understanding emotions leads into the next skill: choosing strategies to help us regulate our emotions. When we understand where our emotions come from, we are better prepared to access support. While chapter 5 supported us with answering "Why am I feeling this emotion?" this next skill, the focus of chapter 6, gives us the answer to "How can I calm down when I am feeling strong emotions?"

Emotion Causes Flip-Book Template

You may choose to print these sample pages, or you can recreate them for your Emotion Causes Flip-Book. You can also make your own unique pages to fit the needs of your group.

I want something.

I wanted someone to play with me.

→

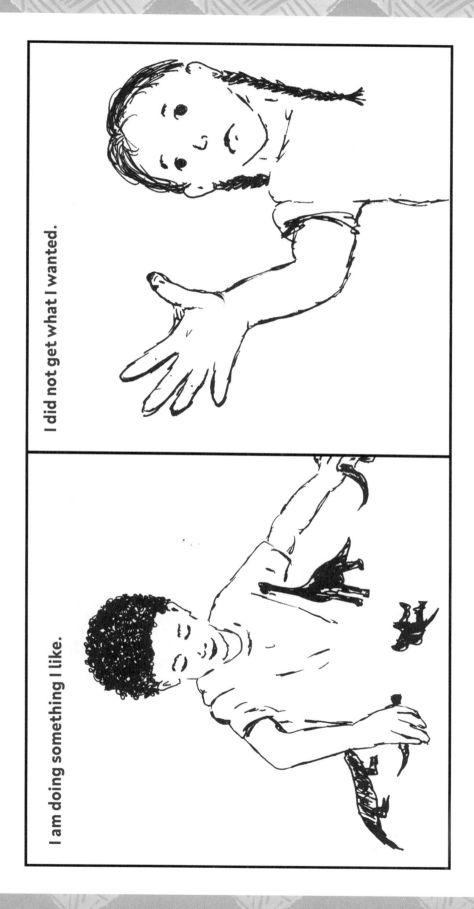

I did not get what I wanted.

I am doing something I like.

From *Create an Emotion-Rich Classroom: Helping Young Children Build Their Social Emotional Skills* by Lindsay N. Giroux, M.Ed. Copyright © 2022. This page may be reproduced for individual, classroom, or small group work only. For other uses, contact Free Spirit Publishing at freespirit.com/permissions.

I expected something different to happen.

My body needs something.

Data Sheet for Recording Children's Thoughts About Causes of Emotions

You can use this data sheet to record your observations about how well children are able to identify causes of emotions—both their own and those of others.

Child's Name	Identifies Causes of Own Emotions	Identifies Possible Causes of Others' Emotions

Chapter 6

Practicing Regulation Strategies

PICTURE THIS Theo is having a rough day. His dad drops him off late to school, and when he realizes he missed morning snack and outside time, he feels disappointed. He goes to small-group time and finds another child using his favorite scissors with the blue handles. Disappointed again, he begins to cry. His tears smudge the ink on his artwork, causing more tears about his streaky picture. What started as silent tears rolling down his cheeks escalates into louder sobbing with heaving shoulders.

Theo's teacher tries to help him calm down. She reaches out to offer him a hug, but he shakes his head. She passes him a tissue and tries to encourage him to dry his tears so he can make a new picture, but he sobs through her words. She offers him the class stuffed animal mascot to snuggle with, but he pushes it away. Next, she asks Theo's classmate Haley if she could rub his back. Haley asks Theo if that would be okay, he nods, and she rubs circles on his back for a minute before getting pushed away. Theo gets up and folds his tiny body into his slender cubby, crying onto his nap blanket and lunch box.

Theo's teacher wonders how to help support Theo with calming down. She felt like she was grasping at straws as she tossed out idea after idea in rapid succession to encourage his regulation. He didn't seem to want her help or the help of a peer. She tried distraction through offering a prop, she suggested supportive physical touch, and she asked for peer assistance. None of these strategies seemed wanted by Theo, and he eventually calmed down by himself in his cubby.

About the Skill of Practicing Regulation Strategies

Dr. Becky Bailey notes that those who can self-regulate are able to handle feelings of distress when their needs are not met. She describes self-regulation as a pause between impulse and action; a person handling the uncomfortable feelings through a pause is beginning to regulate. This pause allows us to access high-level skills, such as using our words to express desires or using problem-solving skills to come up with a new path. Infants first start to build this pause when they have a caregiver who responds to their distress. While they are upset, the child learns that an adult will come when they are needed. They are briefly handling their distress between their cry and a caregiver's response. Those adult responses support infants through coregulation as caregivers and babies calm together through breathing, rocking, swaying, and singing. As children grow, we see additional examples of coregulation. A caregiver holds and breathes with an upset toddler, and the toddler's breathing relaxes to match the caregiver's. Preschoolers often seek out adults for coregulation, like asking a teacher to help them when they feel upset. And yet we also see preschoolers beginning to independently regulate, inserting the pause between impulse and action as they learn to ask for a turn with a toy instead of snatching it, or waiting for their turn during a board game without grabbing the dice or yelling. We also see that pause when a child gets upset and turns to an adult or peer for help, rather than lashing out or kicking.

As teachers, we know there are many children for whom the pause is still short. One child might be able to wait for twenty seconds before sticking his fingers into the birthday cake frosting. Another child might be able to wait for two peers to go down the slide before she impatiently pushes a third peer down so she can have her turn. A child who waits for a teacher to finish a story page before sharing their thoughts is showing steps of impulse control, as is a child who is wiggling with excitement about a special activity without reaching and grabbing it. Teaching, encouraging, and prompting the use of regulation strategies helps give a child something to do during the pause instead of taking that first impulsive action. A child who will storm off and get their blanket when upset instead of kicking the toys off the shelf is showing steps toward regulating their emotions. It's also helpful to remember that the skill of regulation is practiced all day in early childhood classrooms. Waiting for turns, managing emotions, and even pausing during a freeze dance has children practicing regulating.

Like the other skills in this book, regulation is hard work. As adults, we are still working on harnessing this skill in our own lives. We have snapped at a neighbor or yelled at a child when we couldn't successfully pause between our impulse and our action to make a more mindful choice. But as adults we also successfully coregulate others. We talk in a calming tone to a friend who is upset. We bring enthusiasm to a new job, inspiring excitement in others. Our emotions do not exist in a vacuum; they influence those around us as well. This makes it even more important for us to have strategies to regulate our own emotions so that we have the tools to coregulate with children when they need our support.

The Starting Point

Emily and Amelia Nagoski, authors of the book *Burnout*, talk about how completing the stress cycle prevents emotional exhaustion and burnout. Our bodies respond to stressors with physiological changes, in the same way they respond to real or perceived danger. But after the danger has passed, we can take steps to send the message to our bodies that the stress is over, thus finishing the stress cycle. Completing the stress response cycle is part of the process of calming down. Ideas for completing the cycle include breathing, exercising, talking to others, crying, laughing, being affectionate with others, or doing something creative like drawing or storytelling. There are many ways to complete the stress cycle and both you and the children in your class are likely to have preferred ways to release stress.

What helps you calm down when you are upset or overwhelmed? Reflect on the statements below, noting which are true for you.

> I prefer support from others when upset or overwhelmed.

> I prefer to be alone when upset or overwhelmed.

> I choose physical activities, like breathing, running, and stretching, to help me calm down.

> Physical touch, like a hug or a rub on the back, helps me calm down.

> I prefer to not be touched when upset or overwhelmed.

> I choose other sensory ways to calm, like drinking water or listening to music.

> I often choose a favorite hobby to help me calm, such as reading, journaling, drawing, or meditation.

> I feel better after crying to release the stress.

> I feel better after laughing to release the stress.

> I am not sure what I find most useful when upset or overwhelmed.

It is likely that children in your class will have a wide range of preferences. For the class as a whole, it is possible that all ten of the above statements will be true. Remembering this will help as you make decisions about which regulation strategies and choices to teach and offer to children.

Next, take a minute to consider what does not help you calm down. For example, having someone *tell* me I should calm down is unhelpful for me, and being talked to or shouted at feels like sensory overload. Knowing what calms us helps us do some thoughtful planning around tools we might teach children. Knowing what is overwhelming for us can also give us insight into and empathy for how it might feel when we employ those same strategies in our efforts to support children.

Planning to Start

Create a list of regulation strategies and tools you can teach in your classroom. Include what you have seen children gravitating to when upset; if they are going to a certain spot or using certain toys or classroom materials, plan for explicitly teaching related strategies or incorporating those tools. Consider some of the ideas you listed as your go-to strategies. Brainstorm tools that stimulate the five senses (getting a drink of water, squeezing stress balls, watching sensory bottles, smelling a scented flower, listening to music). Also brainstorm regulation strategies that are more active, like squeezing, stomping, or jumping, along with those that are less active, like breathing, yoga, or drawing. Because deep, intentional breaths decrease our heart rate, they begin to stop our stress response system. Make sure to teach children ways to breathe, as this is an effective way to jumpstart the parasympathetic nervous system to calm your body.

Throughout the teaching process, collect children's feedback around the various regulation tools. Gathering their input and ideas, as well as those from families, will help ensure that each child has some helpful tools in their regulation toolbox. There are many possible tools and strategies you might teach. This chapter uses the strategy of deep breathing with a flower and pinwheel as an example, but will also include ideas for teaching other regulation strategies.

Using DAPPER to Teach Regulation Strategies

You've now reflected on tools that might be helpful for encouraging regulation, for yourself and for the children in your care. The next step is to intentionally plan to teach several regulation strategies, using the components of the DAPPER framework.

Demonstrate and Describe

Demonstrating a calm-down strategy has two big components. First, demonstrate and describe how to use the strategy. Second, demonstrate and emphasize how to read body clues (chapter 4's emotional competency) to determine whether the strategy is helping change emotions or physiological sensations. A big takeaway to communicate is that sometimes a strategy doesn't work to get us back to feeling calm, and we need to pick a new one or try the strategy again. So, if a couple of deep breaths don't work, we might need more deep breaths to get to calm, or we might opt to get a hug or listen to music.

There are many creative and effective ways to teach children to take deep breaths to help regulate. Using visual supports enhances the technique's appeal and makes it easier for children to monitor if they are breathing deeply. For example, blowing bubbles requires deep breaths, as does making a pinwheel spin, watching a tissue move as you exhale, or lifting and lowering a small stuffed animal on your stomach while lying down and breathing deeply. Choose a breathing technique with a visual component to help support children's understanding of how a deep breath feels and looks.

One technique I like is to tape a silk or paper flower to the stem or handle of a pinwheel. Teach children to breathe in by taking a long deep "smell" of the flower, and then breathe out by blowing out through their mouth to spin the pinwheel. Model how to do this correctly, labeling the steps for children verbally. "Smell the flower, blow the pinwheel, smell the flower, blow the pinwheel." Consider demonstrating the strategy incorrectly and asking children if you are doing it "right." You can blow the pinwheel first and then smell the flower, you can try blowing the flower and smelling the pinwheel, or you can take such a shallow breath that the pinwheel doesn't spin well. Demonstrating and discussing how *not* to do this strategy helps children engage cognitively with how to do it.

Next, connect the strategy with calming down. Talk about how your body might feel before taking the deep breaths; maybe you are feeling irritated or too excited. Model how taking deep breaths using the pinwheel and flower sends your body messages to relax. Verbally check in with your body: "How do I feel now? Let me check for my body's clues." You can refer to the Body Clues Map to review the ways your body feels calmer. To build reflective practice, we want to teach regulation as a process in which we acknowledge our emotions, try a strategy, and then check in to see if it worked. For other regulation strategies, the modeling would be similar. Describing the strategy and its purpose, modeling how to do it with clearly defined steps, and reflecting out loud about how it helps us will support children in understanding both how to access the strategy or tool and why they might try it.

Planning What Regulation Strategies to Demonstrate and Describe

While there are many calming strategies, challenge yourself to teach at least a couple that are related directly to deep breathing. The flower-and-pinwheel strategy is one example. Other breathing strategies include using a Hoberman Sphere (also called a breathing ball), blowing bubbles, blowing out pretend candles, breathing to make a scarf move, or lying down with a small toy on the belly and taking breaths to make it move up and down.

Ms. Elliott and Ms. Godwin do daily breathing between a movement activity and reading a story in their group time. They plan new strategies that align with content they are teaching, such as wolf breaths when reading "The Three Little Pigs" and dandelion breaths in spring. Children in their class have learned how to take deep breaths as part of the routine, and the variety encourages children's engagement.

Which breathing strategies might be the most engaging for your class? Consider teaching two breathing strategies together, in the same lesson or same week, to allow children some choice when practicing and reviewing ways to calm. If taking deep breaths isn't currently a strategy you use yourself, reflect on ways you can incorporate it into your daily routines for calming so you are more able to explain the benefits to children.

Find other ideas for regulation strategies, along with space to plan out how to teach them, in the Regulation Strategies Planning Sheet at the end of this chapter.

Animate

Visuals are so helpful in times of stress. As adults, we often handle big feelings by making lists, giving us a visual plan. When we are lost in an unfamiliar place, we tackle the problem with maps or GPS or by watching for helpful traffic signs or landmarks. As we attempt to calm down, we often use visuals too, whether that's a soothing picture to look at or visualizing a calmer place. For children, we'll aim to provide visuals to help them access strategies when they most need them.

One example is a calm-down menu. This is a simple visual of calm-down choices, aimed to give children ideas of what strategies they might choose to access. For example, a simple calm-down menu might have a picture of a pinwheel and flower on it to represent pinwheel breathing, a picture of a stuffed animal to represent snuggling something soft, a picture of a book to represent reading, and a picture of a teacher to represent getting help to calm down. A menu can be made in many different formats. For example, printing and laminating pictures creates a static menu where the choices are always the same. Other teachers opt to use hook and loop pieces on pictures so children can pull off a picture to make a choice and other choices can be added or replaced. Other teachers make a calm-down menu of choices they have taught that do not have associated props (such as counting to ten, getting a drink, or singing a song) so children can choose between getting a physical prop such as a pinwheel and using a non-prop option from the menu. A visual menu has the added benefit of being easily portable, allowing children access to strategies in spaces where a range of calm-down props may not be available.

For a gestural component, consider using a gesture to represent calm. The ASL sign for *calm* or *relax* might be helpful. Other teachers create their own gesture so that when they are asking children to practice calming, they can use that gesture as well as their tone to imply slowing down or relaxing. Hearing "let's calm down" said in a supportive tone and accompanied by a supportive gesture feels different than being told to "calm down" when upset. Being mindful of tone and body language can shift the interaction from being directive to supportive.

Planning How to Animate Regulation Strategies

Consider what kinds of visual supports have been successful for your class. For example, are visuals in your classroom primarily displayed left to right, or presented vertically? Do you have interactive supports where children pull off a choice, or do you have static menus where children can look at several options and pick one? Think about your emotion check-in to get more information about how children interact with visuals. Building on their strengths and prior knowledge, decide how to make your calm-down menu. Will you display several options vertically, to match the layout of your classroom schedule, for instance? Or perhaps you will opt to give children a clothespin to mark the strategy they are going to try, in the same way they mark how they feel on an emotion check-in wheel. Using similar systems to those you have already taught will make the introduction and teaching of the new visual a bit easier.

Practice

Practicing calming has many benefits. Like any practice, it helps make skills more fluent so it is more likely that we will be able to access the strategies when we are actually upset or angry. It also builds in time to calm and settle down, which can shift the energy and mood in the classroom. Consider making the daily practice of calm-down strategies part of your routine, both during the weeks when you are focusing on teaching regulation and throughout the rest of the year. This gives both children and staff consistent, daily opportunities to review and regulate.

For example, when teaching pinwheel breathing, consider having each child try with their own pinwheel, or take turns by sharing pinwheels between pairs. If you only have one pinwheel, children can transition out of the whole group by taking a turn pinwheel breathing while the waiting children help by taking their own breaths. Or the children waiting could offer encouragement by repeating "smell the flower, blow the pinwheel" and giving a thumbs-up for deep breathing success. Similar regulation strategies include opening a Hoberman Sphere on inhale and closing it on exhale, or having a child hold up their fingers as candles and taking five deep breaths to blow each one out. Encourage children to use the skill of reading their body's clues. How do their bodies feel when calm? How does their voice sound? What differences do they notice before and after calming?

Ms. Brown, Ms. Bertha, and Ms. Wilson, teachers in a self-contained preschool special education classroom, recognize how important routines and structure are for creating a sense of safety in their classroom. They often use a book of yoga pictures to provide structured movement opportunities during class meetings. When they began brainstorming ways to practice regulation, they opted to create a calm-down yoga book to support regulation using the familiar structure of looking at poses, imitating them, and counting. Rather than teaching an individual strategy, they created a new routine incorporating familiar skills that included identifying the emotion, using calming poses, and then checking to make sure their bodies were calm.

Planning How to Practice Regulation Strategies

How can you make calming practice a regular part of your day? Consider adding it to your daily schedule and your lesson plans. Some teachers opt to give children some voice and choice during this. Can children choose which strategy to practice, such as selecting one off a visual menu? Or are you going to lead the class in learning and practicing a new strategy? Some teachers create a classroom job such as Breathing Buddy or Captain of Calm, where the child in that role chooses a regulation strategy and leads the class in practicing the strategy. The child who holds that classroom job has at least one daily opportunity to lead the class in regulation activities, but also will probably have several more chances as big emotions pop up.

Similarly, there are many opportunities and options for *when* to incorporate this practice. Some teachers work in breathing practice between active movement breaks and stories. Other teachers opt to do slower movement and breathing, like yoga practices, between lunch and rest time. Some teachers have children take deep breaths before they transition to a new activity outside the classroom—such as when they are gathering to head to the music room—to help ease the anxiety of the transition. Think about parts of the day where you often wish for an energy shift and plan some intentional practice of breathing or other regulation strategies during those times.

Jot down notes to yourself as you plan for regulation practice:

➤ What time of day will you intentionally practice regulation with your class?

➤ How will you represent regulation practices on your daily schedule or activity schedule?

➤ Who will choose the regulation strategy to practice?

➤ Who will lead the practice by modeling the regulation strategy?

Planned Opportunities

Of course, the best moments to practice calming down are the natural situations that arise in which we need to access calming strategies to regulate. Offering children choices of strategies that are familiar to them, with props or visual supports to help them choose, allows them to put a strategy into action and feel the benefits in a real-life situation. What a powerful opportunity!

At the same time, we can also think through planned opportunities that give children the chance to practice their calm-down skills. Group opportunities might include times after high-energy activities, such as a movement and music time or coming inside. Another opportunity could be before rest time, as a calming transition into settling down. Consider the power of group calming. When one child is on edge or expresses that they do not feel calm, having the whole class stop to calm helps shift the energy in the classroom and also allows each child to be helpful toward the peer who needs support.

Another planned opportunity is having children create their own breathing techniques. For example, James loved cows. He wanted to do "cow calming." His teacher encouraged him to think about what that would look like and then practice it with the class. James took a deep breath and then exhaled a big "moooooooooooo" breath, while making horns on his head. He taught it to the class, and then the teacher added a cow sticker to the calm-down menu as a choice that James and his classmates can select. Similarly, LaTanja liked ocean animals, so her teacher worked to find ocean movement poses to practice and add to the calm-down menu. Children could choose to jump like a dolphin or stretch their arms and legs out like a starfish. Teachers Tonya and Nichole worked together to envision dinosaur breathing for a dino-loving child who they felt would benefit from increased engagement in regulation practice. These kinds of individualized practices give children the ability to personalize calming down, with supports from their teacher and class, and also allows them to be of service to others by offering their technique and leading the practice.

Planning Opportunities to Regulate

As you plan, ask yourself:

➤ What interests do children in your class have that could be harnessed into calm-down strategies? Are there some interests that might make good props or activities for calming down? For instance, if sensory play is a favorite, could you make sensory bags that children can push, prod, and poke?

➤ If a certain song or book is a favorite, can you develop a calm-down strategy related to it?

➤ How can you work time into the day for children to develop and practice these ideas?

➤ How might you pair children who have similar interests to collaborate on developing strategies?

Extend

One desired outcome of this instruction is to extend the skill from one setting to another. In this case, teaching children calm-down strategies in class would be extended to being able to use these strategies in other situations, other locations, and with other adults. Chapter 7, focusing on the creation of a distinct Regulation Station, also has ideas for how to generalize these skills to a range of situations.

To promote the use of regulation strategies in locations besides the classroom, make sure to have visual supports that are portable and can be used in other places, such as other rooms children travel to in the building. If other adults support children in your class, such as a speech therapist, consider providing them with copies of the calm-down menu so they can encourage regulation using a familiar tool when needed. Encourage children to share their self-created calm-down strategies with other adults, including teachers and family members, so they can also help children remember to access these tools.

If specific strategies help a particular child with regulation, consider turning a small box into an individualized calm-down kit. For example, when Laura is frustrated, she bites or chews on herself or her clothes, or picks at the skin around her fingernails. Her teacher has been encouraging her to access a chew tube or a sensory ball that has small nubs to pick and pull at. Laura's family also shared that she has a favorite song they sing at night, and that it seems to help her calm down as well. Laura's teacher took a pencil box and filled it with Laura's chew tube, textured squishy toys, and a QR code that links to Laura's favorite song. When Laura leaves the classroom to work on climbing the hallway's stairs with her physical therapist, her teacher prompts her to bring her small calm-down box along in case she needs any of those tools. Laura's teacher has done the work of teaching the strategies, celebrating when Laura uses them, and soliciting ideas from her family. Now she wants to ensure that Laura has them even when she is outside of the classroom's four walls.

To further support generalization of skills, coach children during natural moments of strong feelings. Calming is the C in the ICARE coaching framework, and many situations afford children the opportunity to practice calming, revisit situations, and try a more proactive, social approach:

Mrs. Lytton watches from nearby as Ali and Jolene attempt to work out a conflict themselves. They both want to use the same doctor's stethoscope in dramatic play. Jolene has it in her hand, and Ali is asking for it in a pleading tone. Jolene says he can have it when she is finished. Ali yells at Jolene and stomps out of the dramatic play center, swiping all the toys from the shelf onto the floor as he leaves.

Intent: Mrs. Lytton considers Ali's intent. He wanted the toy and couldn't emotionally handle having to wait for it. His act of knocking stuff off the shelf was most likely not intentionally meant to mess up the room or damage the toys, but instead he had angry energy that he had not yet channeled elsewhere. Remembering that his brain is not in the thinking zone helps Mrs. Lytton approach the situation with a tone and demeanor that won't escalate the situation. Rather than a lecture about how he needs to clean up the mess in dramatic play, she knows that helping him regulate will make a bigger impact.

Calm: Mrs. Lytton knows that Ali has several preferred calming techniques on the class's calming menu, including one he added during their days brainstorming and practicing individualized calming techniques. A picture of his superhero doll is on the calming menu, and Mrs. Lytton offers it first. He shakes his head, not wishing to do his superhero breathing today. Since his fists are balled up and he is still stomping, she offers him the stomp mat. He puts his feet on the footprint outlines and stomps and then puts his hands on the handprint outlines on the wall for wall pushups. He stomps and pushes his body until he tires out and sits on the carpet next to his teacher.

Acknowledge: "You really wanted a turn with that stethoscope. Waiting was hard, and your body was so angry. Your feet were stomping, and your arm pushed the toys onto the floor like this." Mrs. Lytton motions with a swipe of her arm so Ali can see what happened when he was feeling angry. He nods at her.

Rewind: Before rewinding to try a different response, Mrs. Lytton encourages Ali to check his body for clues. He confirms that his heart is slower, and his arms and legs are calmer after doing his "exercises" of stomping and pushing. Then she uses role play to help him talk through another way to handle the situation. She plays the role of Jolene, saying that he can have a turn when she is finished. She encourages him to think about how he can successfully wait. Now that he is calm, he chooses to use the pretend thermometer to check the baby dolls' temperature while he waits for the stethoscope. Mrs. Lytton asks if he is going to put the items back on the shelf before the temperature-taking or after. He chooses after the temperature-taking, and Mrs. Lytton checks back in with him in a couple minutes, prompting him to put items on the shelf before his stethoscope turn.

Echo: Jolene finishes her turn with the stethoscope and gives it to Ali. Mrs. Lytton helps echo back the situation. "You found something else to do while you waited, and now it's your turn! You handled it!" She also turns to Jolene and celebrates that she remembered that his turn was after hers, noting how kind and helpful it was to give him a turn when she finished.

As you practice responding with ICARE strategies, reflect and recognize your own patterns when supporting children with calming down.

> How do you approach children who are upset both mentally and physically?

> Are you able to stay calm when children are upset? If not, what strategy can you employ to regulate yourself before stepping in to support a child?

> Do you find yourself talking a lot in these situations? When upset, it's hard for children to process all your language and it can feel even more overwhelming to have additional sensory input. Be mindful of how you are passing information along to children and consider whether you can rely more on visuals or gestures instead of language.

Planning How to Extend Regulation Strategies

Plan for how you will begin to bring regulation strategies into new contexts to extend children's learning. More ideas on this are provided in chapter 7.

> Considering the children in your class and their preferred regulation supports, what props or visuals do you need extra copies of?

> What other adults might need these props or visuals to help children regulate?

> What other locations might need these regulation props or visuals?

> How might you share successful regulation strategies with families?

Reinforce and Reflect

First, think about how you can encourage children to reflect on their ability to calm down. Some possible questions to prompt reflection might be:

- ➤ "What strategy did you choose to help you calm down?"

- ➤ "How did the strategy work? How do you know it worked?"

- ➤ "Why do you think that idea didn't work?"

- ➤ "What might help you next time you are so upset?"

- ➤ "What did you notice in your body as you tried that strategy?"

- ➤ "What other ideas do you have that could help you feel calm?"

- ➤ "What do you think your friend might try to be calm? What could be helpful?"

Asking these questions once children are calm and removed from the situation can allow them to make a new plan if needed, or reinforce that the strategy they tried is indeed helpful and they could choose it again.

Second, offer positive descriptive feedback as children use these strategies. Just like you might comment on a child's effort to build a tall tower or a child's persistence at buttoning their shirt, noticing the effort that goes into regulating their emotions helps children recognize and celebrate that they are doing it.

Anna, a preschool teacher and a mom, had been offering her son support with regulating his emotions since he was tiny. One day, she looked over and saw him pause and take deep breaths without her prompting. She made sure to give him positive descriptive feedback, because while the skills were not new to him, accessing them independently was! Together they celebrated this step toward increased independence.

Planning to Reinforce and Reflect on Regulation Strategies

Intentionally plan when you are going to ask children these types of reflection prompts. Consider how this might look in your classroom by answering these questions:

- ➤ What format for reflection is going to be most helpful for your class? Would this work best, for example, in a closing circle, where children reflect and share about their day?

- ➤ Are there specific children with whom you would want to reflect individually, like during the transition to rest time as you tuck children in?

- ➤ For children who struggle with recall and talking about situations that are not currently happening, would a visual like a photograph or video of them calming down help encourage their recall and reflection?

Teaching Regulation Throughout the Day

Consider the following ideas for integrating regulation skills into the day.

Morning Meeting or Circle Time: Consider working thematic calm-down or breathing strategies into your large group instruction. For example, when Ms. Ronnie is teaching about families, her group does shared writing about ways family members help children feel calm, and then they do visualizations of these strategies, picturing a hug from grandpa or being tucked into bed by mom. When her class is into vehicles, she tries train breathing with long "choo-choo" exhales. What themes or interests will connect regulation and instruction for your group?

Movement and Music: Practice yoga or other calming movement routines. Breathing videos, songs about calming down, and guided movement are all useful for regular practicing of these skills. Adding a calm song, dance, or yoga routine to the end of active dance sessions can also serve to re-center children as they switch to a different type of activity.

Small Group: Have children work together as partners to make pages for a calm-down book. If you have devices that children can access, encourage partners to take photographs of each other calming down. Have children share ideas of what helps them, make or take pictures of these strategies, and decorate the pages with these visuals.

Another small-group activity can be working to make calm-down props. For example, children can make sensory bottles with adult assistance or tape flowers to pinwheels to create their own breathing prop.

Transitions: Transitions are a great time to have children pair up and practice regulation strategies together! These ideas practice social skills like turn taking, leading and following, and gentle touches. For example, have children face each other and ask if their partner is wishing to hold hands. Breathing in, have them raise their linked hands to the sky. Breathing out, have them lower their hands together. Another option is having one child do relaxing yoga or movement poses. Have the other child be their "mirror image" copying their moves. You can also pass out calming props to pairs of children and ask them to figure out how to use these strategies and materials together. This will help as they learn to support each other in the Regulation Station, which is the focus of the next chapter.

Gross-Motor Skills and Outside Time: Blowing bubbles is both fun and a good way to get in some deep breathing. Consider bringing bubbles outside and offering them to children as a way to play *or* as a way to calm down. One creative teacher displayed calm-down ideas along the running and bike track outside. Children in her group could choose to stop as they ran or biked and complete the ideas, like taking deep breaths, stretching, jumping, feeling their heartbeat, and taking a drink of water. Children chose to do these activities whenever they wanted to, sometimes as part of a play obstacle course, as opposed to only when they were actively in need of calming.

However, when children were upset, it was then easy to offer the familiar choices that were already hanging up to see what might help.

Art: Have children each draw or color a cake with five unlit candles on top. Laminate children's cakes and add hook and loop pieces with flames on the top. Now children can use their cake art as a support for taking deep breaths, pulling the flames off the candles as they take each breath.

For many of us, repetitive motion can be soothing. You can encourage children to draw, paint, or color rainbows to use as a calming activity, tracing the rainbow colors from left to right and back again while breathing. Drawing a road to drive a small toy car on can also have a soothing effect. Or encourage children to create artwork depicting calming scenes, and you can hang up these pieces as you create a calming area in your classroom.

Math: Consider using visuals of calm-down strategies in a pattern-focused activity for pairs or trios of children. For example, give one partner pictures of pinwheel breathing, and give the other partner pictures of getting a hug. Encourage partners to take turns putting their pictures on the floor or table, which will create an A-B pattern (or A-B-C pattern for groups of three) with their picture cards. Then have children act out their patterns by following the sequence (such as pinwheel-hug-pinwheel-hug-pinwheel-hug).

You can also embed counting into breathing to add a mathematical element: Breathe in while counting to three, and breathe out while counting to three. Or have children pick a number or roll a die and then try each strategy that many times (four jumping jacks, three sips of water, six deep breaths, and so on).

Story Time: Read stories and use props to illustrate the calm-down strategies that are a focus of the story. For example, in *Little Monkey Calms Down* by Michael Dahl, the little monkey tries several strategies including snuggling with a blanket, singing a song, and using a pinwheel. Use a monkey stuffed animal or monkey sock puppet and have children help you act out the story with the prop. Or offer children the opportunity to act out the story as the monkey and his family, which involves practice calming down (as the monkey) and practice offering support (as the family). *Calm-Down Time* by Elizabeth Verdick is another book with calm-down strategies to read and practice together.

Planning to Teach Regulation Throughout the Day

Which activities to practice regulation appeal to you? What other ideas and materials do you have that build on this skill? As you review activities and materials, plan with the following considerations in mind:

➤ Do you have examples of activities where children practice active ways of regulating (stomping, exercising, moving) as well as less active ones (breathing, snuggling, drawing)?

➤ How can you teach these regulation ideas during classroom activities?

> Spread out your activities across the week and across different settings, including in different centers, during time inside and outside, and as part of activities that are facilitated by different adults.

Formative Assessment of Regulation Skills

The goal of teaching regulation strategies is that children use them—whether alone or with a peer or teacher—to regulate when needed. Collecting data on whether children can regulate using calm-down strategies will give you insights as to who might need extra support, and who has the skills to independently support others. Collecting some simple data allows you to assess your instruction, appropriately pair children for peer support, and share celebrations and emerging skills with families.

Mrs. Lytton collects data on children's use of calm-down strategies. She notes the strategies they choose and how much assistance is needed for them to regain a sense of calm. When Taylor calmed down by jumping on the trampoline and then taking pinwheel breaths, all by herself, Mrs. Lytton notes the strategies Taylor chose and that she was successful independently. Liliana chose to read *Little Monkey Calms Down* and asked Ethan to join her, so Mrs. Lytton notes that too. Ayden picked sensory bottles but threw them; he required teacher support to choose a new strategy and regulate.

Figure 6.1 Sample Data Sheet for Recording Regulation Strategies and Levels of Assistance Needed

Child's Name	Regulation Strategy	Assistance Needed	Notes
Ethan			Read *Little Monkey* with Liliana
Liliana	*Little Monkey*	Asked for Ethan's help	
Ayden	Sensory bottles (not successful); breathing	Teacher support with breathing	
Taylor	Trampoline; pinwheel breathing	Independent	

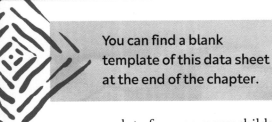

You can find a blank template of this data sheet at the end of the chapter.

After a few days of teaching and recording, Mrs. Lytton decides it's time to use her data. She sits with her teaching partner to review the notes from the week and make an instructional plan for next week. First, they recognized that *Little Monkey Calms Down* was getting a lot of use, as many children chose to look at it when upset. Together they decided to use a monkey mask and take pictures of children doing the steps like the little monkey, and to put these in the library as additional visual supports since the book itself was often in use. Second, Mrs. Lytton decided to work with Ayden to practice asking for help when upset, rather than only accepting help when a teacher initiated the support.

Both teachers had noticed that this was challenging for him during the week, and that he often threw materials toward teachers but then accepted their help when they came over to him. Mrs. Lytton plans on role-play practice with Ayden to support him in asking for help from the get-go when he feels upset.

Planning for Formative Assessment of Regulation Skills

Draft a plan for your formative assessment.

➤ What times of day will work best for gathering data to support your instructional decisions?

➤ What strategies or props will you make sure to have readily accessible for children to use and show you their regulation skills?

➤ When will you review your data so you can use the information to plan your next instructional steps?

When you sit down to review your formative assessment data, note which strategies are commonly chosen in your classroom. Are there other related supports or activities that you can connect to the strategies that have been successful?

Differentiation and Advancement

While some children will be able to access calming strategies after daily practice, some children will need more support. Offering calm-down strategies works best when a child is agitated, but not at peak upset. For children who escalate very quickly, other approaches might be more useful, particularly those that transfer an adult's calm to the child. Some children will let you hold them when upset, and your deep breaths can be used to regulate theirs. Some children will not want you to touch them but will let you be close to them. Continuing to offer steady, deep breathing nearby can help encourage children's breathing to relax and match yours. Children might exhaust themselves when they are very upset. While this is hard to watch, you can track signs of de-escalation, such as slower breathing or movement, or the child starting to talk, and then step in to offer supports for calming down.

For these quick-to-escalate children, considering preventative structures is also helpful. For example, letting a child know via a chart when it is their turn for a preferred object or job can help give time to handle disappointment before the heat of the moment. In Ms. Luy's class, children loved the big red tricycles. When Ayan came onto the playground and was told it was not his day to start outside time on the tricycle, he would become upset very quickly, stomping and kicking the tricycles. Ms. Luy focused on preventative strategies, making a chart showing the days of the week and listing each child under the day when they will start on the tricycle. She started reviewing the chart before transitioning to outside, highlighting whose turn it was and how to get a turn after the first group tires of their tricycle time. Ayan would sometimes still get upset, but the class would breathe together with their Hoberman Sphere and he would return to calm before heading outside. The chart was clearly meaningful to him, as he would come in on Thursdays and announce that it was his tricycle day. The preventative support defused the disappointment by shifting it away from the playground and into the classroom, far away from the trigger of the tricycle itself, and it also built in a planned opportunity to regulate.

For children who struggle with making choices, a visual choice menu of calming strategies can feel overwhelming rather than supportive. A defined calm-down routine can be a more beneficial tool for children who benefit from clear scripts and structures. In this setup, calm-down strategies are combined with visuals and typically arranged in a specific order, to guide children through a consistent, practiced routine when upset. Amy, a four-year-old with autism who has an easy time memorizing practiced routines and scripts, uses a calm-down routine when she gets upset. Her teacher, Mr. Williams, has arranged five calm-down icons representing strategies that he has noticed that Amy will engage with, along with others that her family said are helpful at home. Mr. Williams laminated these pictures onto large paper, in left-to-right order, matching the way Amy's visual schedule is presented. He also made flaps that she can close to cover up the steps as she completes them. Together, they practice the routine when she is calm, going through each step and checking her body's clues to see if she is feeling calm when she finishes. Later, when Amy is upset, she begins to cry. Mr. Williams offers the familiar routine. Amy doesn't engage at first, so Mr. Williams starts the routine himself, softly narrating the steps as he completes them. Amy gradually turns her focus to the calm-down routine and begins to do to the strategies alongside her teacher. When they get to the end of the calm-down routine, Mr. Williams encourages Amy to feel her heartbeat and see if it is fast or slow and listen to her breathing to see if she is calm or needs to work through the routine again.

Some children will come into your class already having the ability to choose effective regulation strategies for themselves. While it's rare that *every* child would not need support in this realm, you might have a couple children who can already tell you what they do to calm down, or whom you observe them successfully calming down on their own. For these children, your focus might be on reflection, encouraging them to articulate how they knew to choose a particular strategy, explain how they knew their strategies worked, or share other times those strategies have worked. Supporting their metacognition about their own regulation brings additional awareness and new ways of thinking.

Ms. Griffin and Ms. Houston worked together to individualize extra regulation supports for a child who needed them. Together, they introduced a volcano with a moving lava ribbon to help him recognize whether he was calm, agitated, or exploding. They modeled how to take breaths and use other calming tools. The child was excited to use "his volcano." He started to access it when upset—pulling the lava to exploding, taking deep breaths and moving the lava down, and then rejoining classroom activities.

Planning for Differentiation and Advancement

Create a plan for children who might need individualization. Use data and observations to identify specific children for whom you will intentionally plan modified or individualized supports.

> Review data and observations for the children who need extra support. How do they currently regulate? Do they accept help from you or a peer?

> What individual regulation strategies might these children appreciate?

> Are there certain situations that are leading to emotional dysregulation and that you can prevent through appropriate supports such as visuals, social stories, or social coaching?

> Review the data and observations for the children who can regulate independently. What reflection questions might you ask to further their own understanding of their skill?

Troubleshooting Around Practicing Regulation Strategies

Consider the following ways to troubleshoot questions or obstacles you might run into as you help children learn regulation strategies.

"I tell children to calm down, but they often do not listen. What should I do to encourage their regulation skills?"

There are three things to consider here. First, consider how you feel when someone tells you to calm down. Depending on the tone, it can feel condescending or demanding, rather than supportive. Rather than using "calm down" as a direction, providing validating statements and an offer of support might be more well received. For example, "You seem really frustrated. How can I help you feel better?" or "Your body is showing me you are really excited. What can I do to help you get out your excitement so that it is safe for you to be next to your classmates on the carpet?"

Second, reflect on your use of "calm down." Are you encouraging children to calm down when their emotions are running high, such as feeling so excited they are jumping or flailing, or feeling so sad they are having a hard time participating in play? Or are you using "calm down" to redirect behaviors that aren't actually related to emotions? For example, are you telling children who have loud speaking voices to "calm down" when a redirection to adjust their volume level would be more descriptive and appropriate? You've taught children to start to recognize when their body clues are suggesting that they are having big feelings. Encouraging them to use calm-down strategies specifically during these instances helps build those emotional competencies.

Third, notice how I use the term *regulation*, rather than *self-regulation*, throughout this book. When we talk about "self-regulation" it leads us to believe that children can do it independently. While older preschoolers are working on increasing independence with regulation, oftentimes coregulation is the goal as children learn the skill. To a young three-year-old, hearing a direction to "calm down" is similar to hearing "tie your shoes." They might understand what you mean but not have the skills to follow through with your direction. Offering your support with clear directions can be more effective in providing information and modeling the skill. "Here's the breathing ball. Let's try deep breaths with it until your body is calm."

Another key part of coregulation is that the adults need to be calm too. Reflect on whether you are calm when telling children to calm down. If you are feeling agitated or annoyed, children are likely to read that and might be hesitant to come over for support. Think through the ICARE steps, including remembering the child's intent and checking for your own calm, before offering support with regulation.

"What do I do to support a child who does not want my help when upset?"
Some children do not want our help using regulation strategies. But since you have taught how to calm down, you have supported the child with many of the needed skills. If a child can regulate without you, congratulations! Independent regulation is a very useful skill to have, and you can celebrate that success. At other times, a child doesn't want our help but cannot regulate independently yet. If this is the case, consider if you are the right person to help. Would the child accept help from another adult? Would they accept help from a peer? When the child is calm, try asking who they want supporting them with regulation.

For a child who isn't wishing for help, consider additional tools that might help them regulate on their own. Would more visuals be supportive? What about individualized calming materials? Some children are so upset that they simply aren't ready to accept help and cannot hear your language and process that you are offering support. In this situation, think through the timing of your help. Is the child just starting to get upset or is the child at the peak of their emotion cycle? You might watch for signs that the child is getting agitated and offer help before they are flooded with big emotions. If you miss that opportunity, you might limit your verbal support and instead sit nearby and take slow calming breaths, offering your support as a calm, steady presence nearby. When the child has begun to calm somewhat, you might turn to other regulation strategies if needed or appropriate.

"I have a child in my class who is almost too calm. He never shows big emotions and rarely gets outwardly upset. I see things that probably bother him, like his tower being crushed by another child, but he doesn't show any reaction. How do I help him get used to his feelings?"

It's important to also consider children who might seem overly calm. We all have emotions, and our bodies all have physiological responses to these emotions. Some children, whether due to individual temperament or personal experiences, handle unpleasant emotions by not outwardly expressing them and not completing the stress cycle. This can lead to a build-up of stress in the body, and in the classroom, it can be challenging to support a child with self-advocacy if they aren't vocal about what they want or what help they need in emotional situations. After all, children getting angry when they are mistreated is natural and can spur them to take action to problem solve or get teacher support.

If a child is used to internalizing emotions, you might take several steps. First, you might talk to the child's family to find out more about how the child shows emotions or copes with them. Families may be in tune with subtle clues the child exhibits that can be helpful for you to know. Family members may also be able to share strategies they use at home to support the child, or might help identify their goals for their child's expression and self-advocacy that you can then plan around together. Second, you might ask your support system for ideas to support the child. If your program has a counselor or a mental health consultant on staff, both may be able to brainstorm with you. And third, you can work with the child individually to practice letting out emotions. This could look like identifying strategies that might work to release stress, or role-playing situations where self-advocacy is important, even if it's as simple as encouraging a child to say "I don't like that" or "I feel sad." If the child isn't ready to say how they are feeling verbally, offering other ways, such as pointing to visuals or drawing, helps provide another mechanism to identify and release emotions.

It's important to note that if a child is anxious about expressing negative or unpleasant emotions, we can be especially intentional about making space for all emotions. We can do that by continuing to normalize the expression of emotions, whether it's sharing examples of a time we were so frustrated we cried to feel better, or making sure we acknowledge how helpful it is to share feelings with others. Pairing with another teacher who can come and observe or record a video of us in the class-room can support our reflection and examination of how we treat emotions, and help us make adjustments if needed.

A teacher was really diving into teaching emotions and wished to ensure that a child who was reticent to express emotions felt safe. She asked me to observe so that we could help plan together. I noticed that during the group's emotion check-in, she typically responded with "I'm so glad you're happy" or "Thank you for sharing that you are excited." For less pleasant or comfortable emotions, she often started with "Oh no." "Oh no, he's feeling sad today," "Oh no, she is feeling frustrated." This language, while not an intentional choice on the part of the teacher, could be interpreted as saying that emotions such as sadness and frustration are problems. Awareness was the first step, and then she was able to respond to all emotions in a way that left out judgment.

Family Engagement and Support

A social and emotional snippet related to teaching regulation strategies might look like this:

> *This week, we practiced different ways to calm down. Two strategies that we worked on were pinwheel breathing and reading Little Monkey Calms Down by Michael Dahl. Both strategies encourage children to take breaths and find props or tools to help them feel more calm or relaxed. We also started working with each child to think about what would help them calm down when they are sad, angry, frustrated, or too excited to keep their body calm. We have been taking pictures of children practicing their calm-down ideas. You can see those up on the wall display above our cubbies in the classroom.*

Videos can be very helpful when teaching regulation. Four different kinds of video clips might be useful to share with families:

> ➤ A child or pair of children demonstrating a calm-down strategy. For example, one child could be doing pinwheel breathing and the other child could be narrating the steps of "smell the flower, blow the pinwheel." Sharing a video of this activity gives families something to watch together and offers coaching around how to use the strategy.

> ➤ A teacher modeling a strategy and discussing why it is useful and how it is being taught at school.

> ➤ A link to an online video that promotes calming. For example, *Sesame Street* has a breathing song and video about belly breathing. Playing videos like this at school and also sending links home so children and families can watch them together furthers the learning and provides video modeling.

> ➤ Lastly, ask families to send you video clips of ways they help their children calm down at home, such as singing a specific song that is calming, doing a calming ritual, or listening to a story or meditation. This allows for another opportunity to connect home and school as you and your class watch the many ways families calm down or relax.

You can also ask families to practice a calm-down routine at home, such as before bed or when children are angry. At family workshops, you can work together to create tools, such as a calm-down menu or visual calm-down routine, that families think would help them. As you discuss calming down with families, solicit feedback about what works for them at home, what they have noticed helps their child, and if their child typically calms down alone or with support. These family insights into children's experience with regulation strategies outside of school can be extremely useful.

And of course, sharing celebrations with families is so important for building a trusting relationship. Families want to hear when their child is doing well and want to see how skills are developing. Letting families know what calm-down strategies their child is gravitating toward, sending home notes celebrating a child's independence in choosing a strategy, or sharing a child's drawing of his family calming down at home are all ways to share your group's work and give families insight into their child's progress.

Wrap-Up

Congratulations on reflecting, planning, and teaching your class developmentally appropriate strategies for calming and regulating! We have all felt so wrapped up in a big feeling, whether sadness or anger or excitement, that we felt like that emotion would consume us forever. But this skill transforms the intensity and confusion of big feelings, making them manageable. Practicing regulation strategies allows children to replace less socially appropriate strategies such as running away, throwing things, or hitting. Teaching and practicing these skills with ample support makes it more likely that a child will pick a familiar supportive strategy when they need it, especially with the help of caring adults.

Practicing regulation strategies leads into the next skill: using a space in the classroom designated specifically for regulation, and doing so with increasing independence. While chapter 6 supported us with answering, "How can I calm down when I am feeling strong emotions?" this next skill, the focus of chapter 7, gives us the answer to "Where can I go to calm down and what supports will I find there?"

Regulation Strategies Planning Sheet

Consider the following materials for helping children learn and practice regulation strategies, and use these as a starting point for creating your own plan for teaching these skills. Keep in mind that it's important to offer materials that provide regulation support in a variety of ways to meet a range of needs and be used in different situations or as part of different regulation strategies. Which of these do you already have in your classroom?

- ☐ breathing tools (pictures of multiple breathing strategies, pinwheels, bubbles, Hoberman Sphere)
- ☐ sensory blocking materials (headphones, dark space, eye mask)
- ☐ sensory seeking materials (various textures, music, vibrating massager, flip-the-sequins fabric)
- ☐ interesting items to look at (books, pictures, liquid timers, sensory bottles)
- ☐ family connections (family photos, family portraits drawn by children, recording of a parent's voice)
- ☐ big body play items (handprints for pushing a wall, stomp mat, pictures of exercises or yoga moves)
- ☐ calming routines (*Little Monkey Calms Down* props to use with the book, chart showing the steps of a calming routine)
- ☐ children's individual favorite items (trains or cars, pictures to represent favorite songs, items from home like a naptime stuffed animal)
- ☐ icons to represent other choices (such as getting a drink or going on a walk)

After reviewing which kinds of regulation strategies you have already taught and which materials are available in your space, what are some additional strategies or materials that would further support the children in your class?

When you've identified additional strategies and related materials to try, use DAPPER to plan out how to teach them.

Regulation Strategy to Teach:	
Components of DAPPER	**Plan for Teaching Regulation Strategy**
Demonstrate and **D**escribe	
Animate	
Practice	
Planned Opportunities	
Extend	
Reinforce and **R**eflect	

Data Sheet for Recording Regulation Strategies and Levels of Assistance Needed

This data sheet gives you a space to record information about children's ability to use the regulation strategies you are teaching. In the "Assistance Needed" column, note whether the child was able to use the strategy independently or needed verbal or physical prompting.

Child's Name	Regulation Strategy	Assistance Needed	Notes

Chapter 7

Accessing the Regulation Station

PICTURE THIS Mia, a four-year-old, is angry. She was line leader last week, and today she proudly walks to the front of the line, ready to lead the class to the playground. Jaime nudges her out of the line, shouting that he is the line leader, and it is not her turn. Mia's face turns red. "Don't take my job!" she hollers as she kicks Jaime in the shins. Their teacher rushes over to the line, standing between the two children. Mia continues to kick and swing her arms, hitting her teacher. Her teacher picks her up and carries her to the classroom's Regulation Station. He tells her to calm down and then returns to the line to get ready for outside.

In the Regulation Station, Mia isn't calm. Her legs are still kicking. Her arms are still swinging. She continues to yell. She picks up a sensory bottle and throws it in the general direction of the line. She picks up a stuffed animal and tosses that too. She hurls a squishy ball and growls. Her teacher continues to tell her to calm down so she can go outside. He calls another teacher to stay with Mia so he can take the rest of the class outside to the playground.

Her teacher wonders what to do differently. Why did it take Mia so long to calm down? What should he have said to help her? He also wonders if having all the calm-down supports is truly helpful, since they were used as projectiles and are now scattered all over the floor. He feels his own mix of emotions: overwhelmed, frustrated, and sad that he isn't sure where to begin when it comes to helping Mia with her emotional regulation.

About the Skill of Accessing the Regulation Station

We have spaces in our room specifically and intentionally designed to support learning. We arrange our library area on soft carpet or rugs, with books thoughtfully

displayed to pique children's interest. We label our shelves so children know where to put the puzzles when they are completed. We arrange the easel close to the sink to make art adventures just a little bit less messy. We save space on the tops of shelves to display children's sculptures, and we label cubbies with children's names and photographs to promote independence. We separate louder, active play areas from quieter ones to allow children to choose a space that meets their sensory needs. In early childhood classrooms, we thoughtfully consider how to make activity areas engaging, organized, and supportive for children's learning.

Many classrooms also have an area for a child to calm down, and there are a multitude of names and setups for these spaces. In some classes it's a "Cozy Corner," or a "Cool Down Spot," or the "Safe Space." In other classrooms it doesn't have a name, but children might seek out a big bean bag to curl into when upset. Regardless of what the center is called, the goal is the same. Just as an art center has supplies for exploring and developing new art skills, the Regulation Station is designed for exploring and developing new emotional regulation skills. If we have similar goals for the Regulation Station as for other classroom centers, then we need to be intentional in treating them similarly. This chapter walks through the intentional planning and teaching process to create a classroom Regulation Station that will support social and emotional development.

The Starting Point

One starting point in fostering regulation strategies in the classroom is to apply the same intentionality that you use when creating other centers in your classroom. When you are creating a Regulation Station, arrangement in your room is important. While some classrooms attempt to keep the regulation space small, or share it with another center, think about what that might mean for children. For example, if your current class space has a bean bag as a cozy space for one, would that allow for a child to help another child calm down? If you have a library that is currently your only space for quiet and calm, would it be conducive to both calming and reading? I encourage you to find a separate, defined space specifically for exploring emotions and regulating. The goal is to create a unique activity area or center with distinct routines, supports, and materials for regulation.

Planning to Start

Identify a possible space for your Regulation Station.

➤ Is there an area where children can have some privacy if needed? Can adults still offer proper supervision of the private space?

➤ Can you make it soft, comfortable, and inviting?

➤ Is it in an area conducive to calming down? For example, if children are overwhelmed by sounds, placing the station away from a loud area might be useful. Choosing an area away from bright lights, busy patterns, and bold colors can also help reduce sensory overwhelm.

> Is the area big enough for more than one child to access?

> Will the area also fit an adult who might be supporting a child?

If you do not have a separate space for regulation, consider where children currently go when they feel upset. Are children sitting in a cubby or crawling under a table? Watching to see where children go tells us what they might prefer—whether that is a small, enclosed space or a dark or private place. These clues can help us set up something similar with intention. Sometimes a small table, an empty cubby, or a giant refrigerator box with a door cut out can offer a supportive space.

If you have children who need to release energy to regulate, consider making sure you have a space for that too. Many teachers combine that into one space, where children can choose active strategies from a range of choices. In this case, ensure that children have enough space to be able to jump, stomp, or do yoga. For example, you might have a space that has room for a three-sided refrigerator box, to provide a partially enclosed area, and is also large enough for a movement space outside the box. Some teachers create two spaces near each other for different types of calming, and some teachers opt to put their active calming ideas into their portable Regulation Station to encourage those regulation options.

Kristen, Kathy, and Christina built two Regulation Stations in their preschool special education classroom. One had a mat to make a defined space for big physical movements to regulate. The other had boxes of props to calm down. They were able to support children who needed movement and sensory input in the active space as they stomped, jumped, or crashed against the mat. When they were beginning to de-escalate and were ready to talk about feelings and problem solve, they'd go with their teacher to the second space. In Shelley's preschool classroom, she put pushing handprints on the wall and ideas for exercises and movement in her one Regulation Station. Consider what works for your class. Either way, ensure that children have access to strategies that are more active—whether that's in your Regulation Station, a separate Active Regulation Station, or a portable Regulation Station for times when the main one is in use by a child who doesn't want active help from a peer.

The Regulation Station Planning Considerations sheet at the end of this chapter can help as you work through the steps of planning and building your space.

Using DAPPER to Teach the Regulation Station

You've already begun to plan where you might build a Regulation Station and how you envision it being used. Now, use the DAPPER framework to plan how to teach your classroom's newest center.

Demonstrate and Describe

Take a moment to review how you teach children about centers or activity areas at the beginning of the year. You probably teach where the center is, what it's called, and what materials are housed there. You probably teach how to know if it is open or closed and how to know if there is room for another child. You show children how to access materials and how to clean up. All these concepts apply to teaching about the Regulation Station as well.

To support this demonstration, begin by choosing several simple calm-down tools to put into the center. You might put a squishy toy to squeeze and a sensory bottle to shake and look at. Start with simple tools that are easy to demonstrate or ones that you have already taught. Then continue to add additional tools as you teach them. (Teaching regulation tools is the focus of chapter 6.) Put a copy of your Body Clues Map in the area as well.

Demonstrating how to access the Regulation Station tends to be most effective when children are engaged and focused on learning about the center. Rather than only talking about how you might use the area, consider staging a little teacher theater session where you or another adult show big feelings, such as being upset or very excited, and then demonstrate how to use the Regulation Station as a tool. Seeing a teacher have large feelings tends to draw children's focus to the Regulation Station and what happens there.

To make your modeling even more effective during this role play, think out loud and describe your behavior. For example, "Ugh, I am so frustrated that my tower keeps falling over. I feel like screaming and shouting. My feelings feel so big. Maybe I should go to the Regulation Station to calm down." Stomp your way over the station, sit down, and continue modeling and describing. Include looking at your choices of tools and picking one to try first. Reflect aloud on whether the tool is working. Label your body clues to help children understand if you are still feeling very frustrated or if you are starting to feel better.

Continue to narrate when you get to calm, and check in with yourself aloud. Reinforce the idea that once you feel calm, you are ready to problem solve. Choose whether you want to try the tower again or start a new activity—which might include sitting and talking with children about the new Regulation Station center!

Ms. Maddi, an inclusive preschool teacher, hung up a chart in her room's Regulation Station displaying pictures of what "calm" looks and feels like. This chart, with hook and loop checkmarks for each picture, helps children remember to check their body's clues to ensure that they are feeling calmer before leaving the Regulation Station. Model using a similar chart or the Body Clues Map to remind children that checking in with your body is one step toward seeing if your work in the Regulation Station is done.

Planning to Demonstrate and Describe How to Use the Regulation Station

Reflect on what you want children to take away from your modeling. Plan how to intentionally work these ideas into your demonstration and how you'll review them afterward. Some big ideas are that you can use that space to help with big feelings, that you choose strategies or tools in the space to help, and that you check in to see if you are calm. What other takeaways do you want children to have about your Regulation Station?

Animate

Visuals and gestures can help animate ideas around using a Regulation Station. Some visual supports will be similar to those in other centers in your classroom. You'll likely begin by making a center sign to label your area. In many classrooms, centers also have visual supports (such as numbers, or spots for hanging a certain number of center tags) to show how many children can be in a center at one time. Putting up a Regulation Station sign and a visual support for the center's capacity will help children remember and understand the center, and also normalize it as simply one more center in the classroom.

Elizabeth and Joan, preschool special education teachers, worked to put up a little clear door for their Regulation Station. They taught their class that leaving the "door" open means you are wishing for help and that closing the door means you want to be alone. This visual symbol helped teachers and peers respond if a child wanted support.

To further animate this idea with a gestural component, think about how you could indicate to a child that taking a break in the Regulation Station might be helpful. One teacher uses the ASL sign for *break* to communicate that some time in the Regulation Station might be needed. Another teacher uses the sign for *relax* to give a gestural cue for the Regulation Station. Keep in mind that a gestural cue to encourage using the Regulation Station can best support a child who is feeling slightly agitated. When at the peak of big emotions, it is unlikely that a child will be able to see and process a gestural reminder to use a new area.

Planning Animations for the Regulation Station

Oftentimes the default is to set a limit of one person at a time in the Regulation Station. Is this because we believe handling big feelings is a private matter? Do we believe that an upset child will make another child upset? Are we worried that, by having more than one child in the center, it will become too exciting? Reflect on your own assumptions about why one child, and one child only, might be the appropriate occupancy for the Regulation Station. Identifying where the idea stems from can help us challenge ourselves as we progress in this work.

Consider making the center a space for two children to collaborate on calming down, with one child being able to support a peer through regulation.

➤ What possible benefits would this have?

➤ What other skills might be reinforced by allowing children to support each other in emotional understanding?

➤ What messages does this help send about recognizing and responding to others' emotions?

You might also make a visual to support choice around this idea. This could be a sign showing that two children can be in the Regulation Station, but also have a component that a child can use to cover the second person and communicate wanting to be alone in that space. Another option is a hanging visual that can be flipped, which has two people on one side (indicating that support would be useful) and one person on the other side (indicating that being alone is the preference). What benefits might arise from giving children a way to reflect and express their wishes around having other children support them? If you choose to make your space for one child but are open to children asking peers for help, how can you explain, demonstrate, and reinforce that idea?

Ms. Xiomara and Ms. Grace teach in an inclusive preschool classroom where they have encouraged children to access their Regulation Station together if needed or desired. On the day of my classroom visit, an upset child went to the Regulation Station with Ms. Xiomara. Another child was nearby in the classroom library with Ms. Grace. He left the library to check in on his friend and offered the upset child strategies including a pinwheel for breathing and a sensory bottle. Rather than Ms. Grace instructing that child to stay in the library, or Ms. Xiomara not accepting his offer to help, the two children passed calming materials back and forth, connecting with each other and talking about how they felt.

Practice

Guided center practice is not a very new concept. To foster new routines, early childhood educators typically take small groups of children into centers at the beginning of the year to practice using materials and cleaning up. You probably already do this when teaching children how to use classroom art materials or how to put blocks back on the shelf. This time, you'll guide children through practicing the Regulation Station. After you've demonstrated the new area, and once you've added and explained the center visuals to children, it's time for children to practice in the center with your support.

One idea for practice is to have children walk a stuffed animal or a puppet through the process of using the center. Peers would work together to help the puppet recognize its feelings, move to the center, choose strategies to regulate, and check in to see if the puppet feels calmer before leaving the center. Another idea for practice is a teacher taking two children to the Regulation Station together to support each other in remembering what to do and exploring the center's materials. By doing this, teachers reinforce how a child can use the center and also how a peer might help, offering children practice in both the roles of the child in need of regulation and the child who is supporting the regulation process. Teachers can use a shared writing activity to make a list of the steps of using the center, and can draw or print corresponding visuals to hang in or near the center.

Planning How to Practice Using the Regulation Station

What steps do children need to remember about using the Regulation Station? Review your notes from demonstrating the center, and then plan for additional learning by listing out each step you'd want children to take as they use the Regulation Station. Think through how to make sure these steps are involved in your practice of this skill. Take a look at figure 7.1 to see some example steps, along with props or visuals children might need to successfully complete them, and brainstorm your own.

Figure 7.1 Steps for Using the Regulation Station with Associated Props and Visuals

Step	Props or Visuals Needed
Recognize you have big feelings.	Body Clues Map, mirror, or emotion check-in chart
Go to the Regulation Station.	Center sign or prop for "signing in" for the center

Planned Opportunities

While we cannot plan when children will be bursting with excitement or simmering with anger, we can be mindful of setting up opportunities for children to use the Regulation Station. Several research studies on science centers in the early childhood classroom looked at how underutilized they were. First, teachers in the classroom did not tend to go into the science center, which meant children who wanted to spend time with a nurturing adult were not drawn to go there. Second, the materials in the center typically were not as familiar as other materials in the classroom and its various centers. For instance, blocks, costumes, and puzzles are most likely familiar to many children, whereas materials like balance scales are less likely to be familiar. Third, there were not many planned or unplanned activities or lessons focused on science and science materials. Researchers also found that a simple intervention in which teachers explained a balance scale and children answered questions and made observations about it drastically boosted children's time in the science center, engaging with the balance scale and also with other materials.

The ideas from the research around science centers can help when thinking about introducing and boosting use of the Regulation Station. First, putting yourself in the area during center time can encourage children to come and explore it. Perhaps you will plan on bringing a new calm-down support, like a sensory bottle, a pinwheel and flower, or a pillow with an interesting texture. Going to a center and introducing a new material would serve as a planned opportunity for children to practice understanding how the station is used.

Second, previewing the center's materials in a large-group format can also encourage children's enthusiasm for using the space and practicing with the materials. As you find additional tools for regulation to put in your space, showing them to the whole class and asking them to practice with you, or asking children questions and prompting them to observe their body clues as they try the materials, might also encourage children to seek out those tools in the Regulation Station during choice time.

Third, consider offering children the opportunity to help you regulate in the center. When you are feeling sad or disappointed, frustrated or overexcited, ask a child to support you in taking a minute in the Regulation Station yourself. Of course, you'll also support children in this work as they have big feelings too.

Last, including the Regulation Station on any choice board or center display you might have will be a reminder that it too is an activity area. For example, Ms. Rachel has a picture of it on her choice board, allowing children to choose it as they transition to their free choice centers. Many days children do choose it, allowing opportunities to engage with the materials and each other, and a teacher often joins to talk about emotions and calming strategies too.

Reflect on how you promote and encourage children to explore other activity areas in your classroom.

➤ Do you preview new materials that are going into the centers?

➤ Do you put out provocations for children to explore and work with?

➤ Do you remember to mention specific centers when describing what children might explore today?

➤ Do you have a centers board or a social story about the centers in your classroom?

Planning to Make the Regulation Station Engaging

Using the reflection questions in the previous section, consider how you can harness these strategies to encourage children to see your Regulation Station as a place to explore and learn. Consider the following planning prompts as you jot down notes to help you intentionally plan for building interest in the Regulation Station:

➤ When during the day will I make a point of going to the Regulation Station?

➤ What new material or visual could I preview and then put into the Regulation Station?

➤ At what time of day might I ask a child to help me regulate my emotions in the Regulation Station?

➤ Which children might benefit most from walking me through the Regulation Station?

➤ How will I make the Regulation Station truly feel like a center children can choose to explore?

Extend

One way we extend a skill is by encouraging a child to use it in more than one setting. Of course, not every room a child is in will have a Regulation Station like the one you have created in your classroom. In fact, most places a child visits will not have these supports in place. To extend this skill of recognizing big emotions and locating a space to regulate, Regulation Station ideas need to be portable. This will allow children to take the idea of the station with them onto the playground, to the local library, or to a restaurant with their family. We often take first aid supplies with us to the playground or to the other rooms in our schools for physical well-being. We can take regulation supplies with us for our emotional well-being.

As you've taught about your Regulation Station, you have probably focused on several key ideas, such as:

➤ The Regulation Station is a defined space in the classroom. You can go to this comfortable space when your feelings are big or when you want to think and explore your feelings.

➤ You can go alone or get help and support to regulate there.

➤ You have choices of tools that will help you regulate.

➤ You check in with your body to see if your strategies are working.

➤ When you are calm, you are ready to explore another area or activity if you choose.

Examining these ideas can help you plan for a portable version of your center. For example, you could have a towel or mat in the portable station that can be used to create a defined space if needed. Similarly, during a visit to the school library you might find a corner in which to post the visual that represents your Regulation Station center, to make a temporary space while your class is at the library. Outside, a hula hoop with a Regulation Station sign on it can provide a small defined space for regulating.

Second, you can consider packing a few example calming materials into a small bag so that the process of choosing a tool can be similar to your classroom. Rather than carrying around heavy materials, you might choose small fidgets or a choice board with pictures of various options that are materials-free (for instance, sing a song, take deep breaths, count to ten, do jumping jacks).

"As a teacher, I found myself rushing to defuse or solve problems for my students, thinking that I was mastering behavior and classroom management, and never realizing that I was denying them the opportunity for critical thinking, problem-solving, emotion regulation, and friendship-building!"

Ms. Pearsall, an inclusive preschool teacher, reflected on this and then began teaching children how to use backpacks of tools to be more independent with regulating and solving problems. Each backpack had pictures of emotion expressions to help children identify how they were feeling, calm-down supplies including pinwheels and favorite stories, and visual reminders of ways to solve problems with peers.

Third, in the bag or other portable station, you can place small reminders of the steps of using the station to make it easier for children to follow the routine in an area that isn't the classroom. One teacher created a small flip-book of index cards on a ring. There are five pages: recognize your feelings and go to the Regulation Station; think about whether you want to be alone or want help; choose tools to help you; check in with your body; leave when you are calm and ready to play. This small script helps support the entire process, offering the child an additional way to be independent and offering those who might be supporting the regulatory process a roadmap for helping.

While allowing two children to coregulate in the Regulation Station can be supportive, sometimes you will have a child who needs to regulate when the center is already in use by a child who does not want a peer there with them. The portable Regulation Station can also come in handy in this case. One child can choose a different spot, with your help if needed, and you can bring the Regulation Station to them. This allows both children to calm with supports, while respecting the desire of a child who wishes to be in the space alone.

The ICARE framework can also be used to coach children around using the Regulation Station. In Mr. Rosenberg's room, he decides to reflect with his team to figure out how the ICARE framework could be useful in situations like Mia and Jaime fighting over the line leader spot. They ask themselves, "What could this situation look like if we approached it with ICARE in mind?" and they talk about what they might have done differently, and what children might have done differently as well.

Intent: Mr. Rosenberg asks himself, as he approaches the situation, "What is Mia's intent in kicking and yelling? What is Jaime's intent in pushing her out of the way?" He thinks about what they are each trying to express. Mia thought her job was taken by another child and wanted to stake her claim to that spot and job. Jaime wanted her to move so he could access the spot to do his job. Both children are trying to be responsible and support their classroom community by doing their class job.

Calm: Mr. Rosenberg reflects that he put Mia in the Regulation Station but did not offer guidance to help her calm down. He plans to either stay with Mia in the center next time to help her calm down, or bring the calm-down supports to her. Additionally, moving the other children outside and sitting with Mia to calm down would eliminate the need to carry her to the other space without her consent.

Acknowledge: He watches as Mia's body starts to relax and offers support through acknowledging. "You looked so angry when you thought Jaime took your job. You really wanted to do that job today." She nods. He acknowledges that she didn't know it was Jaime's job and how it can be scary to not know why a classmate is so upset.

Rewind: He brainstorms that he could rewind the situation when Mia is calm and have her and Jaime work together to role-play the scene where they both believe they are the line leader. Mia suggests checking the job chart if they don't know whose job it is, and Jaime agrees that this would work better. Mia, seeing that it wasn't her turn, gets behind Jaime as they practice.

Echo: Mr. Rosenberg echoes back, "You had a problem together, and you used the job chart to solve it. That was a safer way to solve your problem!" He also reminds Mia of how she calmed down successfully. "You were so upset, and you let me help you calm down. You're calm. You did it!"

Planning to Extend the Regulation Station

Reflect on what you need to make a portable version of the center you have built and taught in your room.

➤ Are there certain children who have individualized calming tools that would be particularly beneficial to have on-the-go?

➤ How will you remember to bring these supplies with you?

➤ How are you going to teach children about the portable Regulation Station?

➤ Will bringing it be a job for an adult? Could it be a job for a child to carry it?

➤ If a child needs the portable station in the classroom because the Regulation Station is otherwise occupied, who will retrieve those supports? Where in the classroom might you help that child create their own Regulation Station?

Reinforce and Reflect

First, consider how to make using the Regulation Station feel celebratory. Oftentimes children are "sent" somewhere as a form of removal or punishment. It's important that going and using the Regulation Station feel different. It should be more akin to accessing a needed tool, like remembering to get the recycling bin when working on a paper-cutting project, or finding the just-right block that will stand upright on the top of your tower. Positive descriptive feedback to support this mindset around the Regulation Station might sound like, "You remembered to go to the Regulation Station when you needed to calm down!" or "You found a tool that would help you calm down. You did it!" It might even sound like acknowledging a supportive peer. "You went with him when he was upset. You were a kind friend to help with calming down."

Some teachers celebrate the use of Regulation Station just as they do any other center. They include it in daily notes to families about centers children engage in, or take photos of children calming or exploring the materials in the station to document what children have been up to. Other teachers have children cheer for each other and themselves at the end of the day for having big feelings and working to handle them appropriately.

Second, having children reflect on their own skills builds greater awareness. For example, asking a child to share how they felt going into the Regulation Station and how they felt exiting it allows them to process how their emotions changed. It can also be helpful to have children share some details of how they calmed themselves down in the station. Asking questions like "What tools did you try in the Regulation Station?" or "Did it work?" or "How did you know it worked?" prompts children to think about the efficacy of their strategies. At other times, it allows teachers to engage in discussions about what happens when we try strategies that don't help, and what we might need to do next if we still have big feelings. Other teachers revisit the emotion check-in several times during the day so children can reflect on how their emotions have changed. This helps reinforce the idea that emotions really do change often, even when it seems like we might feel our current emotion forever.

Planning to Reinforce and Reflect Around Accessing the Regulation Station

As you plan, reflect on how you celebrate children's work in other centers or activity areas.

➤ Which strategies can you use to celebrate children's use of the Regulation Station?

➤ How can you follow up with children after their time in that center to encourage new thinking or idea sharing?

➤ How do you document what children are building in a construction center or creating in an art center? Is there a similar way you'd like to document children's use of the Regulation Station and their reflections about how it helped?

Encouraging Use of the Regulation Station Throughout the Day

The Regulation Station can be a place for assistance—whether it's a teacher helping a child, a child helping a peer, or even a child helping a teacher. Keep this in mind while you practice and encourage its use throughout the day, and intentionally embed some partner experiences into the practice.

Morning Meeting or Circle Time: After teaching the Regulation Station, take pictures of children using the space, whether during practice or in moments when regulation is needed. Show children the photographs and have children share ideas to label them with captions. If desired, you could take photos of the steps in the process (such as going to the station, choosing if you want to be alone or need help, picking a tool to try, and checking in with your body) and then have children work to sequence them, labeling them with numbers. These steps could hang in the station or be accessible elsewhere for children to read and review. If children are in the Regulation Station together, take photos of what helping each other can look like too.

Movement and Music: Try listening to many kinds of music with your class, or playing multiple classroom instruments that you have available while children listen. Have children note whether or not each kind of music is calming or soothing to them. Encourage children to record their answers by putting stickers on a chart to mark calming or not calming, or have children draw how they feel about each kind of music or instrument. This can also lead into conversations about how we respond to things differently as individuals. Then, consider how you can bring elements of calming music into your Regulation Station. Can you put recorded music and headphones nearby? Would certain instruments or noisemakers, like a rain stick, be soothing calm-down props? What class preferences did you discover during this activity?

Small Group: Support children in small groups with drawing where they could make a Regulation Station at home. Help children label their drawings to show where they go when they are feeling big feelings, or where they could go that feels cozy and safe. Rather than only talking to the teacher about their drawings, encourage children to share with their peers, allowing them to learn from each other about different ideas and preferences for calming. You could put the drawings together to make a class book that you send home to families, or hang some of them in the Regulation Station to support children as they work there. A few drawings could also be copied for the portable Regulation Station.

Transitions: When transitioning from one activity to another, consider asking children to share what they chose in the Regulation Station to calm down. Consider turn and talk, having children share their ideas with a partner. Another transition activity could be asking children to share something that helps them calm down and that they think should go into the Regulation Station. Keep a list of children's ideas and consider which ones are feasible to add to the area.

Gross-Motor Skills and Outside Time: Have children support you in setting up a Regulation Station outside. Have them help you draw a boundary with chalk or set up a hula hoop. If you have chalk, children can draw helpful ideas for calm-down strategies. They can also gather and add elements of nature, such as acorns or pinecones with interesting textures, flowers to smell, or dandelions to blow on to practice deep breaths.

Art: Make a sign or display for the Regulation Station and have children decorate it. Consider including on the sign the name of the station, what you can do there, or how many people can go into the area.

> Ms. Broyles-Bello, a preschool teacher of an inclusive classroom, has a large rainbow hanging in her Regulation Station. Each color in this rainbow is made up of smaller construction paper squares. Children can do "rainbow breathing," tracing the rainbow from left to right and back again. Making the rainbow as an art activity, and then teaching children the associated regulation strategy, adds another element to the Regulation Station that children helped create.

Math: Some teachers have children put a sticker on a large piece of paper each time someone handles big emotions in the classroom. At the end of the day, or end of a week, ask children to count the stickers and write down how many times the class has handled feelings in total to share with families. For example, "This week, we handled our big feelings seventeen times! We can calm down!"

Story Time: Consider reading *When Sophie Gets Angry—Really, Really Angry . . .* by Molly Bang. In this book, Sophie gets angry and runs out of her house to a quiet spot in the trees where she can listen to nature sounds and begin to calm down. Have children compare Sophie sitting in the trees to the classroom. Where can your class go that would be a safe, calming spot? What does Sophie do in the trees? What can you do in the Regulation Station?

Planning to Encourage Use of the Regulation Station Throughout the Day

Which activities to encourage the use of the Regulation Station appeal to you? As you review activities and materials, plan with the following considerations in mind:

➤ Do you have activities in which children will work together to brainstorm ideas or plans for using the Regulation Station? If most of your activities are solitary, consider adding some paired or small-group activities to practice coregulation.

➤ Do you have activities that utilize both the Regulation Station and the portable version or outdoor space?

> Spread out your activities across the week and across different settings (in different centers, inside and outside, and facilitated by different adults).

Formative Assessment of Accessing the Regulation Station

In chapter 6, we discussed teaching children about how to try several calming strategies and explored how to support them in doing so. This chapter's skill is similar and closely related, but nevertheless distinct. Its focus is on the actual area of calming. Recording whether children can explain how to use the Regulation Station (in words or by modeling) is useful to know what you may need to reteach. If children can't explain the process while calm, then they will not be able to access it successfully when they are upset.

In Mr. Rosenberg's class, he starts noting which children access the Regulation Station for exploration, including choosing the center during a choice time. For example, Ben has been choosing to go into the center to look at the sensory bottles and read some of the books about calming down; Mr. Rosenberg notes that Ben does this independently. Ben isn't necessarily in need of regulation when he chooses the center, but his teacher watches and realizes that Ben knows how to use the space; he follows the steps that have been taught when he goes there. When Ben is upset or overwhelmed by big feelings during the day, he often needs Mr. Rosenberg to give a verbal prompt or reminder, and this is true during class time as well as when outside or in the gym. Meanwhile, Sura has been going into the portable outside Regulation

Figure 7.2 Sample Data Sheet for Recording Levels of Assistance for the Use of the Regulation Station

Child's Name	Accesses Regulation Station for Exploration	Describes or Models How to Use Regulation Station	Accesses Regulation Station When Needed	Regulates with Portable Center
Ben	Independent; books and bottles	Independent—follows visual steps	Needs verbal prompt from teacher	Needs verbal prompt from teacher in gym, outside
Sura		Independent—follows visual steps outside		Independent outside (tricycle)
Zion	Independent; pinwheel	Independent—shows puppet how to use space		
Tomas		Modeled during small group		

Station every time she is frustrated with having to wait for a turn on the tricycle. Mr. Rosenberg notes that she is regulating with the portable center independently.

At the end of the week, Mr. Rosenberg reviews his data and reflects on what it means for his instructional next steps and children's growth. He observes that the children in his class can all either tell or show him how to use the center. This is a celebration for the class; he knows that all the lessons and support about how to use the center have paid off! He notes that Ben and Zion do access the center for exploration, and he notes that Tomas never accesses the center—not during play, not when having big feelings, and not when one of the portable Regulation Stations is available to him in another space. Mr. Rosenberg plans to bring Tomas into the center for activities and practice this week and plans to also invite Sura as a peer to help model and practice with Tomas, as she's been consistently regulating outside with the portable Regulation Station tools.

For a blank template of this data sheet template, see the end of the chapter.

Examine your data as you are teaching about the new center. Watch for patterns around who can use the center independently and other trends. For example, if no one is using the portable Regulation Station when there are opportunities where that would be appropriate, what can you plan to reinforce this option?

Planning for Formative Assessment of Accessing the Regulation Station

Draft a plan for your formative assessment.

➤ What times of day will work best for gathering data to support your instructional decisions?

➤ How might you collect data about children using the portable space even when you aren't there to observe directly? If children are with other adults (such as in music class or on the playground), how you can you collaborate with those adults to share basic information about children's use of the portable Regulation Station?

➤ When will you review your data so you can use the information to plan your next instructional steps?

Differentiation and Advancement

We offer the Regulation Station as a place to teach and get support with regulation, but it is not a requirement that all regulation happens there. Some children have trouble moving from an interest area into the Regulation Station when their emotions are high, and that is okay. A portable version of the station gives teachers the option to bring the station to a child who might be angry under the lunch table, frustrated in the art or science center, or sobbing in the school's entryway. We can make sure the area the child is in is safe—for example, by moving other children away from the lunch table—and then use the portable tools to support regulation and meet children where they are, literally and figuratively. Remember: building the skill of regulation is more important than where that skill-building happens.

Some children might swiftly pick up these skills and be able to access the Regulation Station and use it appropriately early on. Think about how to challenge them or advance their skills. You might offer them the opportunity to make a video model of the process, narrating the steps and the purpose of the center as though making a Regulation Station advertisement. You might encourage some creative thinking exercises, such as asking them to think about what a book character might choose to do in the Regulation Station, based on what they know about the character's personality and emotions. Another example of creative thinking could be having children build or create Regulation Stations for baby dolls in dramatic play or for the dollhouse figures or other figurines in a block center, making little scenes through which children can show what they know about the Regulation Station.

You might also encourage a child who is able to use the Regulation Station appropriately to identify which tools are the most helpful for them in calming down. Is there a way to access those tools at times when the Regulation Station isn't available? This could be through the use of portable tools, or it could just be through mental practice. Supporting a child to access the tools in their head, without necessarily needing physical props, is a natural next step for some children.

Nichole, an inclusive preschool teacher, had a child in her class who had intense emotional responses to songs at group time. Rather than eliminating songs from the preschool classroom, Nichole focused on teaching individualized coping skills, including a social story about recognizing her upset, going to their classroom Regulation Station, and returning when she was ready. "She began to leave when upset, use strategies to calm, and independently return to the group. Teaching her how to access and use the Regulation Station meant that she had a way to take control of the difficult feelings that she was experiencing. I'll never forget the first day that she heard a song, jumped up, and ran over to our cozy corner."

Planning for Differentiation and Advancement

Reflect on your data for the week and whether your Regulation Station props are portable enough to bring to a child who needs them in various settings. What changes do you need to make to ensure you can meet children where they are?

Create a plan for children who might need individualization. Use data and observations to identify specific children for whom you will intentionally plan modified or individualized supports.

➤ Where does the child currently go when upset? How can you use that space to support regulation?

➤ What regulation tools or props is the child drawn to? How can you make sure these are easy to access when needed?

➤ Which children have this skill? Which advancement strategies would support them in thinking more deeply or creatively about the Regulation Station?

Troubleshooting Around Accessing the Regulation Station

Consider the following ways to troubleshoot questions or obstacles you might run into as you help children learn to access the Regulation Station and its tools—whether the classroom center or the portable version.

"What if a child in my class chooses to be in the Regulation Station all day long?"
This is a common worry. Let's brainstorm what information we can gather from a child who is opting to spend much of their day in the Regulation Station and what it might reveal about their reasons for this:

➤ The child might be tired and wishing for a cozy and quiet place to rest.

➤ The child might prefer being alone or with one other child, rather than in the bustle of other classroom centers and activities.

➤ The child may prefer the activities of the Regulation Station to those elsewhere in the room.

➤ The child might be having emotions that they feel need to be regulated.

➤ The child might not understand the purpose of the Regulation Station.

As teachers responsible for the environment and instruction, it's essential to our problem-solving process that we observe the child and figure out which one (or two, or more) of these possibilities is true. Or perhaps the child's behavior is due to a reason that's not even on this list. In any case, we must identify how the child is benefiting from being in the Regulation Station, even if their time there doesn't seem like a benefit from our perspective. For example, if a child misses circle time, that likely won't feel like a benefit to us as teachers. Still, if the child is consistently choosing the Regulation Station instead of engaging in classroom routines, we can conclude that it feels safer or better for the child to be there.

Based on our observation, we can choose strategies or solutions to try. Perhaps we re-teach the Regulation Station to make the expectations clearer. Maybe we offer multiple spaces to work alone or quietly rest in the classroom, such as a center designed to be used by one child at a time. Perhaps we embed preferred activities into group times or other centers to make them more engaging and encourage participation. Offering additional supports for the child to navigate play and group interactions could also help, if the Regulation Station is the child's chosen spot because interactions are overwhelming or expectations for other areas are confusing.

Don't forget that the goal is for the Regulation Station to be just another center in the classroom. How would you approach the problem if a child only wanted to be in dramatic play all day? What strategies might you try to broaden the child's engagement? Would you be concerned if a child had a preferred interest center and desired to be there often? If not, then why does this feel different to you? Examining why it feels different can help you better understand the child *or* yourself.

"I have children who seem worried, nervous, or embarrassed to go to the Regulation Station." You might have children in your group who resist going to the Regulation Station. Some children might be embarrassed about using the Regulation Station if they feel like it puts their problems on display in a way that isn't comfortable for them. Some might confuse it with a punishment until we teach and reinforce it as another center in the classroom. I remember when a preschooler told me, "I'm not going to go to Time-Out over there" as she pointed to the Regulation Station. Teachers had never referred to it as Time-Out, nor was it used as a response to undesirable behavior. Nevertheless, she had this idea or notion that it was the time-out space. Wherever the idea had come from—whether at home or in another setting outside the classroom—it was a challenge to reframe it for her at school. These experiences make the job of normalizing the Regulation Station as a learning center even more important, as we coach children to see the use of regulation strategies as a strength and point of pride, rather than as a weakness or source of shame.

One way to support a child in understanding this distinction is to talk openly and clearly about it. When working with this preschooler, hearing her describe time-out as "where you go when you are in trouble" and "you sit there until they say you can come out" was helpful in addressing misunderstandings and explaining the purpose of the Regulation Station. After all, it's a space for calming, not punishment, and a child can choose another center or activity when their body is ready. The child's teacher and I discussed the issue and then reviewed the use of the Regulation Station by classroom staff to ensure no one was sending children there who didn't want to go, or speaking about the Regulation Station as if it was a punishment or consequence, rather than a center for learning and practicing new skills. Working together with the teaching staff on a list detailing how the Regulation Station was different in purpose and in structure from a time-out area was also helpful in making sure the "time-out" message was not accidentally coming through in adults' use of or language about the Regulation Station. Last, we invited the child to come with adults to the Regulation Station in moments of calm, to engage together with materials in a way that was playful. Together, the teachers and the child rewrote the child's story about the area and helped her associate it with positive memories and feelings of connection.

Family Engagement and Support

Having an area to calm down is a concept that is applicable not only for school but also at home. Children might already have preferred spots at home where they like to go, or families might wish to set up something similar once their child has learned additional tools and strategies for calming down.

A social and emotional snippet related to the Regulation Station might look like this:

> *This week, we opened a new center in our classroom, the Regulation Station! This center is a great choice when children are having big feelings and need a space with tools to help them calm down. We practiced going into the Regulation Station, deciding if we wanted to be alone or if we wanted help with calming down, using calming tools and strategies, checking to see if our bodies were calm, and then rejoining class activities. To help children continue practicing regulation, we have a special blue bag that we bring outside and to the library and gym to create a portable Regulation Station. Look at the picture of our Regulation Station and ask your child to tell you about it.*

A video of a child modeling the regulation process when calm, or of a child using the center with your support when upset, can be beneficial in engaging families. Sometimes it's hard to know what using a center looks like when you haven't seen it with your own eyes. Consider sending videos home to families so they can see the Regulation Station in action. If you have an in-class workshop or family event, consider giving families a tour of the center, sharing what children learn there and how the props and structures support calming down.

For related family activities, consider asking families to share pictures of where their child calms down at home. Asking for feedback from home and gathering ideas that families have found successful can be a great asset. If a family says their child likes to crawl under the bed when upset, you might consider offering a small private space as part of your Regulation Station. If a parent shares that their child's calm-down habit is snuggling with them on their bed, you might be more mindful of asking the child if they would like your support in using the center.

You can also ask families if they would welcome support in planning out how to make a Regulation Station at home. Some teachers work on this through home visits, using materials the family has to create cozy areas and also bringing familiar visuals or simple calm-down tools from school to put in these at-home spaces. Other families might want your support in making a portable Regulation Station, like the one you use at the playground, to support their child when they are having a hard time in other locations like the store or grandma's house.

Remember to share your data and celebrations with families! What teachers choose to share often influences what families see as important. Just as you share photos of children's artistic masterpieces and tall towers, sending photos of children in your Regulation Station taking deep breaths together implies that the social and emotional growth of children is important and worthy of celebration too!

Wrap-Up

Congratulations on reflecting, planning, and teaching your class a brand-new center! You've done the work of creating the space, teaching the new routines, practicing, and making the center inviting enough to interest children. Those are not small tasks. Establishing a Regulation Station as a formal center changes the perception of the area. Your work in this chapter has normalized the calming down process. It's not a "bad" thing to need to regulate. It's helpful—and so is having a specific space to do this calming work. Our classroom environment reflects our values and beliefs as teachers. Having a center with a focus on regulation sends the message to children, families, staff, and visitors that emotional regulation needs to be taught, nurtured, and explored, and that it is important enough to devote your precious classroom real estate to.

Chapters 3 through 7 have focused primarily on looking inward to recognize and label and regulate our emotions. Chapter 8 shifts the focus to more intentionally using some of these skills with others. While chapter 7 focused on "Where can I go when I need to calm down and what supports will I find there?" chapter 8 answers the question, "How can I respond to someone else's emotions and help them with these regulation skills?"

Regulation Station Planning Considerations

Reflect on the following questions and considerations as you prepare to add a Regulation Station to your classroom.

Where can you put a Regulation Station?

Where could you create a private space that can be appropriately supervised?

Are there spaces you've noticed children are drawn to when upset, like a nook or a cubby?

Would the areas around the Regulation Station be noisy and active or less active and quiet?

How will children know how to access the center?

Will you create a center sign to designate the space?

How will children check into your Regulation Station?

How do children check into other centers? If you use a center board, will you add the Regulation Station to it?

Who can access the Regulation Station?

How many children can go into the space at a time?

How can children ask for help from others?

Is there enough space for you to support a child in the Regulation Station?

If the Regulation Station is occupied, where should another child go if they need regulation support?

→

What regulation strategies and props will live in the Regulation Station?

What visuals or props do you have for emotion identification (emotion dolls, pictures to help children identify how they feel, a shatterproof mirror)?

What visuals or props do you have to support calming down?

How will children know what is in the center? What additional cues or support might they need to use these strategies and props within the center?

How will you make a portable version of your Regulation Station?

What container can you use to bring regulation strategies to other places?

What props make the most sense to put in a portable Regulation Station?

How will you remember to bring it with you?

How will children transition out of the Regulation Station?

How will children know where to put supplies when finished?

How will children recognize if they are calm and ready to transition to another activity or space?

What activities might you offer as children transition from the Regulation Station to the class?

Data Sheet for Recording Levels of Assistance for Use of the Regulation Station

As you observe children's use of the Regulation Station, you can use this sheet to record whether children complete these steps independently, or if they needed verbal prompting or other support from adults or peers, along with any other observations that may be helpful in guiding your ongoing instruction.

Child's Name	Accesses Regulation Station for Exploration	Describes or Models How to Use Regulation Station	Accesses Regulation Station When Needed	Regulates with Portable Center

Chapter 8

Responding to Others' Emotions

PICTURE THIS — Three-year-old Luca arrives at school. His mom leaves, and he stands next to his cubby, crying and looking at the door where his mom exited. His teacher goes over to comfort him. She pats his back and repeats, "You're okay; you're okay." When she looks up, several other children are watching him and her, with concerned expressions. The teacher tells the nearby children, "He's okay." The children continue to look worried about Luca as he cries.

In this situation, the teacher's intent is to soothe the child and quiet the worries of his classmates. Luca hears that he is okay, but he recognizes his feeling as sadness, not a feeling of "okay." His peers hear from the teacher that Luca is okay, but his facial expressions, body language, and tears are sending them a different message. The children remain bystanders as the teacher attempts to support Luca. Opportunities to grow the emotional understanding of both Luca and his peers, and to encourage kindness, are accidentally quashed through this interaction.

Through practice with identifying and recognizing their own emotions, children have studied how facial expressions vary with emotions and how emotions feel in their bodies. This knowledge of their own emotions, and the intentional practice of discussing and modeling emotions, has prepared children to also recognize emotions in others. Once children can recognize how another person is feeling, responsive caregivers can support them in responding to others' emotions appropriately. This changes their role from bystanders of others' feelings to being helpers or cheerleaders, growing their emotional understanding and relationships.

About the Skill of Responding to Others' Emotions

As adults, we often recognize emotions in others and are tasked with choosing how we will respond. For example, you notice a coworker seems both despondent and distracted. Recognizing that he is handling some bigger feelings, you check in to see if he is okay. He explains that his mother is ill and he is feeling worried about her. You then have to decide whether to express sorrow ("I'm so sorry to hear that."), offer encouragement ("With that great team of doctors, I'm sure she'll recover soon."), offer support ("Can I bring you over a meal to ease the burden while you take care of her?"), or choose another option from a ton of other possible responses. The truth is, even as adults we often find it challenging to know what to do or say when responding to others' emotions. Sometimes we flub this, offering solutions when a friend just wants to feel heard or offering a kind of help that might not actually be helpful after all. We may offer encouragement or a positive outlook when a more empathetic response would supply validation and acknowledgment that the situation is genuinely difficult.

Despite this being a challenging skill even for adults, young children are hardwired to recognize and respond to others' emotions. Infants begin to cry when other infants cry, and this kind of motor mimicry is often credited as forming the roots of empathy. However, between ages two and three, motor mimicry fades as toddlers begin to recognize that it is someone else's pain, rather than their own. This development, in turn, leads children to the realization that they can attempt to comfort others. They might start by offering an item or response that *they* find comforting; for example, a toddler offering her special blanket to an upset classmate. We can teach and support children in asking for others' insight into what they find supportive and helpful. This skill, just like other skills, is not equally present in all children. Children who have been guided or directed to notice others' emotions, or who have witnessed examples of people responding to others' upset, have more practice and tools around an empathetic response.

You'll notice the goals of this chapter are twofold. First, we want children to recognize emotions in others, which pulls in the skills from chapter 3 on labeling emotions and from chapter 4 about recognizing various emotion clues.

In addition, as we teach children possible ways to respond to others' emotions, you'll notice one focus is asking the other person what would help them feel better. We're teaching children to respect the wishes of others, to not make assumptions, and to offer help that another person wants to receive. The ideas in this chapter focus on both of those empathy-building steps: encouraging children to be intentional in noticing the emotions of others, and practicing socially appropriate ways to respond to others' emotions. We will teach sample responses so children have options in their toolbox, just as they do for regulating their own emotions, when someone is feeling gleeful or angry or a range of emotions in between.

The Starting Point

Like the other emotion skills in this book, the first challenge in teaching this competency is identifying how, exactly, we want children to respond to the emotions of others. How do we figure out what responses to teach and encourage? One way to begin exploring this is by watching how we, ourselves, respond to children's or other adults' emotions. What do we want to hear when we are sad? How do we support children when they are angry? What are some of our responses when children share their excitement with us?

A second way is to watch and see what skills children currently have. If children play "family" and pat a crying child on the back, we might build on this skill to teach children to offer gentle touches when a peer is upset. If a three-year-old claps for himself when he kicks the ball into the net, we might encourage him to clap for others when they are showing the same feelings of pride and excitement.

Some popular responses to teach children might include:

➤ clapping when another child is proud or excited

➤ giving a compliment or encouragement ("Way to go!" or "I like when you chase me because you are fast.")

➤ offering a gentle touch to a peer who is sad, after gaining the child's consent

➤ helping someone choose a way to calm down when angry or upset

➤ asking, "How can I help you feel better?"

➤ offering a tangible object, like a tissue, an ice pack, a bandage, or a toy that brings comfort

Planning to Start

Take these ideas and create a simple script that outlines what you want to teach children to do. For example, "When a classmate is proud of their work, I can clap and say, 'way to go!'" Or "When a classmate is sad or angry, I can ask, 'How can I help you feel better?'" Consider at least two scripts: at least one for joy, happiness, or excitement, plus at least one for anger, sadness, or disappointment.

Using DAPPER to Teach Responding to Others' Emotions

You've begun to create scripts to teach children simple ways to respond to the emotions of others. Next, you'll work to specifically plan opportunities to intentionally teach and reinforce how to respond to others' emotions by using the DAPPER framework.

Demonstrate and Describe

Review the scripts you have created and choose one to demonstrate and describe first. Rather than demonstrating and describing only the script you have created, brainstorm with children to come up with multiple possible ways to respond. Then demonstrate your script, followed by inviting children to act out their other ideas.

You might role-play with another teacher in a teacher theater session, having your partner act out feeling sad and then showing a way you can help them feel better. Or you might have a child act out feeling sad or angry and then model what to do. To keep the focus on responding to emotions, be sure to draw attention to the emotion expression both before the helping and after. While not every attempt will work to help another child handle big feelings, when you are first teaching this skill, highlight successful responses. Later you can give examples of what to do when a response *doesn't* work.

This demonstration might look like this:

➤ Set the stage: "When a classmate is feeling sad or upset, there are things we can do to help them."

➤ Ask children to share ways they could help a peer who is sad, and record their responses.

➤ Teacher role play, beginning with noticing the emotions of another person. "See Ms. Lawrence's face? She seems really sad. Her mouth is frowning, and her eyes are down."

➤ Describe your script out loud. "One thing I try is asking if she wants a hug. I'm going to ask before touching her, like this. 'You seem sad, Ms. Lawrence. Do you want a hug?'"

➤ Demonstrate how to wait for consent before helping or touching someone else. "She nodded yes and put her arms out. That means she is wishing for a hug, and I can give her one."

➤ Describe the impact on the person. "Look at Ms. Lawrence's face now. It seems like the hug helped. Her mouth isn't frowning anymore."

Teaching the skill of responding to others' emotions also teaches how to respect people's wishes and boundaries and how to get consent before touching or helping others. As part of this work, explicitly talk about and model how we wait for someone to tell or show us that it is okay for us to help them. Point out when a child makes a choice communicating a need or a boundary. For instance, "Look. He pointed to a hug on our chart. That means he is saying he wants a hug, so we can offer one." Or "She signed *no*, so that means she doesn't want our help right now. That's her choice so we are going to listen to her words and move over here." To further teach and reinforce this skill, we also need to make sure we are consistently modeling asking children for consent around touch and assistance, and accepting children's responses when they do not want us to help them or do not want us close to them when upset.

Planning to Demonstrate and Describe How to Respond to Others' Emotions

In a teacher training session, teachers jotted down their ideas for how children can respond to the emotions of others. Then we played charades with their ideas, picking one and acting it out. This is a great self-test to see if a skill or behavior is described with enough detail. After all, if we can't act it out in a game with our colleagues, we probably can't describe and model it clearly enough to teach children. Reflect on your scripts. Would they pass the charades test? If you are unsure, try acting out a script and seeing if you need to be more specific or if you know exactly what behavior you would model and teach, and how.

Animate

To support children's learning, create visuals to reinforce the scripts you are teaching. Three possible visuals include a social story or poster with visual scripts, a How Can I Help You Feel Better? Card, and a Feel-Better Basket.

You can find a How Can I Help You Feel Better? Card at the end of this chapter.

The goal of animation is to flesh out the steps a child would need to take to be successful in responding to the emotions of others. For example, you might make and hang up a poster that shows these steps:

➤ Notice a classmate is sad.

➤ Show them the How Can I Help You Feel Better? Card.

➤ Have them pick an option.

➤ Follow through with their choice.

You might make a social story with pages showing various emotion expressions, using icons or pictures of children in the class. "When a classmate is sad, we can ask how we can help them feel better." "When a classmate is proud, we can give a thumbs-up and tell them 'Way to go!'" A story can outline many ways to support each other. You can also consider a personalized book, outlining strategies that children identify for themselves. "When Caryn is sad, a hug helps her feel better." "When Miles is angry, giving him headphones helps him feel better."

Another visual support is a choice menu of options to help a classmate feel better. This How Can I Help You Feel Better? Card is a sheet of picture options, which could include gentle touches (such as a hug, handshake, or high-five) as well as other ideas. Icons for "help me fix it," "breathe with me," or "something else" are all visual choices that can be presented on a card. Essentially, the card serves as a menu a child might offer to a peer who is sad, worried, angry, or frustrated. The upset child then picks an option, using words or pointing, to indicate a choice that would help them feel better.

This card is both a way to empower children to support each other through feelings and a tool for making amends. If Kristen knocks over Max's tower, Kristen can bring the card to Max to help with restitution, replacing an insincere apology with a helpful course of action to "make it right." Rather than us telling Kristen to help Max rebuild, when that might not be what Max is hoping for, the tool allows Max to self-identify the kind of assistance or action that would feel helpful to him.

Similarly, other visual structures to encourage responding to emotions of others may include collections of comforting objects. A Feel-Better Basket provides a tangible way for teachers and children to access helpful tools. Items teachers and children might place in the basket typically include tissues, bandages, stickers, a stuffed animal, paper and pencil, a small photo album with pictures of children's families, and breathing or regulation tools. A How Can I Help You Feel Better? Card might also go in the Feel-Better Basket. When a child or teacher is disappointed, frustrated, mad, or sad, a classmate can offer them the basket of supplies or a single item from it to help with the calming process. Teaching these visual supports involves the same overarching strategies of demonstration: setting the stage for when children might use these visuals, modeling how to use the card or basket, and choosing a place where children can access the tools independently.

To further animate this concept, think about what gesture might support children in remembering what to do when they respond to others' emotions. Animating "how can I help you feel better?" might look like holding your hands up like you have a question and then bringing them close to your heart. Singing "How can I help you" with your hands up and open to the sky and then "feel better" while bringing your hands to your heart is another way to help children learn the phrase more easily than using words alone.

Planning How to Animate Ways to Respond to Others' Emotions

Reflect on the options described for visual supports. Consider how children have responded to similar supports. Would social stories work well with your group? Do they enjoy physical props, like a Feel-Better Basket? Would the How Can I Help You Feel Better? Card be the most effective support? Perhaps you'll choose a combination of supports as you reflect on children's strengths and prior knowledge.

Choose which visual support you are going to start teaching first.

➤ What materials do you need to make it?

➤ How many copies will you need? Consider how children will access the support, and whether they will need it in other locations beyond the classroom, such as outside or in the cafeteria.

➤ Where will you keep the visual support so children can easily access it? Plan out how you will show children where to get it.

Practice

When introducing a skill, structured practice gives every child a chance to be successful. In fact, with encouragement, immediate feedback, and prompting during their initial attempt, children are almost guaranteed to experience some success! When you first introduce and model this skill, consider having at least one child try it in front of the group. This gives every child another example beyond your own modeling, and allows a child to feel successful as a leader and helper. You might pick a child who needs extra support with social interactions to give it a try, or you might pick a child who is "ready" to do it with little prompting.

For example, Parker is a four-year-old who struggles to understand the emotions of others, and often laughs when others are upset or when they get hurt. Ms. Elliott picks Nina to look sad, and picks Parker to model the skill of responding. She prompts Parker to look at Nina's face while asking, "How might she feel, Parker?" He notes that she is sad, and Ms. Elliott asks Parker if he can help her. She offers the How Can I Help You Feel Better? Card to Parker, prompting him to say the script she has modeled: "Nina, you seem sad. How can I help you feel better?" He holds up the card to her, and she points to the picture for a hug. He gives her a hug, and she smiles. Ms. Elliott prompts Parker to look at Nina's face again to see that his hug helped her feel better. She asks Nina how she feels; she says "happy." Ms. Elliott asks, "Did Parker's solution work?" The whole class shouts yes and claps for the actors. Parker and Nina sit back in their spots, smiling. Ms. Elliott doesn't let the last interaction go unnoticed. "Parker and Nina looked proud of the acting they did for the group, and you clapped and cheered to encourage them; that's another way we respond to the emotions of other people. We cheer with them when they feel proud!"

In this example situation, Ms. Elliott thoughtfully chose a child who could benefit from extra support and practice. She was able to prompt him and celebrate his success with the class. Ms. Elliott lets the other children who want a turn know that at small-group time she will call them over to practice with her so that everyone will have a chance to use the new visual supports.

In his classroom, Mr. Moore opts to have each child use the How Can I Help You Feel Better? Card as they transition to centers. Rather than calling children to leave the carpet based on what color they are wearing, he chooses to call two children at a time, hands one the card, and has that child ask the other, "How can I help you feel better?" The child being asked points to an icon, the pair follows through, and then both transition to centers after hearing from their teacher that they did it. Instead of acting out a whole scenario, the focus during transition time is on practicing the words and using the card quickly, but consistently.

Planning How to Practice Responding to Others' Emotions

Reflect on the practice ideas you have implemented from other chapters. Which were the most successful? Does your class engage best through transition activities? Do the children attend well to modeling?

Decide how to structure the practice for this skill. Considerations may include:

➤ Do you want to pair children up so each one can try it with a partner simultaneously? Do you have enough materials for every pair to use?

> Do you want a specific child to work with you so you can provide more support?

> Do you want every child to observe the other children practicing this skill?

> Do you have time allotted in your schedule to practice in a small-group setting shortly after introducing the skill?

Planned Opportunities

At this point, you've decided on the scripts and tools you are going to teach your class. You've demonstrated how to use the script or tool to respond to others' emotions, and you've given children the opportunity to practice. Now children have an idea of the new skill, but it is likely not fluent for most of them yet. To ensure that it becomes an easy and natural way of life in the classroom, children will need plenty of opportunities to practice the skill, in situations facilitated by teachers as well as in naturally occurring opportunities.

One planned practice opportunity is using a game such as bowling or basketball. Both games typically provoke a range of feelings. For example, children knock over the bowling pins and feel elated, or they miss the basketball hoop and feel disappointed or frustrated. Setting up these games provides an opportunity for practicing the scripts you have taught. Before starting, consider reviewing the scripts and modeling them as part of a game. For instance, take a turn bowling yourself and miss the pins. Encourage children to think about what they might say or do to respond to your emotions. Take another turn and knock over some pins. What could children do to share in your joy? After reviewing with children, encourage them to respond to their peers' emotions as they take turns in the games.

Consider other planned opportunities where you could provide children with materials that encourage a range of emotions. This could be using a collaborative board game during small-group lessons or reading specific books and responding to the emotions of the characters.

Planning Opportunities to Respond to Others' Emotions

How might you plan additional opportunities for practice? Take a copy of your daily schedule and jot down ideas next to each activity or routine to see where opportunities might fit in. For example, you might note next to story time that while reading a book you will ask children what they could do to help a sad character, stopping for brainstorming or role play. You might note next to mealtime that you could encourage peers to notice and respond when a child is frustrated about not liking the lunch choices. While this may or may not happen, planning out likely scenarios makes us more mindful to respond with practice and encouragement of the new skill if the opportunity does arise.

While you might write your notes on one day's schedule, in real life, the ideas would be stretched out over a longer time span than a day. These and other planned opportunities might occur on several days to give every child a chance to practice.

Ms. Patti, a preschool special education teacher in a classroom of young children with autism, taught her group strategies for helping others feel better. One child picked up a feelings doll with a sad expression, gave the doll a hug and started singing to it. When she taught these skills virtually to children during the COVID-19 pandemic, she had her box of calming supports nearby. When a child got frustrated, Patti's preschool-age daughter came over and brought the calming box to the screen to help the upset class member. Consider intentionally putting out materials, such as dolls with various facial expressions, to encourage practice with these skills. Keeping tools easily accessible allows for peers to help each other.

Extend

Because the goal of extending is to encourage children to use a skill in new contexts, this first requires that children know how to access the visual reminders you have used or created. For example, if a class has been taught to use the How Can I Help You Feel Better? Card, keeping these cards in the teacher-materials box means that children wouldn't have access to them when they need the support. Place these tools and materials instead in an area where children have access, such as hanging them on a wall, posting them on shelves in centers, or having a social and emotional resource shelf or Feel-Better Basket. This allows children to access supports and extend their learning into naturally occurring situations.

As children start to access the materials independently, the teacher's role shifts from facilitator to coach to cheerleader. A child may notice a peer is sad, ask them how they can help, and follow through. Adults are left to be a cheerleader, noticing and celebrating the use of emotional competencies. Some children may notice a child's emotion, walk over to a visual support and grab it, and then need coaching from you to do the next steps independently. In that case, seeing the child with the visual support is a prompt to the classroom staff to be aware and mindful of the need for a coach. A third group of children may need you to draw their attention to the other child, prompt them to get the visual materials, and provide support during the interaction that follows. The goal for teachers is to continue to practice and socially coach children as needed while they try these skills. Teachers can also model using strategies and supports in context when children are upset and need emotional support from adults.

Children in Ms. Elliott's classroom are working on gardening at a sensory table, poking seeds and fake flowers into dirt. Javier asks Sarah if he can help her plant; she says she doesn't need help. He tells her, "You're not my friend anymore," and plucks her flowers out of the dirt, tossing them onto the floor. Ms. Elliott can use ICARE to help Javier and Sarah access their skills of recognizing and responding to others' emotions.

Intent: She asks herself, as she approaches the situation, "What is Javier's intent in plucking the flowers and yelling at Sarah?" She realizes that Javier was angry or sad at being rejected from Sarah's play. Realizing that the incident is about emotional expression allows Ms. Elliott to focus on that in the social coaching interaction, rather than focusing only on the behavior (by saying things such as "destroying work isn't helpful" or "we use kind words," for instance).

Calm: When she approaches the children, she notices both Javier and Sarah are upset. She pulls the How Can I Help You Feel Better? Card off the wall, and turns to the children, modeling the skill she's been teaching them. "I notice you are both upset. How can I help you feel better so that we can feel calm and solve the problem?" Sarah chooses a hug; Javier chooses a high-five, and Ms. Elliott gives each of them their preferred gentle touch.

Acknowledge: She watches as their bodies start to relax and offers support through acknowledging. "Javier, you seemed frustrated when Sarah didn't want you to play with her, and you pulled the flowers out. Sarah, you looked sad that your garden was messed up." Both children nod at Ms. Elliott's description of the situation.

Rewind: She asks them to do a "rewind" with her and try to handle the situation in a better way. She prompts Javier to support Sarah by asking, "Do you remember what you can do when you recognize that a classmate is sad? What tool could you get for Sarah?" Javier asks for the card and uses it with Sarah. Sarah picks the picture for "jellyfish fist bump," they do the silly greeting, and they laugh.

Echo: Ms. Elliott echoes back, "You helped Sarah feel better about her garden. That was helpful. Next time you feel left out or upset, what could you do that is helpful?" Javier suggests walking away to the Regulation Station, and his teacher celebrates that he thought of a safer and more socially appropriate choice.

In this situation, Ms. Elliott is able to respond to socially coach Javier and Sarah effectively because she had the visual support she had been teaching, the How Can I Help You Feel Better? Card, readily accessible as children were in need of it. Similar to making a portable Regulation Station, making a small How Can I Help You Feel Better? Card or a tiny pencil-box version of a Feel-Better Basket can ensure that you'll have the strategies you've taught children to access available when you need them.

Planning to Extend Responding to Others' Emotions

Part of extending this skill involves having the materials readily accessible. Plan where you might be when children need to be coached through those supports.

➤ Are your visual supports, like your social story or How Can I Help You Feel Better? Card, readily accessible for social coaching?

➤ If not, where do you need extra copies? Are there specific areas that would benefit from having these materials?

➤ Do you need to have them on you, like on a lanyard or clipped to a belt loop?

➤ What about when a child is in need of help but other children do not notice and therefore do not respond? Will you model how to respond to the child's emotions yourself, or will you encourage a nearby peer to respond? What response would be most helpful for children's understanding and growth in this skill?

Reinforce and Reflect

Positive descriptive feedback supports children by giving them language that matches their behavior. It draws their attention to their own actions and behaviors and can direct their focus to the impact their behavior has on the classroom and on others. Giving positive descriptive feedback for responding to others' emotions ties together the child's behavior and the reaction from the peer. Positive descriptive feedback might sound like, "You noticed she was sad and tried to help. You gave her a tissue and now her face is clean." "You asked him what would help him feel better and you helped! He smiled when you gave him a hug." For the other child in the situation, positive descriptive feedback might focus on responding and allowing help. "You made a choice of what would help you feel better." "Wow, you really listened to your body. You picked a hug and it calmed you right down!"

We also want to notice children who are recognizing and responding to children's joy and pride. Another opportunity for giving positive descriptive feedback is when children cheer on others or when they celebrate another's effort or skills, such as cheering when a peer kicks the ball into the goal. "You noticed her effort and cheered for her! That's friendly!"

If you have an established way of celebrating children's accomplishments, such as a bulletin board showcasing acts of kindness, consider putting examples of children responding to the emotions of others on the board. Ask children to reflect: "How did you help a classmate feel better?" Add their reflections to the board and give positive descriptive feedback as a response, reiterating what they did and how it helped. As children become familiar with your language around positive descriptive feedback, they will often be able to use that same kind of language in their reflections, noting what they did and how it supported the other person.

> Many teachers have very creative ways of celebrating kindness. Ms. Kathy and Ms. Amy use a wreath hoop. They help children choose colorful ribbons and tie them on the wreath to celebrate how classmates worked together. Ms. Nichole changes her system with the class's area of study, adding celebration leaves to a tree when they learn about trees and adding bricks to a house when they study buildings. Other teachers write positive feedback on shapes or put stickers on a display to match their classroom themes, like alligators or rocket ships.

Planning to Reinforce and Reflect Around Responding to Others' Emotions

Plan to reflect and give children positive descriptive feedback for kind and helpful behaviors as they practice responding to others' emotions.

If you already have a way that you reinforce kindness (like a kindness tree, marbles in a jar, celebrating super friends, or notes about kindness to send home), plan how you can add intentional reflection and positive descriptive feedback to this process.

➤ When in your day will you ask children to reflect on who helped them and how they felt (or who they helped and how it worked out)?

➤ How will you make sure to give positive feedback as you track acts of kindness?

➤ Will you record the acts of kindness, such as writing the positive feedback down on a leaf to add to the tree? Or will you give feedback verbally and then have the child add to your kindness display?

➤ How might you share these acts of kindness with others in the school community or with families?

Having a system to celebrate kindness is not required, and there are other valuable approaches you might choose, such as giving feedback immediately after the situation or taking time at a closing circle to have children share how they have been helpful. If you do not have a system for celebrating kindness and are not looking to create one, be intentional about planning positive descriptive feedback and chances for children to reflect through other means. When will you give positive descriptive feedback? How will you make sure to notice children who are helping their peers?

➤ What will your class need to successfully reflect and remember how they were helpful? Will they need you to take photos to be able to reflect on who they helped and what they tried? How might you get this documentation?

Responding to Others' Emotions Throughout the Day

Consider the following ideas for helping children practice this skill during a range of activities and respond to others' emotions throughout the day.

Morning Meeting or Circle Time: Have the class brainstorm ideas for what children might put in a Feel-Better Basket. Display documentation of children's ideas as you build your basket.

Encourage sharing opportunities, such as Questions of the Day, that focus on children sharing their feelings about certain situations. Encourage discussion of how our reactions and emotions vary from person to person. Ask children to take the perspective of others, a key skill for empathy. For example, "Kate said that having a babysitter was exciting. Why do you think she might feel excited about it?" Next, ask Kate to share why she was excited. Then consider asking the class why a peer might feel sad about the same situation.

Music and Movement: Sing and act out a new version of "London Bridge Is Falling Down." Have one child "fall down" and have other children offer ideas for helping their classmate. Act out the ideas as you sing. For instance:

➤ *Rachel* is falling down, falling down, falling down

➤ *Rachel* is falling down, how can we help her?

➤ Offer to help and *pick her up, pick her up, pick her up*

➤ Offer to help and *pick her up,* so kind and helpful.

Other verses could replace "pick her up" with "get a bandage," "get an ice pack," "tell a teacher," "give a hug," or any other helpful ideas children can come up with. Before touching the child who has fallen, encourage them to nod or say yes to model asking for and receiving consent. This might mean pausing after "How can we help her?" to ask "Would a hug help?" or "Can I help you up?" before singing the next lines.

Small Group: Consider playing a basic picture matching game, pairing "emotions and needs" cards with "help and support" cards. Matches might include a crying face and a tissue, a scraped knee and a bandage, a child not being able to reach something and an adult retrieving the item. Limiting options to one match for each picture supports children in thinking of possible solutions without being overwhelmed with choices. Encourage children to ask for help from another child if they cannot find the match.

Make a video model of children acting out this skill. Stage a small role play where one child is sad, proud, or upset. Have another child offer the tools your classroom is using. Record a video of this interaction. Consider adding narration over the situation (such as, "he notices she is sad and wants to help"). Then watch and discuss the video with children. Consider also sending it to families to watch and talk about at home.

Transitions: Create a transition activity using emotion pictures and a Feel-Better Basket. Include pictures of feelings like hurt, sad, angry, proud, and excited. Have children practice picking a card and acting out the emotion on their face. Have another child pick out something from the Feel-Better Basket that might help. Then the pair can transition together to the next activity.

Gross-Motor Skills and Outside Time: Practice specific games such as soccer, where one child takes a turn kicking the ball, and the job of the other children is to clap and cheer when the ball makes it into the net. Practicing the roles (kicker and cheerleader) can help young children stay engaged while waiting for a turn in a social game and also encourage them to pay attention to the actions and successes of others.

Art: Develop a class book with a page for each child's picture. On each page, write the prompt, "When I feel _____ (emotion), _____ (tool or strategy) helps me." Children can decorate, write and draw ideas, or take photos of classroom supports for their page.

Math: Lay out six emotion visuals in a row across a table or rug. Have children take turns rolling a die and counting to the corresponding card. Ask children to work together to think of several ways they could respond to someone's emotions if they were feeling that way.

Story Time: Read books where characters respond to each other's emotions in different ways. For example, in *How Much Is That Doggie in the Window?* by Iza Trapani, a boy who hopes to buy a dog spends his money trying to help his family, buying things including a treat for his sister and tissues for a family member who is sick. In *The Very Cranky Bear* by Nick Bland, a group of animals tries to cheer up the bear in their own ways, and they find success when they ask the bear what would help him feel better. This reinforces the idea of asking, "How can I help you feel better?" rather than guessing.

Planning to Respond to Others' Emotions Throughout the Day

Which activities focusing on responding to others' emotions appeal to you? What other ideas and materials do you have that build on the skill of helping others through their emotions? As you review activities and materials, plan with the following considerations in mind:

➤ For which activities will children practice offering physical support (hugging, rubbing a peer's back, holding an ice pack on a hurt child's knee, and so on)? How will you model and encourage children to ask for consent before touching another child?

➤ Review your activities and consider if you have some where children respond to others' joy, pride, and excitement as well as activities where children respond to sadness, disappointment, or anger. Aim to include a range of emotions—both uncomfortable and comfortable—across your activities.

➤ Spread out your activities across the week and across different settings (including in different centers and rooms, inside and outside, and as part of activities that are facilitated by different adults).

Formative Assessment of Responding to Others' Emotions

The skill of responding appropriately to others' emotions has several components. Children need to know how to read emotions and look for body clues (chapter 4). It also helps if they can make sense of these clues and apply an emotion label (chapter 3). Knowing how the other person is feeling then allows them to choose a way to respond that is supportive of the emotion. Because of the multiple steps and skills involved, focusing on task analysis and level of assistance recording can both help as you collect formative assessment data.

The sample data sheet shown in figure 8.1 lists four steps in columns, with space to record how independent the child was in completing these steps. For example, Kristian needed Ms. Elliott's prompting ("Look at Samantha's face, Kristian. She is crying.") to recognize Samantha's feelings. When asked how Samantha feels, Kristian independently noted that she looked sad. Then, he went to get the How Can I Help You Feel Better? Card independently but needed verbal prompting to show it to Samantha. One more thing to consider recording is whether Samantha responds when Kristian asks her how he can help her feel better. Getting a response from a peer adds social reinforcement to the interaction. Samantha did respond to Kristian's offer of support without needing teacher prompting, so Ms. Elliot marked that as independent.

Figure 8.1 Sample Data Sheet for Recording the Assistance Needed for Responding to Others' Emotions

Child's Name	Recognizes Others' Feelings	Labels Feelings	Chooses a Strategy	Implements Strategy	Responds When Supported by Peer
Kristian	"Look, she's crying" (verbal prompt)	Labels sad (independent)	How Can I Help? Card (independent)	Needed a verbal prompt to show Samantha the card	
Samantha	"How does he feel?" (verbal prompt)				Chose something from the How Can I Help? Card (independent)
Giovanna	Independently approaches peers	Labels sad Labels excited Labels angry (independent)	Feel-Better Basket (independent)	Independent	Responded to peer when prompted verbally to answer their question

Ms. Elliott reviews her data after collecting it for several days. She looks for trends and patterns and works to identify children who might need additional support. For example, Giovanna is independently recognizing others' feelings, labeling them, and most often is independent in offering the Feel-Better Basket to a peer and asking what would help them. However, when peers try to support her, she tends to need adult prompting to respond. Ms. Elliott watches the interactions and Giovanna's body language to realize that she often doesn't want the help of another child. She prefers to get her own tools for feeling better. Ms. Elliott meets with her and talks about saying, "no thank you" if she doesn't want a peer's help. For Kristian, the step that is the least independent for him seems to be knowing what to say when he has the Feel-Better Basket, so Ms. Elliott practices a script with him to support his growing independence.

For a blank template of this data sheet, see the end of the chapter.

Remember to reflect on your data. What supports do children need? If the whole class knows to get the How Can I Help You Feel Better? Card but they do not know independently what to say next or how to present the card to another person, plan whole-class or small-group opportunities for everyone to practice the language.

Are there children who have the skills to identify and address others' emotions but don't consistently respond when peers offer help? They might need additional support with responding, including telling peers they aren't wishing for help. Or are there children who don't get responses from other children when they are trying new skills? Plan to support children with the interaction skills needed to be able to finish these interactions positively and, in turn, motivate children to keep using these skills.

Planning for Formative Assessment of Responding to Others' Emotions

Draft a plan for your formative assessment.

➤ What times of day will work best for gathering data to support your instructional decisions?

➤ Task analyze the steps for responding to others' emotions. For example, clapping or cheering for a peer or giving a compliment when a proud classmate shows you a picture they drew might only have two steps to record (what emotion they noticed and how they responded). Recognizing an emotion, getting the How Can I Help You Feel Better? Card or a Feel-Better Basket, and interacting with a peer to offer support might involve all the steps on the sample data sheet.

➤ When will you review your data so you can use the information to plan your next instructional steps?

Differentiation and Advancement

You might need to modify your approach to teaching this skill to meet a wide range of developmental needs in your class. For instance, this might look like creating talk buttons that say, "How can I help you feel better?" for children who aren't able to articulate or speak the phrase yet. For some children, you might reduce the number of choices on the How Can I Help You Feel Better? Card. Rather than using a laminated card with eight choices, a system of hook and loop choices would allow teachers and peers the ability to offer one choice or two choices if children need fewer options to successfully choose. For a child who needs more structure, you might script out the whole interaction in a social story, including the words the child might say. For children who do not yet understand representational pictures, using a Feel-Better Basket with props could help them offer a tangible tool.

You might also have children in your classroom who are advanced at recognizing and responding to others' emotions. You may observe this as they recognize subtle shifts in other children's emotions, or you might notice that they are keenly aware of what other children are interested in or find helpful. Maddi, a four-year-old, had this skill. She knew the other children's favorite colors, and she knew the characters and books they enjoyed. When she saw Emmett crying, she knew to offer him the red sensory bottle because red was his favorite color. When she saw Angel get hurt, she would offer a wet paper towel because Angel disliked wearing bandages. Her teacher encouraged this skill and talent. As other children were just beginning to use the class Feel-Better Basket, Maddi was given the job of supporting children who needed additional help. The teacher put a card with a photo of Maddi and the words "I need help" next to the basket and modeled how a peer could take the card to Maddi if they were unsure of how to use the basket. The teacher worked with Maddi to ensure that she wanted that responsibility, but also worked with her to practice the steps of peer support, including giving directions without taking over the process. Maddi learned to prompt peers to label how a classmate was feeling, encourage them to take the Feel-Better Basket to the classmate, and verbally prompt them to ask if something in the basket would help. Later, when adding individualized supports to the Feel-Better Basket, Maddi helped add four more ideas based on items she recognized her classmates appreciated.

Planning for Differentiation and Advancement

Create a plan for children who might need individualization around learning this skill. Use data and observations to identify specific children for whom you will intentionally plan modified or individualized supports.

➤ Who in your class is fluent in the skill of recognizing and responding to others' emotions?

➤ How can you harness their strengths to support children in the class who need extra help?

➤ What strategies might encourage growth in this area: modeling, making video models, pairing up peers to work together to help others? If one child guides a peer through responding to others' emotions, it will enhance both children's skills.

➤ When it comes to children who are struggling with this skill, what materials or visuals have been successful for them in the past? Consider whether your How Can I Help You Feel Better? Card or Feel-Better Basket aligns with the other visuals these children have had success with. If not, how can you modify these supports to be more similar to other visuals or materials that have worked well?

➤ How can other staff members, related service providers, or families collaborate with you to develop ideas for these children?

Troubleshooting Around Responding to Others' Emotions

Consider the following ways to troubleshoot questions or obstacles you might run into as you help children learn and practice ways to respond to others' emotions.

"I have a child who is visibly disturbed when other children are upset. She shouts at them to 'stop it' or pushes them if they are crying loudly near her. How can I support her with responding appropriately?"

This can be quite common in classrooms, which makes sense as everyone comes into the classroom with differing levels of comfort with emotion expression. There are several possible ways to support this child, depending on what her upset is communicating. Talking to the child when she's calm and brainstorming with her family can give you insight that in turn will help you decide on next steps. For some children, the issue is sensory; the noise of a crying or shouting child is very overwhelming. If a child feels like big emotions are too much sensory input, teaching a strategy to lessen the noise is helpful. In some classrooms, this means that the child who doesn't like hearing others cry will move to the Regulation Station and use strategies to keep calm. In other classrooms, teachers have headphones for children to access if it's too loud. In this case, teaching about this support and offering access to headphones could help the child begin to independently request what would be helpful for her when the noise is too much.

On the other hand, perhaps this child's distress isn't related to noise but instead is related to discomfort about expression of certain emotions. Strategies that might help work through this issue include reminding the child that all emotions are okay in the classroom (and beyond); providing a mantra as a way to lessen the discomfort ("He seems sad. It is safe to be sad at school."); or offering reassurance that the upset child will be okay soon ("Ms. Elliott is helping him to feel better.").

Above and beyond feeling discomfort, perhaps the child needs to know what she can do other than admonishing a child who is upset. In this case, it might be useful to role play with puppets or peers, placing a specific focus on validating the idea that it can feel scary when a classmate is upset, and then practicing concrete ways to respond. A teacher offering the child choices of how to help might also be useful to get her get "unstuck" from the situation. This could sound like, "Maxwell is really missing his auntie today. I'm going to check to see how I can help him feel better. Would you like to come or would you like to stay here?" Some children who would be distressed in this situation alone may feel it isn't so scary or out of control when they are working alongside their teacher to take a proactive step to help and support an upset child.

"I have a child who gets easily embarrassed and doesn't like when others cheer for him. The other children in the class are trying to be encouraging but it ends up upsetting him."

When my son was younger, I remember him learning how to ride a two-wheeled bicycle. When he finally learned to use the brakes to stop instead of dragging the tips of his sneakers on the ground, I called out to him, "You stopped! You did it!" He turned to me quickly and said, "Don't cheer for me. Everyone looks at me." I was trying to give some enthusiastic and positive descriptive feedback, and he was clearly saying, "No thank you."

The strategy that we practiced after that was twofold. I practiced asking him if he wanted that kind of encouragement or not, and I mostly stuck with less exuberant feedback—especially in public. At the same time, I encouraged him to keep telling and reminding me, "Please don't cheer for me."

For a child who doesn't wish to be cheered for, you might ask what kind of response they do want. Perhaps a smile or a thumbs-up, both of which are a lower energy level and less attention-getting, would be more acceptable. You can then work together to teach the rest of your group about how this classmate would prefer to be encouraged. You can also practice how that child can give a reminder to others, such as "Just a thumbs-up," when it's his turn in a game. This helps him practice advocating for the kind of support and acknowledgment that works best for him.

This is a great opportunity to talk as a class about how we all have different feelings and different comfort levels. Using our words to tell others how we feel, and having others hear us and respect our wishes, are skills to practice and celebrate, even if that celebration is a quiet thumbs-up or a private conversation. We often encourage and guide children to treat each other fairly. Expanding our idea of "fairness" to include the concept of each child getting what they need to be successful and feel comfortable will, ultimately, support children—and us—in understanding and creating a more equitable classroom.

Family Engagement and Support

Recognizing and responding to the emotions of others is a skill with plenty of opportunities for use in a home setting. Family members have so many different feelings and different preferences for help or support. Sending home information on this skill allows children to transfer their abilities to their home setting and have supportive interactions with their family.

A social and emotional snippet in a newsletter or weekly email might look like this:

This week, we practiced recognizing and responding to the emotions of others. We cheered for others when they were proud of their accomplishments, and we offered to help classmates when they felt sad or angry. Now, if a child notices a friend crying, they can use the How Can I Help You Feel Better? Card to ask their friend what would help them (such as a hug or high-five). One reason we are practicing this skill is so that we can read the emotions on others' faces and learn how to be empathetic, caring friends. To practice, we have cheered up puppets who were "feeling sad," and we have taken turns being the kicker and the cheerleaders during soccer. We are recording ways we have helped our peers feel better on the bulletin board in the hallway. Come check it out!

Consider sending home video clips to further explore or explain the new emotional competency. For example, you could show two children role playing with the How Can I Help You Feel Better? Card. Explain the strategy to families when you send a video of the role play. Also send home a copy of the card for children and families to use at home. Consider having children decorate or color their cards to make them personalized for home use. Including a video model of the process can help families to see this skill in action before they try to use it at home.

In addition, gather family feedback about how they help their child feel better at home. Use family responses to add to items to a Feel-Better Basket or to add picture choices to the How Can I Help You Feel Better? Card. You can also add ideas to pages in a class book of "ways our family helps us feel better." Similarly, you might ask families to send in ideas for how they cheer and celebrate accomplishments with their child, and you could add these to a class book or make a simple display of ways families cheer us on. If your program has family events where families watch their children, you can take photos of families clapping and hugging their children during these events and include these photos in class books or displays. Using family feedback can enhance the tools you are using at school and encourage children to access supports or review concepts.

Wrap-Up

Congratulations on reflecting, planning, and teaching your class specific tools so they can offer others help with understanding, recognizing, and regulating emotions. Specifically teaching children strategies for responding to others' emotions transforms their role from passive bystanders to active supporters.

Now children have the skills to identify when they are feeling emotions, to label those emotions with a nuanced vocabulary, and to understand why they are feeling the way they are. They can seek regulation tools when needed and know how to access the classroom space designed to support them with regulating. And as they gain greater understanding of their own internal states, they are also learning to respond to others' emotions with caring and compassion. They can do all these things because of the instruction and environment you've created: an emotion-rich classroom!

How Can I Help You Feel Better? Card

You can print and laminate this one-page visual and use it as your How Can I Help You Feel Better? Card. You can also create a card made up of your own ideas and images, customized for your group's needs and preferences.

Breathe together

Something else?

Make a plan with someone

Go to the Regulation Station

Fix it

Help

Hug

Handshake

Data Sheet for Recording the Assistance Needed for Responding to Others' Emotions

On this sheet, you can note whether children are able to take these steps independently or need verbal or physical prompting as they use the skill of responding to others' emotions.

Child's Name	Recognizes Others' Feelings	Labels Feelings	Chooses a Strategy	Implements Strategy	Responds When Supported by Peer

Concluding Thoughts

In my years of coaching teachers, one trend has emerged. Teachers talk with pride and enthusiasm about the growth children in their classroom have shown. And yet, they neglect to connect that growth with the role *they* have played—arranging the environment, planning instruction, building relationships, and coaching children—all of which led directly to children's growth.

Child growth is certainly a reason to celebrate! A celebration of how your actions and strategies as a teacher have fostered and encouraged the emotional growth you have seen in your classroom is also well deserved. Let's review the six beliefs from chapter 1 and reflect on how they played out in your classroom over the course of this work:

Belief 1: Emotional intelligence matters and can be enhanced through teaching. Teaching emotional competencies enhances teachers' emotional intelligence as well.

Did you see children's growth in emotional intelligence because of your teaching? What skills do they have now that they didn't have at the beginning of your emotion work? Which of your strategies were most effective?

How did your own emotional intelligence grow through this journey? You might choose to review your Social and Emotional Skill Reflection Checklist (page 8) to see areas in which you have grown more comfortable. What skills have you been able to model authentically for your class?

Belief 2: Preschool is an ideal time to focus on social and emotional learning.

What made this year an ideal time for children to learn new skills? How will these skills help them in the years to come, after they have left your classroom? In what ways did your preschool classroom environment, schedule, and structures support this learning?

Belief 3: Focusing on either social and emotional learning **or** *academics in preschool is a false dichotomy.*

How did you teach cognitive skills such as referencing print, observation, comparing and contrasting, reflecting on behavior, and communicating with others? How will these skills help children with academic learning? How will having the skills to regulate and read others' emotions support them with school success?

Belief 4: Understanding identity and family background will help teachers plan instruction that can be supportive for more children.

What did you learn about children's families, cultures, and beliefs through this work? How did connecting with your families and sharing data and celebrations benefit you as a teacher? How did learning about classroom emotion instruction benefit families?

Belief 5: Instruction in social and emotional skills reduces challenging behavior.

Did you see behavioral changes in children as they gained new skills? Thinking about your social coaching using ICARE, were you able to see positive intent behind behaviors? How did your coaching reduce challenging behavior? How did shifting your mindset help you reframe challenging behavior?

Belief 6: Creating an emotion-rich classroom is both a lot of work and a lot of reward.

Consider the work you put into planning, implementing, and sharing your teaching. What part of the work was your favorite? Did you discover that certain parts of DAPPER really played to your strengths? What part of the work required the most growth for you? Thinking about the rewards of this work, what moments with children particularly encouraged or inspired you?

Consider recording some of your reflections so you can revisit them as you plan for teaching these emotional skills to a new group of children. Reflecting on children's progress, as well as what your role was in that growth, can help you remember why the work is important to you as you gear up to do it again.

Take one more look around your classroom with this book. As you've worked through these chapters, you've created an emotion-rich classroom. You have been intentional in your planning, using best practices to illustrate new emotional concepts. You've offered your class many activities, materials, and opportunities to use their new skills, rather than limiting social and emotional teaching to one SEL timeslot in your schedule. You've built new habits around the language you use to notice children's skills and to encourage children to reflect about their own behavior, thinking, and strategies. And next school year, you'll have new children entering your emotion-rich classroom. You'll use the habits you've built and the plans you've made to grow their emotional competencies, and you'll use data to create individualized supports reflecting the needs and strengths of these new children. Thanks to your ongoing effort to create, maintain, and improve your emotion-rich classroom, these skills and habits will stay with you and with the children in your care, helping them grow into more emotionally intelligent adults. Congratulations on your emotional journey.

References and Resources

Abraham, Cathy. 2003. "Literacy: Creating a Print-Rich Environment." *Texas Child Care Quarterly* 6 (3): 10–17. childcarequarterly.com/pdf/fall03_literacy.pdf.

Adams, Sarah. 2020. "School Mental Health for All." *Management in Education* 34 (1): 28–30. doi.org/10.1177/0892020619881111.

Adams, Susan, Janet Kuebli, Patricia A. Boyle, and Robyn Fivush. 1995. "Gender Differences in Parent-Child Conversations About Past Emotions: A Longitudinal Investigation." *Sex Roles* 33: 309–323. doi.org/10.1007/BF01954572.

Aznar, Ana, and Harriet R. Tenenbaum. 2014. "Gender and Age Differences in Parent-Child Emotion Talk." *British Journal of Developmental Psychology* 33 (1): 148–155. doi.org/10.1111/bjdp.12069.

Bailey, Becky. 2000. *Easy to Love, Difficult to Discipline: The 7 Basic Skills for Turning Conflict into Cooperation.* New York: William Morrow.

———. 2011. *Creating the School Family: Bully-Proofing Classrooms Through Emotional Intelligence.* Oviedo, FL: Conscious Discipline, Inc.

Bettencourt, Amie F., Deborah Gross, Grace Ho, and Nancy Perrin. 2018. "The Costly Consequences of Not Being Socially and Behaviorally Ready to Learn by Kindergarten in Baltimore City." *Journal of Urban Health* 95 (1): 36–50. doi.org/10.1007/s11524-017-0214-6.

Blais, Caroline, Rachael E. Jack, Christoph Scheepers, Daniel Fiset, and Roberto Caldara. 2008. "Culture Shapes How We Look at Faces." *PLoS ONE* 3 (8). doi.org/10.1371/journal.pone.0003022.

Boldt, Gail. 2020. "Possibilities and Problems in Trauma-Based and Social Emotional Learning Programs. Occasional Paper Series 43." *Bank Street College of Education.* eric.ed.gov/?id=ED606413.

Brackett, Marc. 2019. *Permission to Feel: Unlocking the Power of Emotions to Help Our Kids, Ourselves, and Our Society Thrive.* New York: Celadon Books.

Bridgeland, John, Mary Bruce, and Arya Hariharan. 2013. "The Missing Piece: A National Teacher Survey on How Social and Emotional Learning Can Empower Children and Transform Schools. A Report for CASEL." Civic Enterprises. casel.org/the-missing-piece.

Brody, Leslie R., and Judith Hall. 1993. "Gender and Emotion." In *Handbook of Emotions*, edited by Michael Lewis and Jeannette M. Haviland, 447–461. New York: Guilford Press.

Burton, Neel. 2014. "What's the Difference Between a Feeling and an Emotion?" *Psychology Today* blog. December 19, 2014. psychologytoday.com/us/blog/hide-and-seek/201412/whats-the-difference-between-feeling-and-emotion.

Campbell, Susan B., Susanne A. Denham, Grace Z. Howarth, Stephanie M. Jones, Jessica Vick Whittaker, Amanda P. Williford, Michael T. Willoughby, Monica Yudron, and Kristen Darling-Churchill. 2016. "Commentary on the Review of Measures of Early Childhood Social and Emotional Development: Conceptualization, Critique, and Recommendations." *Journal of Applied Developmental Psychology* 45: 19–41. doi.org/10.1016/j.appdev .2016.01.008.

Cordaro, Daniel T., Dacher Keltner, Sumjay Tshering, Dorji Wangchuk, and Lisa M. Flynn. 2016. "The Voice Conveys Emotion in Ten Globalized Cultures and One Remote Village in Bhutan." *Emotion* 16 (1): 117–128. doi.org/10.1037/emo0000100.

Crosson-Tower, Cynthia. 2003. *The Role of Educators in Preventing and Responding to Child Abuse and Neglect.* Washington, DC: US Department of Health and Human Services, Administration for Children and Families, Administration on Children, Youth and Families, Children's Bureau, Office on Child Abuse and Neglect. childwelfare.gov/pubpdfs/ educator.pdf.

Darling-Churchill, Kristen E., and Laura Lippman. 2016. "Early Childhood Social and Emotional Development: Advancing the Field of Measurement." *Journal of Applied Developmental Psychology* 45: 1–7. doi.org/10.1016/j.appdev.2016.02.002.

Dawson, Joe. 2018. "Emotions in Context: What We Know About How We Feel." *Observer* 31 (2): 25–26. psychologicalscience.org/observer/emotions-in-context-what-we-know-about-how-we-feel.

Denham, Susanne A., Hideko H. Bassett, and Susanne L. Miller. 2017. "Early Childhood Teachers' Socialization of Emotion: Contextual and Individual Contributors." *Child & Youth Care Forum* 46: 805–824. doi.org/10.1007/s10566-017-9409-y.

Denham, Susanne A., Kimberly A. Blair, Elizabeth DeMulder, Jennifer Levitas, Katherine Sawyer, Sharon Auerbach-Major, and Patrick Queenan. 2003. "Preschool Emotional Competence: Pathway to Social Competence?" *Child Development* 74 (1): 238–256. doi. org/10.1111/1467-8624.00533.

Durlak, Joseph A., Roger P. Weissberg, Allison B. Dymnicki, Rebecca D. Taylor, and Kriston B. Schellinger. 2011. "The Impact of Enhancing Students' Social and Emotional Learning: A Meta-Analysis of School-Based Universal Interventions." *Child Development* 82 (1): 405–432. doi.org/10.1111/j.1467-8624.2010.01564.x.

Ekman, Paul. 2003. *Emotions Revealed: Recognizing Faces and Feelings to Improve Communication and Emotional Life.* New York: Times Books.

Farnsworth, Bryn. 2020. "How to Measure Emotions and Feelings (and the Difference Between Them)." *Imotions* blog. April 14, 2020. imotions.com/blog/difference-feelings-emotions.

Ferro, Jolenea, Lise Fox, Denise Binder, and Meghan von der Embse. 2022. *Pyramid Model Equity Coaching Guide.* National Center for Pyramid Model Innovations. challengingbehavior.cbcs.usf.edu/Implementation/Equity/Guide/index.html.

Fivush, Robyn, Melissa A. Brotman, Janine P. Buckner, and Sherryl H. Goodman. 2000. "Gender Differences in Parent-Child Emotion Narratives." *Sex Roles* 42 (3): 233–253. doi. org/10.1023/A:1007091207068.

Fox, Lise, Glen Dunlap, Mary Louise Hemmeter, Gail E. Joseph, and Phillip S. Strain. 2003. "The Teaching Pyramid: A Model for Supporting Social Competence and Preventing Challenging Behavior in Young Children." *Young Children* 58 (4): 48–52. jstor.org/stable/42728957.

Goleman, Daniel. 1995. *Emotional Intelligence: Why It Can Matter More Than IQ.* New York: Bantam Books.

Grimm, Beca. 2015. "11 Feelings There Are No Words for in English." *Bustle.* July 15, 2015. bustle.com/articles/97413-11-feelings-there-are-no-words-for-in-english-for-all-you-emotional-word-nerds-out.

Gunter, Leslie, Paul Caldarella, Byran B. Korth, and K. Richard Young. 2012. "Promoting Social and Emotional Learning in Preschool Students: A Study of Strong Start Pre–K." *Early Childhood Education Journal* 40 (3): 151–159. doi.org/10.1007/s10643-012-0507-z.

Halle, Tamara G., Elizabeth C. Hair, Margaret Buchinal, Rachel Anderson, and Martha Zaslow. 2012. *In the Running for Successful Outcomes: Exploring the Evidence for Thresholds of School Readiness Technical Report.* US Department of Health and Human Services. aspe.hhs.gov/basic-report/running-successful-outcomes-exploring-evidence-thresholds-school-readiness-technical-report.

Hemmeter, Mary Louise, Lise K. Fox, and Patricia Snyder. 2014. *Teaching Pyramid Observation Tool for Preschool Classrooms Manual, Research Edition.* Baltimore: Brookes Publishing.

Hemmeter, Mary Louise, Michaelene Ostrosky, and Lise Fox. 2006. "Social and Emotional Foundations for Early Learning: A Conceptual Model for Intervention." *School Psychology Review* 35 (4): 583–601. doi.org/10.1080/02796015.2006.12087963.

Humphrey, Neil, and Michael Wigelsworth. 2012. "Modeling the Factors Associated with Children's Mental Health Difficulties in Primary School: A Multilevel Study." *School Psychology Review* 41 (3): 326–341. doi.org/10.1080/02796015.2012.12087513.

Isik-Ercan, Zeynep. 2017. "Culturally Appropriate Positive Guidance with Young Children." *Young Children* 72 (1): 15–22. naeyc.org/resources/pubs/yc/mar2017/culturally-appropriate-positive-guidance.

Ivcevic, Zorana, and Marc Brackett. 2014. "Predicting School Success: Comparing Conscientiousness, Grit, and Emotion Regulation Ability." *Journal of Research in Personality* 52: 29–36. doi.org/10.1016/j.jrp.2014.06.005.

Jack, Rachel E., Wei Sun, Ioannis Delis, Oliver G. B. Garrod, and Philippe G. Schyns. 2016. "Four Not Six: Revealing Culturally Common Facial Expressions of Emotion." *Journal of Experimental Psychology: General* 145 (6): 708–730. doi.org/10.1037/xge0000162.

James, Colin, Miles Bore, and Susanna Zito. 2012. "Emotional Intelligence and Personality as Predictors of Psychological Well-Being." *Journal of Psychoeducational Assessment* 30 (4): 425–438.

Jones, Paul Anthony. 2019. "15 Obscure Words for Everyday Feelings and Emotions." *Mental Floss.* March 14, 2019. mentalfloss.com/article/502463/15-obscure-words-everyday-feelings-and-emotions.

Jones, Stephanie M., and Emily J. Doolittle. 2017. "Social and Emotional Learning: Introducing the Issue." *The Future of Children* 27 (1): 3–11. jstor.org/stable/44219018.

Joseph, G., Strain, P., and Ostrosky, M. M. 2005. *Fostering Emotional Literacy in Young Children: Labeling Emotions. What Works Brief No. 21.* Center on the Social and Emotional Foundations for Early Learning. csefel.vanderbilt.edu/briefs/wwb21.pdf.

Kosonogov, Vladimir, Elena Vorobyeva, Ekaterina Kovsh, and Pavel Ermakov. 2019. "A Review of Neurophysiological and Genetic Correlates of Emotional Intelligence." *International Journal of Cognitive Research in Science, Engineering and Education* 7 (1): 137–142. doi.org/10.5937/IJCRSEE1901137K.

Mahoney, Joseph L., Joseph A. Durlak, and Roger P. Weissberg. 2018. "An Update on Social and Emotional Learning Outcome Research." *The Phi Delta Kappan* 100 (4): 18–23. doi. org/10.1177/0031721718815668.

McClelland, Megan M., Shauna L. Tominey, Sara A. Schmitt, and Robert Duncan. 2017. "SEL Interventions in Early Childhood." *The Future of Children* 27 (1): 33–47. doi.org/10.1353/foc.2017.0002.

Nagoski, Emily, and Amelia Nagoski. 2019. *Burnout: The Secret to Unlocking the Stress Cycle.* New York: Ballantine Books.

Nahigyan, Pierce. 2015. "17 Words We Don't Have in English that Describe Feelings We Have Every Day. *Thought Catalog.* December 17, 2015. thoughtcatalog.com/pierce-nahigyan/2015/12/17-words-we-dont-have-in-english-that-describe-feelings-we-have-every-day.

Nayfeld, Irena, Kimberly Brenneman, and Rochel Gelman. 2011. "Science in the Classroom: Finding a Balance Between Autonomous Exploration and Teacher-Led Instruction in Preschool Settings." *Early Education and Development* 22 (6): 970–988. dx.doi.org/10.1080/10409289.2010.507496.

Neuman, Susan B. and Tanya S. Wright. 2014. "The Magic of Words: Teaching Vocabulary in the Early Childhood Classroom." *American Educator* 38 (2): 4–13.

Ng Fei-Yin, Florrie, Catherine Tamis-LeMonda, Hirokazu Yoshikawa, and Irene Nga-Lam Sze. 2015. "Inhibitory Control in Preschool Predicts Early Math Skills in First Grade: Evidence from an Ethnically Diverse Sample." *International Journal of Behavioral Development* 39 (2): 139–149. doi.org/10.1177/0165025414538558.

Paul Ekman Group. n.d. "Universal Facial Expressions." Accessed January 19, 2022. Paulekman.com/resources/universal-facial-expressions.

Pogosyan, Marianna. 2016. "Emotion Perception Across Cultures: How Culture Influences the Way We Interpret Facial Expressions of Emotions." *Psychology Today* blog. October 9, 2016. psychologytoday.com/us/blog/between-cultures/201610/emotion-perception-across-cultures.

Pons, Francisco, Paul L. Harris, and Marc de Rosnay. 2004. "Emotion Comprehension Between 3 and 11 Years: Developmental Periods and Hierarchical Organization." *European Journal of Developmental Psychology* 1 (2): 127–152. doi.org/10.1080/17405620344000022.

Posner, Jonathan, James A. Russell, and Bradley S. Peterson. 2005. "The Circumplex Model of Affect: An Integrative Approach to Affective Neuroscience, Cognitive Development, and Psychopathology." *Development and Psychopathology* 17 (3): 715–734. doi.org/10.1017/S0954579405050340.

Price, Charis Lauren, and Elizabeth A. Steed. 2016. "Culturally Responsive Strategies to Support Young Children with Challenging Behavior." *Young Children* 71 (5): 36–43. naeyc.org/resources/pubs/yc/nov2016/culturally-responsive-strategies.

Reyes, Maria R., Marc A. Brackett, Susan E. Rivers, Mark White, and Peter Salovey. 2012. "Classroom Emotional Climate, Student Engagement, and Academic Achievement." *Journal of Education Psychology* 104 (3): 700–712. doi.org/10.1037/a0027268.

Richburg, Melanie, and Teresa Fletcher. 2002. "Emotional Intelligence: Directing a Child's Emotional Education." *Child Study Journal* 32 (1): 31–38.

Rubin, Gretchen. 2015. *Better Than Before: Mastering the Habits of Our Everyday Lives.* New York: Crown Publishing.

Sam, A., and AFIRM Team. 2015. "Task Analysis." Chapel Hill, NC: National Professional Development Center on Autism Spectrum Disorder, FPG Child Development Center, University of North Carolina. afirm.fpg.unc.edu/task-analysis.

Schonert-Reichl, Kimberly A. 2017. "Social and Emotional Learning and Teachers." *The Future of Children* 27 (1): 137–155. eric.ed.gov/?id=EJ1145076.

Schwartz, Katrina. 2019. "Nine Ways to Ensure Your Mindfulness Teaching Practice Is Trauma-Informed." *KQED: MindShift.* kqed.org/mindshift/53228/nine-ways-to-ensure-your-mindfulness-teaching-practice-is-trauma-informed.

Statman-Weil, Katie. 2015. "Creating Trauma-Sensitive Classrooms." *Young Children* 70 (2): 72–79. naeyc.org/resources/pubs/yc/may2015/trauma-sensitive-classrooms.

Strickland, Dorothy S., and Lesley Mandel Morrow. 1988. "Creating a Print Rich Environment (Emerging Readers and Writers)." *The Reading Teacher* 42 (2): 156–157. eric.ed.gov/?id=EJ381760.

Taylor, Rebecca D., Eva Oberle, Joseph A. Durlak, and Roger P. Weissberg. 2017. "Promoting Positive Youth Development Through School-Based Social and Emotional Learning Interventions: A Meta-Analysis of Follow-Up Effects." *Child Development* 88 (4): 1156–1171. doi.org/10.1111/cdev.12864.

Torres, Marcela M., Celene E. Domitrovich, and Karen L. Bierman. 2015. "Preschool Interpersonal Relationships Predict Kindergarten Achievement: Mediated by Gains in Emotion Knowledge." *Journal of Applied Developmental Psychology* 39: 44–52. doi.org/10.1016/j.appdev.2015.04.008.

Wu, Ling, and Minkang Kim. 2019. "See, Touch, and Feel: Enhancing Young Children's Empathy Learning Through a Tablet Game." *Mind, Brain, and Education* 13 (4): 341–351. doi.org/10.1111/mbe.12218.

Yates, Tweety, Michaelene M. Ostrosky, Gregory A. Cheatham, Angel Fettig, LaShorage Shaffer, and Rosa Milagro Santos. 2008. "Research Synthesis on Screening and Assessing Social-Emotional Competence." The Center on the Social and Emotional Foundations for Early Learning. csefel.vanderbilt.edu/documents/rs_screening_assessment.pdf

Index

Italics denotes information in figures

A

Academics, 18–21, 212
Acknowledge step (ICARE framework), 44, *45, 46,* 101, 127, 151, 176, 199
Adolescents, emotional intelligence in, 14
Adult reflection. *See* Reflection (educator)
Adults. *See also* Educators; Family and family engagement
    benefit of emotional intelligence in, 14
    with high emotional intelligence, 14
    responding to others' emotions, 191
Advanced skills
    accessing/using Regulation Station, 182–183
    emotion vocabulary acquisition and, 83–84
    recognizing emotions and, 107–108
    regulation strategies and, 158–159
    responding to others' emotions and, 205–206
    understanding causes of emotions and, 132–134
Aggression, 25
Anger
    biological response, 93
    child-friendly description of, *89*
    as emotion to teach, 71
    in emotion vocabulary to teach, 66, 67
    facial expression of, 66
    ways of showing up in yourself, *95*
Animate (DAPPER framework), 38
    in action, *41, 42*
    causes of emotions and, 122–123
    emotion vocabulary acquisition and, 72–73
    recognizing emotions, 96–97
    regulation strategies, 147–148
    on responding to others' emotions, 194–195
    on using Regulation Station, 170–171
Anxiety/anxious, 14
    child-friendly description of, *89*
    as emotion to teach, 67
    understanding causes of, 118, 123
Art (activities)
    calming activities used with, 155
    emotion vocabulary acquisition and, 79
    for Regulation Station, 179
    related to causes of emotions, 129

related to recognizing emotions, 104
related to responding to others' emotions, 202
Asking for something, *26*
ASL (American Sign Language), 73, 123, 147, 170
Assessment. *See* Data recording sheet; Formative assessment
Autism spectrum disorder, 25, 83, 110, 158
Avoidance (of emotions), 28, 33

B

Bailey, Becky, 135
Baltimore City Public Schools, 25
Bar graph, 104
"Be happy" classroom rule, 52
Belief (component of emotional development), *16*
Belief 1, 12–15, 212
Belief 2, 15–18, 212
Belief 3, 18–21, 212
Belief 4, 21–24, 212
Belief 5, 24–27, 213
Belief 6, 27–29, 213
Biases, 55–56
Blame/blaming
    avoiding statements of, 44
    talking about causes of emotions without, 135–136, *136*
Body clues, 44, 95, 96–99
    planning how to practice recognizing, 98–99
    recognizing emotions in yourself and, 98
    self-regulation and, 145, 146
    sharing information with families about, 111–112
    trauma-sensitive emotion coaching and, 108–109
Body Clues Map, 96, 101, 102, 112, 114
Books. *See* Handmade books; Story time (books)
Book study group/format, 6, 7
Brackett, Marc, 5
Breathing techniques, 145–147, 148, 149–150, 158–159, 179
Bubbles, 35, 145, 146, 154
Building a Habit of Positive Descriptive Feedback, 90–91

C

Calm
    child-friendly description of, *89*
    as emotion to teach, 71
    in your emotion vocabulary to teach, 67, 71
"Calm down," 55

Calm-down book, 154
Calm-down kit, 151
Calm-down menu, 147, 150, 151, 162
Calming strategies, 44. *See also* Regulating emotions
Calm step (ICARE framework), 44, *45, 46,* 101, 126, 151, 176, 199
Cause and effect, understanding of, 21
Causes of emotions, 117–137
    child identifying *abuse, neglect,* or *maltreatment,* 134–135
    DAPPER framework for understanding, 120–128
    differentiation and advancement around, 132–134
    discussing throughout the day, 128–131
    Emotion Causes Flip-Book, 123
    offering genuine responses to, 119–120
    overview, 117–119
    talking about without blaming or shaming, 135–136, *136*
Challenging behavior, 24–27, 213
Charades, 78, 194
Check-in charts. *See* Emotion check-in charts
"Checking in" with your body, 96
Cheering other children in the class, 200, 205, 207–208, 209
Child-friendly explanations of emotions, 69
Children
    deeply human needs of, 2–3
    disclosing traumatic experiences, 28–29
    misidentifying their emotions, 110–111
Choice boards, 173, 175
Circle time. *See* Morning meeting and circle time
Coaching. *See* ICARE framework
Coaching, trauma-sensitive emotion, 108–109
Collages, 74, 129, 137
Colleagues, using the DAPPER framework with, 41
Comparing and contrasting, 21
Confusion, child-friendly description of, *89*
Coregulation, 143, 160, 175
COVID-19 pandemic, 3
Crying
    cultural beliefs about males, 22
    labeling pictures of sad as, 85
    reframing messages about, 53, *54*
Cultural beliefs about emotions, 21–24, 94

Empathy, 4, 12, 44, 120, 191
Enjoyment
    in emotion vocabulary to
        teach, 66, 67
    facial expression of, 66
Environmental print, 34
Evidence-based strategies. *See*
    Pyramid Model
Excitement
    child-friendly description of, *89*
    as emotion to teach, 71
    in emotion vocabulary to teach, 67
    recognizing in oneself, 98
    ways of showing up in yourself, *95*
Executive functioning, 18
Explicit instruction, 69
Expressing emotions. *See* Emotional
    expression
Expressive understanding of emotions,
    81, *82*, 92
Extending new skills (DAPPER
    framework), 39
    in action, *41, 42*
    for calm-down strategies, 150–152
    emotion vocabulary acquisition
        and, 75–76
    identifying causes of emotions
        and, 126–127
    portable version of Regulation
        Station, 174–176
    recognizing emotions in yourself
        and, 100–102
    for responding to others' emo-
        tions, 198–199
External cause (component of emotional
    development), *16*, 17
Eye gaze, 22

F

Facial cues, 35
Facial expressions
    associated with anger, *95*
    associated with excitement, *95*
    associated with sadness, *95*
    connecting emotion vocabu-
        lary to, 66
    differentiation around, 83
    emotional development in
        preschoolers and, 17
    recognized in cultures around the
        world, 66–67
    as same across different cultures, 94
    teaching children to recognize, 12
    understanding family's com-
        fort with, 23
    used for child-friendly descriptions
        of emotions, *89*
Family and family engagement, 50
    communicating with, 5–6
    educator biases and, 55, 56
    emotional display rules in, 22
    emotion recognition and, 111–112
    emotion vocabulary acquisition
        and, 86–88
    gender-related differences in
        emotion learning in, 23–24
    involved in extending new skills
        (DAPPER framework), 39

receiving input from fami-
    lies, 112–113
regulation strategies and, 162–163
responding to others' emotions
    and, 208–209
sharing information about
    Regulation Station
    with, 185–186
understanding cultures and beliefs
    of, 21–24, 212
when talking about causes of
    emotions, 136–137
Fear
    child-friendly description of, *89*
    as emotion to teach, 71
    in emotion vocabulary to
        teach, 66, 67
    facial expression of, 66–67
    minimizing, 64
Feedback. *See* Positive descrip-
    tive feedback
Feel-Better Basket, 195, 198, 201,
    202, *204*, 205
Feelings. *See also* Emotions
    classroom rules dictating a
        child's, 52
    definition, 50
    emotions *versus*, 50–51
    examples of, *51*
"Feelings chart," 50
Flip books
    Emotions Causes Flip-Book,
        123, 125, 128, 129, 131–132,
        133, 138–140
    for Regulation Station, 175
Formative assessment
    of accessing/using Regulation
        Station, 180–181, *181,* 189
    data collection, 47
    of emotion vocabulary acquisi-
        tion, 80–83
    levels of assistance recording,
        47, 48–49
    of recognizing emotions,
        105–107, 116
    of regulation skills, *156,*
        156–157, 165
    of responding to others' emotions,
        203–205, *204,* 211
    task analysis, 47–48, *48*
    of understanding the causes of
        emotions, 131–132
Four primary/universal emotions, 67
Freeze dance, 78
Friendship skills, 18
Frustration
    child-friendly description of, *89*
    as emotion to teach, 71
    in emotion vocabulary to teach, 67
    reframing behaviors from, *26*

G

Games
    emotion vocabulary, 74, 79
    exploring causes of emotions with,
        125, 130, 137
    responding to others' emotions
        during, 194, 197

that involve responding to others'
    emotions, 202
during transitions, 129
Gender/gender differences
    educator biases and, 55
    in emotion learning, 23–24
    expression of sadness/crying
        by boys, 22
    teacher biases and, 55
Gestures and signs
    animate step (DAPPER
        framework), 38
    for Regulation Station, 170–171
    to represent *calm,* 147
    when responding to others'
        emotions, 195
    when talking about causes of
        emotions, 133
    when using the Body Clues
        Map, 96–97
Graphs, 104
Greeting peers, 36
Grief, 22
Gross-motor skills. *See* Outside time
Guided meditations, 96

H

Handmade books. *See also* Emotion
    Causes Flip-Book
    about body clues, 100, 104
    about emotion words, 74
    calm-down book, 154
    flip books on causes of emo-
        tions, 129
    for Regulation Station, 178
    for regulatory process, 175
    on responding to others' emo-
        tions, 194, 202
Happy
    associating acceptable classroom
        behaviors with, 52–53
    child-friendly description of, *89*
    as emotion to teach, 71
Hiding (component of emotional
    development), *16*
Home, the. *See also* Family and family
    engagement
    emotion check-in chart for, 112
    making a Regulation Station in, 185
How Can I Help You Feel Better? Card,
    194–195, 196, 198, 199, *204,*
    205, 208, 210

I

ICARE framework
    about, 37, 43
    coaching children around using
        Regulation Station and, 175–176
    components of, 43–45, *45*
    DAPPER compared with, 43, 45
    emotional regulation and, 151–152
    example of components of, *46*
    identifying causes of emotions
        and, 126–127
    putting into action, *45*
    recognizing emotions and, 101–102
    reframing how we talk about
        emotions using, 54

About the Author

Lindsay N. Giroux, M.Ed., specializes in coaching pre-school teachers on implementing the Pyramid Model to promote social and emotional development and prevent challenging behavior. She is a contributing author of *Connect4Learning*®: *The PreK curriculum* and the ChooseFi Pre-Kindergarten financial literacy curriculum. Her professional interests include teacher training, social skill instruction, and inclusion of preschoolers with special needs. Lindsay received a B.A. from Wellesley College and an M.Ed. in Early Childhood Special Education from Peabody College of Vanderbilt University. She is currently the Social Emotional Foundations for Early Learning (SEFEL) Coordinator for the Wake County Public School District and a North Carolina Preschool Pyramid Expert Coach. She resides in Raleigh, North Carolina, with her husband and son.

Other Great Resources from Free Spirit

Uncover the Roots of Challenging Behavior
Create Responsive Environments Where Young Children Thrive
by Michelle Salcedo, M.Ed.

For early childhood educators.

192 pp.; PB; 8½" x 11" includes digital content
Free PLC / Book Study Guide
freespirit.com / PLC

Big Conversations with Little Children
Addressing Questions, Worries, and Fears
by Lauren Starnes, Ed.D.

For early childhood educators.

192 pp.; PB; 1-color; 8½" x 11"; includes digital content

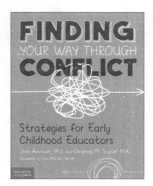

Finding Your Way Through Conflict
Strategies for Early Childhood Educators
by Chris Amirault, Ph.D., and Christine M. Snyder, M.A.

For early childhood educators.

176 pp.; PB; 1-color; 7¼" x 9¼"
Free PLC / Book Study Guide
freespirit.com / PLC

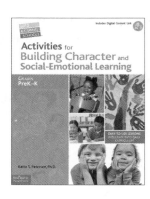

Activities for Building Character and Social-Emotional Learning, Grades PreK–K
Safe and Caring Schools Series
by Katia S. Petersen, Ph.D.

For educators, group leaders, caregivers.

160 pp.; PB; 8½" x 11"; includes digital content

Mindful Classrooms™
Daily 5-Minute Practices to Support Social-Emotional Learning (PreK to Grade 5)
by James Butler, M.Ed.

For educators, grades preK–5.

192 pp.; PB; full-color; photos; 8½" x 11"

Intentional Teaching in Early Childhood
Ignite Your Passion for Learning and Improve Outcomes for Young Children
by Sandra Heidemann, M.S., Beth Menninga, M.A.Ed., and Claire Chang, M.A.

For early childhood teachers and providers, instructional coaches, directors, and administrators.

216 pp.; PB; 7¼" x 9¼"; includes digital content
Free PLC / Book Study Guide
freespirit.com / PLC

Interested in purchasing multiple quantities and receiving volume discounts?
Contact edsales@freespirit.com or call 1.800.735.7323 and ask for Education Sales.

Many Free Spirit authors are available for speaking engagements, workshops, and keynotes. Contact speakers@freespirit.com or call 1.800.735.7323.

For pricing information, to place an order, or to request a free catalog, contact:

Free Spirit Publishing • 6325 Sandburg Road, Suite 100 • Minneapolis, MN 55427-3674
toll-free 800.735.7323 • local 612.338.2068 • fax 612.337.5050
help4kids@freespirit.com • freespirit.com